SILVER OF THE
POSSESSED

SILVER OF THE POSSESSED
Jewellery in the Egyptian zār

SIGRID M. VAN ROODE

~ To Nefertari Tadema in loving memory ~

© 2024 Sigrid van Roode

Published by Sidestone Press, Leiden
www.sidestone.com

Imprint: Sidestone Press Dissertations
This book was originally written as a dissertation and successfully defended at Leiden University in 2024

Lay-out & cover design: Sidestone Press
Artwork cover: 'Red Wind: Fire' in the series 'Palimpsets: Presences of Others' by Salma Ahmad Caller

ISBN 978-94-6428-072-2 (softcover)
ISBN 978-94-6428-073-9 (hardcover)
ISBN 978-94-6428-074-6 (PDF e-book)

DOI: 10.59641/z8c4w5x6y7

CONTENTS

Preface — 9
    On the title — 10
    On the cover art — 11
    On the artist — 11

1 Introduction — 13
    1.1 Aims and approach — 13
        1.1.1 Collected context — 13
        1.1.2 Living context: ritual — 14
        1.1.3 Living context: jewellery — 15
        1.1.4 Historic context — 16
        1.1.5 Limitations of this study — 17
        1.1.6 Terminology — 18
    1.2 Sources: sample collection — 19
        1.2.1 Challenges in the sample collection: definition and bias — 19
        1.2.2 Composition of the sample collection — 21
        1.2.3 Challenges in the sample collection: dating — 21
        1.2.4 Challenges in the sample collection: size — 22
    1.3 Sources: literature — 23
        1.3.1 Parameters — 23
        1.3.2 Written sources combining jewellery and *zār* — 24
        1.3.3 Discussion — 28
    1.4 Structure of this thesis — 29

2 Spirits and women in Egypt — 33
    2.1 Origins and dissemination of *zār* — 33
        2.1.1 An African phenomenon — 33
        2.1.2 Taking the world by storm: the rapid spread of *zār* — 34
    2.2 Spirit engagement and the world of women — 37
        2.2.1 Understanding the spirit world — 38
        2.2.2 Spirit influence in the world of women: fertility, marriage, and childbirth — 39
        2.2.3 Spirit possession — 41

    2.3 *Zār* 42
        2.3.1 The ritual specialist 43
        2.3.2 General configuration of *zār* 43
        2.3.3 Elements of *zār* 47
        2.3.4 Inviting and averting: a dual approach to dealing with spirits in *zār*   48

3 Collected Objects   51

    3.1 The curious case of the missing jewellery: published objects 51
        3.1.1 A century of publications 51
        3.1.2 19th century – 1950s: first publications 51
        3.1.3 1960s: a changing perspective 52
        3.1.4 1980s: from academia to the wider public 53
        3.1.5 1990s: information circulation in social networks 53
        3.1.6 2000s: the Siwa-effect 55
        3.1.7 A timeline of publishing 56
    3.2 To have and to hold: collected objects 57
        3.2.1 Buying: museum collections from 1960 onwards 57
        3.2.2 Buying: museum collections before 1960 58
        3.2.3 Buying: private collections 60
        3.2.4 Selling: vendors 61
        3.2.5 Life as collected object 62
        3.2.6 A timeline of collecting 63
    3.3 Disassociation from the primary life 63
        3.3.1 Reuse within *zār* 64
        3.3.2 Reuse beyond *zār* 64
        3.3.3 *Zār* jewellery on the fringes of Egypt 68
        3.3.4 Telling damages 70

4 Living objects   73

    4.1 Challenges with interpreting decontextualised objects 73
        4.1.1 Jewellery in written sources pre-dating the collection phase 73
        4.1.2 Purpose-made *zār* jewellery in the sample collection 78
        4.1.3 Other jewellery ascribed to *zār* in the sample collection .. 82
        4.1.4 The spirit world in Egypt: the Blackman collection of amulets 86
        4.1.5 From generic to specific 88
    4.2 Humans, spirits, and objects 90
        4.2.1 *Zārs* ancestors: possession cults in Africa 90
        4.2.2 *Zārs* cousin: candomblé 91
        4.2.3 Purpose-made jewellery in *zār*: an interpretation of its role 93
        4.2.4 Roles of jewellery in and beyond *zār* 94
        4.2.5 Converging worlds 101
    4.3 *Zār* jewellery in everyday life 103
        4.3.1 Costs 103
        4.3.2 Marriage dynamics 104
        4.3.3 *Zār* as integral part of life 106

5 Historic Objects — 109

5.1 Materialised memory — 109
- 5.1.1 The performance of cultural memory — 109
- 5.1.2 Challenges in identifying individual spirits — 111
- 5.1.3 The pivotal role of the ritual specialist — 113
- 5.1.4 Time is of the essence: changing narratives — 114
- 5.1.5 A collective representation: the personal front — 115

5.2 Three case studies — 118
- 5.2.1 Direct reference: khedive Abbas Hilmi II — 118
- 5.2.2 Indirect reference: the maḥmal festivities in Cairo — 119
- 5.2.3 Indirect reference: women and their world — 122
- 5.2.4 The limits of *zār* images — 124

5.3 The sample collection as historic source — 124
- 5.3.1 Distribution over time — 124
- 5.3.2 Techniques — 125
- 5.3.3 Execution — 126
- 5.3.4 Variety in images — 127
- 5.3.5 Wear pattern — 129
- 5.3.6 Undated pieces — 129

6 The world of *zār* jewellery — 133

6.1 The people of *zār* — 133
- 6.1.1 The lower classes — 133
- 6.1.2 The 'others' — 134
- 6.1.3 Changes in the visualisation of the people of *zār* — 135

6.2 Long-term changes in *zār* — 136
- 6.2.1 Political and economic changes — 137
- 6.2.2 Religious peer pressure — 138
- 6.2.3 Syncretizing worlds: the pivotal role of the ritual specialist over time — 139

6.3 The origin of the Egyptian power objects — 140

7 Conclusions — 145

Bibliography — 151

Captions to the photographs at the beginning of each chapter — 164

The costs of a *zār*: a case study from 1913 — 165

Glossary of Arabic terms — 169

Summary — 171

Acknowledgements — 175

Catalogue 177

Zār jewellery with spirit images 1900-1920 — 178
- Water spirits — 178
- Male spirits — 180
- Human spirit pairs — 181

Zār jewellery with spirit images 1920-1940 — 182
- Water spirits — 182
- Male spirits — 184
- Female spirits — 188
- Human spirit pairs — 190
- Camels — 193

Zār jewellery with spirit images 1940-1960 — 194
- Water spirits — 194
- Male spirits — 195
- Human spirit pairs — 196
- Camels — 196

Zār jewellery with spirit images 1960-1980 — 197

Jewellery with spirit images, different iconography — 198

Jewellery often associated with *zār*, but not exclusive to *zār* — 199
- Coin jewellery — 199
- Regular jewellery — 200
- Regular amulets — 206

PREFACE

I vividly remember purchasing my first piece of *zār* jewellery. It was late in Summer of 1995. At that time, I was working as a young student of Egyptology on the excavation of Deir Anba Musa al-Aswad, a Coptic monastery in Wadi al-Natrun. On one of our weekly days off, the project director, dr. Karel Innemée, took us to Cairo's Khan el-Khalili to show us the jewellery store of a friend. As we entered the tiny shop, he asked for 'the bag', upon which the owner reached under the counter and pulled a dusty fabric bag into view. Its contents were poured on a large platter and we spent a good time sifting and sorting through broken bits and pieces, pendants, rings, bracelets...I had never seen jewellery like this, and Karel explained to us that this was traditional Egyptian jewellery. That day, I purchased a Bedouin bracelet and a pendant with a mermaid on it. I wore it often, strung on a necklace, and happily explained when asked what I was wearing that this was a *zār* pendant from Egypt. I had no idea what *zār* was.

That afternoon in Cairo also marks the start of my collecting of jewellery. Every year, when working in Egypt, I would explore in Khan el-Khalili, searching for old silver jewellery. Initially, on a student budget, I would select pieces that I liked and that I could wear: they were a material form of Egypt to take home with me. Later, when I finally had landed a job, I could afford larger pieces. Between the late '90s and the early years of the new millennium, I steadily collected jewellery (among which many pieces of *zār* jewellery). However, I found that there was not much available in terms of background information on these pieces. I wanted to know more about the world it came from, and in turn share that information. I read what I could find, and when I was asked for a few *zār* pieces on loan to the exhibition Egyptian Magic in 2010 in the National Museum of Antiquities in Leiden, I was more than happy to oblige. I provided a few pieces that depicted a sphinx and an obelisk, remnants of ancient Egyptian beliefs lingering until today – or so I thought.

That same year, my first book *Desert Silver* was published. In it, I aimed not so much to provide a catalogue of jewellery items with their descriptions but rather to give an overview of the world these pieces come from and the various roles they played in everyday life. Because jewellery, to me, is not a stand-alone object; it belongs in the context of its wearers. I used my collection, which had steadily expanded by then, in exhibitions and on the emerging social media platform Facebook, to provide glimpses into the lives of their wearers. These collected objects, like the archaeological artifacts

I studied as an Egyptologist and later as an archaeologist, belong to the wider material culture of a community. They have stories to tell, and by studying them closely, one may learn what those stories are.

But in order to do that successfully, it is imperative to look beyond one's own world view. Looking at *zār* jewellery and seeing ancient Egyptian shapes is exemplary of that need: I saw what I *wanted* to see, not what was actually there. It is equally important to be aware of the double-edged sword that collecting can be. On the one hand, collecting is the reason that many items still survive today. On the other hand, it is only those objects that collectors consider desirable, often from an aesthetic standpoint, that are collected. An example is the general dislike for damaged goods, while it is in damages that stories reveal themselves, as this book will illustrate. And finally, collecting operates along the lines of demand: objects that are desirable are collected, published and shared, and so end up in higher demand still, because these are the objects that are known and asked for. Collecting is inevitably selecting.

While my understanding of jewellery in general grew, *zār* jewellery remained elusive to me. In 2017, the first seeds for this study were sown, as I decided to look into *zār* jewellery seriously. While working my way through both written sources and collections in Europe and abroad, the potential of these pieces began to dawn on me. A year later, I drafted a research proposal for this study and, much to my joy, was accepted as external PhD candidate in 2019. And at a certain point during the years I have worked on this study, I have stopped wearing my *zār* pendants. It was not a conscious decision; I only noticed after a while that it no longer felt right to wear them. It was not to put a professional distance between myself and my research topic, rather the opposite. Instead of merely jewellery items, they have become living things to me. Individually, each pendant is an incredibly personal piece that was not even meant to be seen by outsiders. When together, these pieces whisper stories of Egypt around the turn of the last century as experienced by women. They tell of the relation between people and their land, they speak of oppression and dissent, they share the bounty, but also the terrors of living with a mighty river. Jewellery can be a historic source – and so much more than that, as this thesis will show. Looking at jewellery in its cultural and in its collected context provides not only new information about their lives, but hopefully also new ways of using jewellery as medium to share these histories. I hope my exploration into the world of *zār* jewellery inspires collectors and curators alike to collect not only objects, but also information, and that it inspires not only to collect these, but even more so to share and to pass them on.

ON THE TITLE

'Silver of the Possessed' is derived from the introductory chapter in 'Zar. Spirit possession, Music and Healing Rituals in Egypt' (2016) by dr. Hager el-Hadidi. Here, she describes how her encounter with silver *zār* jewellery, in Arabic called 'silver of the possessed', set her on her path of both ritual specialist and scholarly ethnographer. I chose this title because in English, it has a double meaning that appealed to me in relation to a study into the value of collected objects: while it refers to the silver of those possessed by spirits, it may also be explained as the silver of those possessed by the desire to collect.

ON THE COVER ART

The artwork on the cover is 'Red Wind: Fire' in the series 'Palimpsets: Presences of Others' by Salma Ahmad Caller. Salma writes about this in the note accompanying the print I purchased in 2019: 'The colour red is associated with the spirits of the Zar, and in particular with Ethiopian spirits. The Zar ritual is thought to have originated in what is now Ethiopia and Eritrea, before it reached Egypt through enslavement of Ethiopian women sold in Cairo as highly prized beauties in the 18th century. These women then became part of Egyptian families. With projections from photographs of 18th century Ottoman mashrabiyya from Cairo and refractions from vintage glass.'

During this research, I encountered so many presences of others in both the objects and literature studied: of spirits and possessed, of colonial views and emic lived experiences, of collectors and sellers, and not to forget my own presence, inserted into this study through my own choices and understandings. This artwork to me visualises not only the fluid nature of *zār* itself, but also the many layers of the beholder: the highlights drawing our attention and the world outside that frame, the selections, prejudices and repeated (mis)information to be aware of, dissected and peeled back, in order to reach what *zār* jewellery might be - and what it could reveal about the women that once wore these pieces.

ON THE ARTIST

Salma Ahmad Caller is an artist, art historian and writer, born in Iraq to an Egyptian father and a British mother, she grew up in Nigeria and Saudi Arabia, and now lives in the U.K. The focus of her work is on cross-cultural exchange, and particularly mixed-race identities, experiences and embodiment, with an art practice that embraces collage, drawing, watercolour, photography, projection, installation and film. Salma also writes art theory, poetry and creative non-fiction, drawing on her theoretical background in research on the meanings of ornament in non-Western cultures through frameworks of anthropology of art and cognitive science. Her aim is to contribute to the decolonisation of art history and theory, and to break down hegemonic colonial and patriarchal formations in ideas and language.

1

INTRODUCTION

1.1 AIMS AND APPROACH

What is 'zār jewellery'? That question is at the heart of this study. At first glance, it seems to be a matter of straightforward terminology and definition, but that belies the multifaceted character of these objects and the contexts in which they existed over the course of a century.

These contexts started around the second half of the 19th century when an African possession cult called zār spread through Egypt, gaining immense popularity among women of the Egyptian Nile Valley. Jewellery formed part of zār, as German doctor Klunzinger noted already in 1878.[1] Silver jewellery with images of spirits started to appear in the early 20th century and played a role in zār for over seven decades, until they ceased to be made in the 1980s. These jewellery items show hand-engraved, frontal views of male and female spirits as well as mermaids, surrounded by a zigzag border. From the late 1950s onwards, the hand-engraved pieces were gradually replaced by machine-tooled, much thinner and lighter pieces. Currently, jewellery items with spirit representations are in collections of private collectors and museums, along with a wide variety of other items called 'zār jewellery'. Despite jewellery in zār having a history of over a century and pieces with spirit images having been collected in large numbers, it is surprisingly vague what makes jewellery into 'zār jewellery', and what role it played in zār.

1.1.1 Collected context

My starting point to unravel the question of what zār jewellery is, is its current context: as collected items. As such, I have used an artefactual approach,[2] in which material culture is central to my observations and conclusions, rather than relying on the first-hand experience of attending one or more zār rituals. I chose this approach because, although zār itself is still practised in Egypt, its use of jewellery has changed considerably. To begin with, the jewellery under study in this volume is older than zār as it is carried out in the present: it was manufactured and used between 1900 and 1980 approximately, so in a timeframe spanning around half a

---

1 Klunzinger 1878, p. 388.
2 Houlbrook and Armitage 2015.

century to a century ago. The period under study in this thesis is a little wider: from the first mention of *zār* in Egypt in 1869 until today, encompassing a little over 150 years.

The collection history of *zār* jewellery coincides with its publication history. In other words, our view on *zār* jewellery, and notably that of jewellery with spirit images, has largely been shaped by both publications about jewellery that had already been collected and, prior to that, by the choices made in the act of collecting itself. As Ter Keurs points out, it is in the act of collecting that the first instances of meaning getting 'lost in translation' occur: there is a difference in understanding of these jewellery items between local networks producing and using them, and the world of foreign collectors that noticed and then started to collect them.[3] One of the first aims of this study is to unravel how collections of *zār* jewellery have come into being, and what the current interpretations of these items are based on.

The fact that this particular material culture of *zār* takes the form of jewellery in my view is relevant. And so, in this study, two contexts intersect: that of ritual and that of jewellery. I will go into both next.

1.1.2 Living context: ritual

The primary context in which I have studied *zār* jewellery as living objects is that of ritual. *Zār* is a possession cult with its own rituals and community, which I will introduce in more detail in chapter 2. For understanding the context and the inner workings of *zār* itself, the works by Boddy[4] and Hadidi[5] have been instrumental. However, this present study focuses on objects used in *zār* – objects that are material remnants of acts and transactions with, or by, invisible beings.[6] Like archaeological finds, that makes them very suitable for tracing changes in ritual itself: seemingly small changes in the material record can indicate the onset of a substantial change in acts in, or even interpretation of, ritual.

A closely related aspect is that of 'agency'. The concept of agency is diffuse and generally pertains to the meaning or power objects can have, or be given, in a certain context. The most relevant aspect of agency in relation to *zār* jewellery is that as put forward by Gell[7]: the emotional impact objects have on humans. Jewellery with spirit images has had a profound emotional impact, not only on its original wearers, but also on its later collectors. Exploring what that agency was and is, is another aim of this study, as is explaining the difference in perception.

Zār itself is not an isolated phenomenon: it exists in the context of spirit engagement in Egypt in general. The large number of 'regular' amulets in the jewellery I studied for this volume testifies to this larger landscape of spirit engagement. Spirits play a role in many informal practices[8], and these practices themselves change over time[9]. Hansen argues that these are part of dialectic processes, in which oral traditions and acts are

---

3   Ter Keurs 2014, p. 50-51.
4   Boddy 1989.
5   Hadidi 2006 and 2016.
6   Keane 2008, p. 110.
7   Gell 1998.
8   Drieskens 2008 for an overview of spirit engagement in Cairo.
9   Hansen 2006 for an overview of spirit engagement in Cairo from ancient Egypt until the present.

transmitted from one generation to another.[10] With every generation, these traditions and acts change as they adapt to new circumstances, but they retain elements as well. Given the period under study in this book, approximately 150 years, placing these changing and surviving elements of spirit engagement for both *zār* and other forms of spirit engagement in their temporal context is essential. To provide 'temporal anchors' I have used Lane 1842, Blackman 1927 and Drieskens 2008. Lane wrote his *Manners and Customs of the Modern Egyptians* before *zār* arrived in the Nile Valley, and Drieskens researched spirit engagement in Egypt in a period when *zār* was still practised, but after the last hallmark date of the jewellery pieces with spirit representations.

Lane, being a man, would not have been allowed into the female domain, so we need to bear in mind his notes on the beliefs and acts of women are based what male informants told him about such matters. This brings me to the perspective of gender. Interaction with spirits itself is not necessarily a gendered domain[11], but the use of jewellery <u>is</u>. While we may see more material evidence from the domain of women, that does not imply the absence of interaction between spirits and men, or a stronger belief in such interactions among women. For both men and women, the interaction with spirits focuses on navigating the important transitions in life as well as on the desire to have children: spirits may prevent this from happening in many ways.[12] Women make use of jewellery in a variety of ways to ward off evil spirits. As objects worn on the body, they provide a barrier between the self and outside influences. Many jewellery items have amuletic capacities one way or another, be it in the choice of materials, colours, form and decoration, or their placement on the body, their smells or sounds. But there is more to jewellery in a woman's life.

1.1.3 Living context: jewellery

Just as *zār* is not an isolated ritual but firmly embedded in the wider context of spirit engagement in Egypt, jewellery is not an isolated category of material culture either. Apart from its amuletic capacities, jewellery plays an important economic role in a woman's life. This is because of its amount of silver or gold: it is her main asset and the basis for her financial independence.

The processes of singularization and commoditization, as outlined by Kopytoff, are applicable to this intersection of jewellery and ritual.[13] Singular objects are objects precluded from exchanging or selling; such an object is literally a non-commodity. Among these often are ritual objects and rare items that convey status or power. Not all non-commodities carry ritual or other powers, however; some non-commodities are too worthless to carry any significance or even value. Opposed to singular objects are objects that are meant to be sold or exchanged: they are common, general things. A hybrid form are singular objects that still need to be purchased, but are forbidden

---

10 Hansen 2006, pp. 111-112.
11 Lane 1842 recounts male attitudes towards spirits, Blackman 1927 presents both male and female beliefs and acts with regard to spirits; Drieskens 2008, pp. 16-17 discusses how a gender-based approach does not reflect Cairene reality.
12 Hansen 2006 focuses on this.
13 Kopytoff 1986, p. 74-75.

to be resold or gifted away, for example, personally tailored medicine. These are called 'terminal commodities'.[14] one could also say such an object is a single-way commodity.

Jewellery, in general, is first and foremost a commodity. Gifts of jewellery are common during every transition in life, such as engagement, marriage and childbirth, as well as on religious celebrations.[15] These gifts hold strong financial significance, and women increase their jewellery collection throughout their life as a means of securing capital. Inflation renders actual currency worthless, while precious metals can be exchanged against the current rate when the need arises.[16] Jewellery is sold to cover major expenses, such as the wedding of sons or hospitalisation. This economic aspect extends into the *zār* community. *Zār* jewellery, like regular jewellery, is primarily made of silver. Silver has no particular capacities that would make it the material of choice for ritual purposes: it was the expenses that mattered most, as I will address in chapter 4; instead of silver, more affluent people would use gold jewellery in *zār*. Apart from ritual, *zār* is a business, as Hadidi 2006 explained.[17] The ritual specialist and her staff are paid for their services, as were the silversmiths creating these items, but the network stretches further to suppliers of incense, candles, and foodstuffs used in *zār*.[18]

The economic aspect of jewellery is fundamental for our understanding today. Appadurai links the commodity aspect of an object to its social life: there are moments in the object's life where its main social function is to be exchanged in return for something else, and those are the moments in which an object moves from one situation to the next.[19] This notion of movement underlays the chain of events from the initial production of a piece of jewellery to its current presence in a collection, often in another country. It ended up there as a result of the choices made by the women who used these items: the economic aspect of jewellery influenced household politics, formed a part in their decision to eventually sell these items, and as such is tied in to the collection history of these pieces.

1.1.4 Historic context

It is this larger community created by *zār* that continues to speak through the jewellery with spirit images. For this, we need to turn to the origins of *zār*. Just as *zār* forms part of a larger context of spirit engagement in Egypt and the jewellery used has other aspects than just adornment, *zār* itself as a phenomenon did not appear out of thin air. *Zār* is not particular to Egypt, but in the words of Hadidi is a 'transnational hybrid phenomenon.'[20] More specifically, *zār* as practised in Egypt is an African possession cult with roots in Ethiopia and Nigeria.[21]

---

14 Kopytoff 1986, p. 75.
15 Bakker & McKeown 201, p. 200.
16 As already mentioned by Blackman 1927, p. 47.
17 Hadidi 2006, p. 80; p. 102 where the ritual specialist is considered a business partner of the silversmiths; p. 108 where the money made in the *zār* community circulates back into this community. See also 'Abd er-Rasoul 1955, p. 2, who mentions that the ritual specialist is connected to the goldsmiths and the herbalists.
18 'Abd er-Rasoul 1955, p. 81; Hadidi 2006, pp. 80-81.
19 Appadurai 1988, p. 13-14.
20 Hadidi 2006, p. 47, note 12.
21 See chapter 2 and 5 for further discussion.

An element of many African possession cults is the capacity to store and transmit collective memory,[22] and *zār* possesses that same capacity. The works of Behrend & Luig[23], Kramer[24] and Lewis[25] have shaped my understanding of African possession cults as carriers of memory, and the study by Megerssa & Kassam[26] has shed light on the knowledge structures present within those possession cults. The mnemonic capacity of *zār* has been noted for Egyptian *zār* as well,[27] but where this is often explored in *zār* songs or the identity of *zār* spirits[28], its presence in jewellery has gone unnoticed. In the larger family of African possession cults, *zār* in Egypt is the only member that uses material culture with spirit images in the form of jewellery. I argue that these images form a historic source in two ways. They reflect actual historic events in approximately 3% of the pieces with spirit images, but mostly, they visualise the world of the *zār* community. For this last capacity, the concept of the 'personal front' as formulated by Goffman[29] has been most helpful to catch a glimpse of that world.

1.1.5 Limitations of this study

This study focuses on Egyptian *zār* jewellery. It does not aim to be a study into the theory of agency, ritual and materiality, nor into the many layered and thoroughly adaptive nature of *zār* itself. Rather, it concentrates on one object category of the Egyptian *zār*: jewellery at the intersection of collecting, ritual and economics in a diachronic perspective.

As we shall see, there is no such thing as 'the' *zār* in the wide geographical area in which *zār* is practised. *Zār* as practised in Sudan differs from that of Egypt, which differs from the Arabian Peninsula, and so on. In this study, I have focused on Egyptian *zār*.

As I have worked with collected jewellery in a secondary context, the study is undertaken from a supra-regional perspective. This means that I have studied the collected jewellery from Egypt on a national level without making subdivisions into regional styles, the existence of which Hadidi refers to but which I have not been able to observe myself.[30] That same limitation applies to the religious background of the participants; I have not been able to discern explicitly between *zār* jewellery used by Christian or Muslim participants. As Islam is the main religion in Egypt, my main focus is on *zār* in an Islamic context. I have attempted to present the general context of *zār* jewellery, which may possibly serve as starting point for conducting more detailed regional analyses in the future.

---

22 See Behrend & Luig 1999, p. xviii-xx 'Spirit possession as performative ethnography and history 'from below'' for an introduction. Also Motta 2005, p. 298 for an example of an Indian spirit in Brazil, referring to a rebellion leader, and Della Subin 2021 for both *zār* and an introduction into similar phenomena worldwide.
23 Behrend & Luig 1999.
24 Kramer 1987.
25 Lewis et. al. 1991.
26 Megerssa & Kassam 2019.
27 Sengers 2003, p. 105-106; Hadidi 2016, pp. 127-144.
28 As for example elaborated upon by Kenyon 2012, and also noted by Hadidi 2006, Sengers 2003.
29 Goffman 1959.
30 Hadidi 2016, p. 22 indicates a difference in Upper Egyptian and Cairene *zār* amulets. Weeks 1984 also mentions local differences in *zār*.

Within the focus on Egyptian *zār* jewellery, there is a further emphasis on the jewellery with spirit images. This is the only type of jewellery that can with certainty be ascribed to *zār*.

There are also limitations in the sources used. I have not used Arabic sources because of my own inadequacy in this language. That means that all written source material is derived from Western publications and thus, unavoidably, one-sided.[31] I have maintained transliterations of Arabic as I have found them in the literature quoted: a glossary at the end of this study presents a standardized rendering of the most important Arabic words used, following the dictionary by Hans Wehr.

Finally, this artefactual approach revolves around a specific category of the material culture of *zār*: the jewellery used. Obviously, this is not the only material culture present in *zār*: each spirit has its own material demands such as particular perfumes, certain foods and drinks, or specific objects. In addition, musical instruments are used, as are dishes, bowls, and other utilitarian objects. These will also not be discussed in this study, although they will be referred to where needed.

1.1.6 Terminology

I would like to address a few words most often found in publications about *zār*: 'amulet', 'jewellery', and 'cult', and explain how I interpret and use these throughout this study.

The vast majority of publications refer to jewellery with spirit representations as '*zār* amulets'. They are called *ḥijāb* in Egyptian Arabic, often translated as 'amulet' as well.[32] As Garcia Probert has shown in the context of the Tawfiq Canaan-collection of amulets, *ḥijāb* is a generic term covering a variety of amulets, each with their own agency.[33] However, using vocabulary like 'amulets' may influence our understanding of that agency. There are many definitions of what an amulet is expected to do, none of which necessarily align with the functions of *zār* jewellery. I have avoided the use of 'amulets' for jewellery items with spirit images and instead indicate them based on their appearance: pendants with spirit images, bracelets with spirit images, rings with spirit images. Where other authors use the word 'amulet' I have continued that use in quotations or references to their work. In this book, I consider an amulet to be an object believed to contribute to future events that have not yet come to pass. Those can be either bad or good: an amulet may help keep evil, sickness and other negativity at a distance, and it may be directed at obtaining blessings, good health, and other positive things.

The word 'jewellery' itself may also be limiting for our grasp of these objects. Unger, in her multidisciplinary framework for the study of jewellery, presents as definition of jewellery 'a piece of jewellery is an object that is worn on the human body, as a decorative and symbolic addition to its outward appearance'.[34] However, as I will demonstrate in this study, pieces with spirit images, for the most part of their life,

---

31 The work of scholars from the Arab world has of course been used insofar as these publications were accessible and available in English, French, or German, but still many more in Arabic remain. See for an overview for example Natvig 1988.
32 Kriss & Kriss-Heinrich 1962 refer to them as *higab qalb*, 'heart amulet'. Weeks 1984 uses the word *hafessa*.
33 Garcia Probert 2021, p. 55.
34 Unger 2019, p. 18.

were not part of an 'outward' appearance, and their significance goes beyond that of an 'addition' – are they, then, 'jewellery'? Interestingly, a difference between 'jewellery' and 'amulet' is noted in 1955 by Abd er-Rasoul, who writes about the pieces with spirit images: 'They are also symbolically called 'Sigha' (jewelry) because they are made of silver or gold, although they are amulets'.[35] Another role not included in Unger's definition, but one that jewellery in Egypt certainly has as I introduced above, is that of a portable asset. The sample collection consists of items we would indeed recognise as jewellery, such as bracelets, rings, anklets, made of metal (including silver) or beads and visually indistinguishable from regular, i.e. non-*zār*, jewellery. For lack of a better word, I use 'jewellery' throughout this study for all objects designed to be worn on the human body as an addition to dress. These objects, in turn, have their own roles: they may be amulets, but also practical dress accessories such as belts, they are wearable assets, and, of course, they can be embellishments in the aesthetic sense of the word.[36]

And finally, I have chosen to refer to *zār* as 'cult', following Natvig 1987. He defines 'cult' in the sense of a 'small, often local, more loosely organised and more individualistic group'[37] and states that 'cults are often little concerned with doctrine, and belonging to a cult is independent of allegiance to a particular set of doctrines, and does not preclude membership in other kinds of religious groups'.[38] It is precisely this flexibility of *zār* that I wish to emphasise by using the word 'cult'.

1.2 SOURCES: SAMPLE COLLECTION

For this volume I have studied a substantial collection of jewellery items identified as *zār* by their curators and collectors. In this section I will introduce the sample collection and discuss its main challenges. Throughout this book, pieces from the sample collection are referred to as 'sample coll.'.

1.2.1 Challenges in the sample collection: definition and bias

First, how certain can we be that the jewellery in the sample collection is indeed '*zār* jewellery'? After all, what is, and what is not, *zār* jewellery is one of the primary questions this study seeks to answer. The only jewellery items that can unequivocally be ascribed to *zār* are those with spirit images. In the collections that I have studied for this thesis, many other pieces of jewellery were present as well, identified by their collectors as *zār*.[39] I have chosen to include everything without imposing my own ideas of what *zār* jewellery should be.

A complicating factor is that the collection- and publication history, addressed in chapter 3, reveals that most jewellery present in collections today, believed to be *zār*, has been acquired <u>after</u> the two major publications on *zār* jewellery[40] had seen

---

35 'Abd er-Rasoul 1955, p. 7.
36 A personal observation is that the words used for jewellery items may reflect these different roles. I have heard *sīga* or *masāg* for jewellery in general: when called simply *dahab* 'gold' or *fidda* 'silver' this appears to me to be used more in the context of its value, and when an amulet is meant it is called *higāb*.
37 Natvig 1987, p. 670.
38 Natvig 1987, p. 670.
39 I have asked collectors, so people who already obtained jewellery they believe to be *zār*. They may base their opinion on information sellers provided them with, or in later research of their own.
40 Kriss & Kriss-Heinrich 1962 and Bachinger & Schienerl 1984.

Collection	Studied as
Schienerl (Landesmuseum Oldenburg)	In person
Schienerl (Staatliche Kunstsammlungen, Dresden)	In person
Schienerl (Weltmuseum Wien, Vienna)	In person
Blackman (Pitt-Rivers, Oxford)	Photographs
Nationaal Museum Wereldculturen (The Netherlands)	In person
Indiana University Museum (USA)	Photographs
Medelhavsmuseet (Sweden)	In person
Reem Maguid Amin (Egypt)	In person
Beads of Paradise (USA)	Photographs
Giovanni Bonotto (Italy)	In person
Jolanda Bos/Wearable Heritage (The Netherlands)	In person
Rene Cappers (The Netherlands)	In person
Derek Content (UK)	In person
Sarah Corbett (UK)	Photographs
Qilada Foundation – Eric and Marion Crince Le Roy (The Netherlands)	In person
Patricia Deany (USA)	Photographs
Cornelia Demaree (The Netherlands)	In person
Yasmine el Dorghamy (Egypt)	Photographs
Aleksandr Emelyanov	Photographs
Janny Haverhals (The Netherlands)	In person
Marlise Hof (The Netherlands)	Photographs
Karel Innemée (The Netherlands)	In person
Remke Kruk (The Netherlands)	In person
Inge Lagerweij (The Netherlands)	In person
Sylvie Lebars (France)	Photographs
Arna Mendonca Ferreira (Kazakhstan)	Photographs
Jocelyne O'Krent (USA)	Photographs
Sigrid van Roode (The Netherlands)	In person
Savanna Storm Russo (Australia)	Photographs
Nefertari Tadema (The Netherlands)	In person
Tesori Orientali (USA)	Photographs
Vonda Adorno (USA)	Photographs/in person
Sylvia Walters Jenette (USA)	Photographs
Carry Zaghow Offers (Egypt)	Photographs
Anonymous	Photographs

Table 1.1. Composition of the sample collection: collections under study and whether I have studied them in person or through photographs.

the light of day in the 1960s – these collections are therefore inevitably biased, as they have been based on published notions of what *zār* jewellery should look like.[41] This leaves the possibility that jewellery with spirit representations may be present in collections acquired before these publications were released, but not labelled as *zār* because they were not recognised as such. I have reached out to museums with older collections of Egyptian ethnography and requested to see everything they have on Egyptian jewellery, in search of pieces with spirit representations. I have found only three pieces with spirit representations collected before 1960 and not identified as *zār* in museum collections.[42] Table 1.1 shows the collections used for this study.

1.2.2 Composition of the sample collection

The sample collection consists of 1,239 pieces of jewellery identified as *zār* jewellery by their respective owners, within larger collections. Of these, 681 feature spirit images, while 558 do not. These collections include both museum and private holdings. The collection of dr. Peter W. Schienerl and his wife Jutta Schienerl, now housed in the Ethnological Museum in Dresden, the Weltmuseum in Vienna and the Landesmuseum Natur und Mensch in Oldenburg, has been of considerable importance. The Schienerls amassed thousands of objects of popular culture in Egypt during the second half of the 20th century.[43] I had the opportunity to study this collection in person in all three museums. The extensive collection of Dee Birnbaum, currently in the Indiana Museum of Archaeology and Anthropology, was generously offered for study in the form of high-resolution photographs.[44] In addition to the museum collections, many private collectors provided access to their collections. Most of these I studied in person, while collections outside of Europe have been made available to me through photographs. Table 1.1 indicates which collections I examined in person, and for which I had to resort to photographs.

1.2.3 Challenges in the sample collection: dating

As this study aims to be diachronic, dating jewellery items with images of spirits has been of great importance. The dates of these items are based on the hallmarks they carry. Towards the end of the 19th century, silver occasionally bore an Ottoman stamp. The first true hallmarks were introduced in Egypt in 1914.[45] From 1916 onward, a hallmarking system was implemented, marking silver objects with the grade of silver content, the location of the assay office, the official mark for silver, and the year of marking.[46] Although hallmarking may also occur upon selling a previously unmarked piece, this has been attested only a few times in the sample collection.[47] In compliance with the law, most pieces have been hallmarked around the time of

---

41   Theoretically, this also opens the door to new productions of old jewellery to satisfy the demand of collectors. I have not come across such productions, and given the carefully guarded hallmark system in Egypt, I have no reason to suspect otherwise.
42   These will be discussed in chapter 3.
43   See Gerber 2008 for a history of these collections.
44   Many thanks go to dr. Emily Bryant for her help in making these available for this study.
45   Nicklewicz 2016, p. 90. This system was based on the British hallmarking system.
46   Niklewicz 2016, p. 90.
47   These instances are presented and discussed in chapter 5.

their production and sale. The year of marking provides the most precise date, though the applicable range of the hallmarks varies over time. From 1916 onward, hallmarks changed each year, generally halfway through the year, placing the item within the range of two calendar years. After 1949, Egyptian hallmarks were sometimes in use for longer periods, dating the object within the range of several calendar years, generally within 3 to even 7 years. The official mark for silver provides a broader date: before or after 1946. Up until 1946, the official mark for silver took the shape of a cat, and from 1946 onwards a lotus flower has been used. For the purpose of this study, I have referred to the hallmarks chart as included in Niklewicz 2016.[48] One particular mark was not included in Niklewicz 2016, but occurred repeatedly: twelve times on jewellery with spirit representations, fifteen times on other jewellery pieces, and in both cases only in association with a cat stamp, marking it before 1946. I have discussed this particular mark with Danusia Niklewicz of the Hallmark Research Institute, who also was unable to explain this hallmark definitively despite her extensive research into hallmarks.[49]

Of all jewellery items carrying representations of spirits in the sample collection, 120 lack a hallmark. I have dated these on stylistic grounds, based on comparison with dated specimens.[50]

1.2.4 Challenges in the sample collection: size

For this study, I have been dependent on the cooperation of museums and collectors, as I have worked with the jewellery made available to me. That raises the question of the relevance of this dataset from a statistical point of view. The primary data of relevance consists of items with spirit images, which are the only items that can be attributed to *zār* with certainty. To study this dataset over time, items with spirit images also will need to be dated or datable, as discussed above. This narrows the main dataset to dated items with spirit representations. Within this main dataset, a smaller dataset exists that I used to trace reflections of socio-political events and developments in Egypt. When the dataset of dated items with spirit representations had reached 300 pieces, only 3 % were found to be related to specific events. At that point, I have calculated the necessary sample size by zooming in on the desired frequency of jewellery items with spirit representations related to actual events: if the proportion of this particular jewellery is indeed around 3%, how many individuals would the dataset need to confirm this proportion?[51] To calculate the sample size for a confidence interval around a proportion, I have used the following formula:

$$n = \frac{4 Z crit^2 \, p \, (1 - p)}{D^2}$$

---

[48] This is the most recent overview of Egyptian hallmarks, developed in close cooperation with the Cairo Assay Office. Earlier overviews of Egyptian hallmarks such as in Fahmy 2007, also found on hallmarkwiki.com, are less complete.

[49] Email correspondence between May 14, 2018 and May 26th, 2019.

[50] See chapter 5.

[51] Eng 2003. Although this publication is written to calculate sample sizes for radiology study purposes, the underlying principles are the same.

The results of this formula are to be regarded as the estimate of an absolute minimum.[52] The width of the estimated proportion is set at 3%, as has the confidence interval (p). Confidence (z) and statistical significance have been set at 1,96 and 0,05 respectively. This approach resulted in n = 497 dated jewellery items with spirit representations.[53] With a sample of this size, the chance of missing an object with spirit representation related to actual events is 0,025. The number of dated pieces with spirit representations is 561, meeting the absolute minimum criterion.

1.3 SOURCES: LITERATURE

Besides the sample collection, I have based this thesis on written sources. A challenge in this regard is that the best-known publications dealing with jewellery in *zār* have been written with <u>collected</u> jewellery as their starting point, and there are only a few publications that describe jewellery within the ritual itself. I will introduce these publications below. Before I do, I address several parameters against which I have read these publications: discernible bias, gender, authenticity of the events described and descriptive detail.

1.3.1 Parameters

Many of the earlier studies into *zār* display a clear religious or cultural bias. They consist of notes and articles in mission publications and chapters in early anthropological observations on local culture. As the interest in psychological studies increased in the 19th and 20th centuries, *zār* also was noticed as potential research topic. However, it took some time for *zār* to be seen and studied in its own right: early studies mainly relate the trance-stage of *zār* to the, at that time, popular and much researched subject of hysteria in women. In addition, *zār* posed a challenge for Muslim scholars: including it as a topic in the field of mental health implied accrediting the ritual with some form of merit, which was not very desirable from a formal religious viewpoint.[54] So, even though early literature has the advantage of being contemporary with the jewellery under study, the scientific, cultural and social predilections of the period in which it was written need to be taken into account.

To complicate matters further, the majority of anthropological studies published in the first half of the 20th century were written by men. As *zār* was, as it still is, mainly a women's affair, male observers would not have been granted access as easily.[55] The number of eye witness accounts, therefore, is rather limited. In one tantalizing case, an eye witness account by a female attendee was available but deliberately left out of the publication.[56] Following the developments in the western world concerning female

---

52   Eng 2003, p. 312.
53   Using the sample size calculator developed in addition to Eng 2003 http://www.rad.jhmi.edu/jeng/javarad/samplesize/, accessed on August 26th, 2019.
54   See Khouri 2005, p. 119.
55   Macdonald 1911, p. 332-333 for example writes that 'Men are never supposed to see it, and only by the rare chance and possibility of an intelligent woman taking part in it could the knowledge of it come to us in the West'. Kahle 1912 relates on p.5 how a *zār shaykha* did not follow up on his question to explain the *zār* songs to him out of fear, although of what exactly is not mentioned. McPherson vividly describes the consternation caused by his presence outside the room where a *zār* was held in the 1920's in Carman & McPherson 1983, p. 239 ff.
56   Littmann 1950: see below in section 1.4.1.

scholarly independence in the second half of the 20th century, the number of studies by women increased. Access to *zār*, its participants and its officiating women became less difficult and the phenomenon received more, and more thorough, research.

The reports of *zār* events also differ in the method of their execution. Some descriptions are by eyewitnesses, while others have been translated from manuscripts by others. Not all *zār* events described are actual, original *zār* ceremonies: some have been staged for the occasion. Lastly, some reports have been published years to decades after the event they describe, which may affect the accuracy of details presented.

A final challenging factor in compiling the present volume is the apparent lack of descriptive detail in existing literature when it comes to jewellery used in the Egyptian *zār*. Although thousands of jewellery items with spirit images survive to the present day, remarkably little is stated about these in publications on *zār*.[57] It appears to me the focus of the studies often lies with elements that are notably different from the cultural background of the observer: much is written about the trance, the sacrificing of animals and the use of blood, the rhythms drummed and the spirits invoked. If at all mentioned, jewellery is treated in passing, almost as a given factor, nothing exquisitely exotic or to get too excited about. None of the publications studied for this volume provide clear statements about how, where and when this jewellery was acquired, how it was used during and after an Egyptian *zār* and what its role in the broader scenery of the *zār* world is.

1.3.2 Written sources combining jewellery and *zār*
The focus of this research is the use of jewellery, and so my starting point, has been those publications that include jewellery.

Klunzinger 1878
Written by a male quarantine doctor and biologist stationed in Quseir between 1863 and 1875, this work is included in a larger publication on Upper Egypt and the Red Sea. The publication is based on his experiences in Egypt during his stay. Klunzinger devotes two pages to *zār*, here spelled as *Sâr*. The report is remarkably neutral in its wording (even though it is part of the chapter on superstition, and other passages in the book evidence bias towards superstition over science) and describes the various stages of *zār*. The jewellery is noticed as well, with some attention for detail. The second edition of publication appeared in 1878, three years after his sojourn in Egypt ended. As his publication spans over a decade of observations during the formative stages of *zār*, it is a valuable resource for these early *zār* varieties.

Le Brun 1902
This early publication by a female author, operating under the *nom de plume* Niya Salima, this book sheds light on *zār* as practised at the end of the 19th/beginning of the 20th century. The author attended two ceremonies and surrounds her report with observations on the importance and beliefs attached to *zār* by its participants. It is unclear in which particular year the events took place, as the publication carries the

---

[57] An exception is Littmann 1950, who provides two manuscripts in German translation about *zār* with notes about all details the original writer, Mahmud Sidqi, included, and annotations of his own.

form of letters in style only: none of them are dated, and they are to be regarded as general letters for a non-specific audience. At the beginning of the letters describing *zār*, she clearly conveys her opinion that the idea of possession is preposterous, but the sincerity with which one of her servants regards *zār* and the jewellery she wears as a result convinces her that, at least to the participants, there is meaning in both the ritual and the objects connected with it.

Kahle 1912

Written by a male author who is convinced that accounts on *zār* by 'Orientals' cannot be taken at face value[58], and that it is very difficult to obtain a reliable account of *zār*. In order to provide such an account, he himself sought and found sources that were reliable to him. This publication offers two accounts of a *zār* and some background information based on other literature. The first is written down by the author himself in Luxor, where a *zār shaykha* and a *zār shaykh* invited him to a performance that was arranged just for him. To show him what a *zār* looked like, they had even gone through the trouble of arranging a man that represented the audience. Technically this would be an eyewitness account, but of a staged event.

The second is a translation by the author of a manuscript produced by an Egyptian friend, who had, at the request of Kahle, found a *shaykha* willing to walk him through him the proceedings. This is not an eyewitness account, nor a description from an authentic event. Oddly enough, the author mentions having visited an authentic *zār* after quite some trouble, but does not include an account of this in his publication.

Thompson & Franke 1913

An article by two female authors associated with the Christian mission in Cairo. The first half of the article is by Thompson, who attended various *zār* events in Coptic homes, but these are not discussed. She describes a *zār* in a Muslim home as an eyewitness account, in which jewellery also is described.

The second part of the article is by Franke. Here, her Christian point of view is more present than in Thompson 1913 and serves as the main reason to describe *zār*, so that missionaries may better understand Egyptian women in order to help them to 'open the blind eyes'.[59] The author presents a literature study of *zār*, including eyewitness accounts of others, but not of herself.

Blackman 1927

Written by a female author, based upon her research and personal experiences among the rural population in Upper Egypt during the 1920s and included in her book on the same topic. *Zār* is presented in the chapter dealing with magic and magicians. Interestingly, she discerns two different ways of treating spirit possession: closely related, but carrying different names. From the text, it is clear the author has witnessed several *zārs*. The proceedings as well as costume and jewellery are described in general. One photograph of beaded *zār* jewellery is included. Only in the last sentence of the

---

58   Kahle 1912, p. 1.
59   Thompson & Franke 1913, p. 289, quoting the Bible.

chapter does her ambivalence show, upon remarking that 'officials are quite rightly trying to put an end to the holding of the *zār*'.[60]

Winkler 1936

Written by a male author in his endeavour to document Egyptian customs. The author set out with a systematic approach to ask the same questions on a given topic in villages throughout the country. *Zār* is mentioned briefly, but because of his systematic enquiries, this is the only publication detailing where *zār* was, and was not, practised at the time of this field research. Winkler has not observed a *zār* himself, but notes on jewellery that the possessing spirit demands 'any one piece of jewellery', without further specification.[61]

Littmann 1950

Written by a male author, this publication presents two translated texts by another male, Egyptian author named Mahmud Sidqi. The first text dates back to 1911, the second from 1930. Both were compiled and published together in 1950, accompanied by remarks from Littmann. The 1930 text, forwarded to Littmann by another professor, includes an eyewitness account of a *zār* by the professor's wife along with three photographs of costumes, that, unfortunately, were not published.[62] The texts provide a detailed description of jewellery in great detail and are valuable for understanding of jewellery of their respective timeframes, although it remains unclear whether these are eyewitness accounts or general descriptions.

'Abd er-Rasoul 1955

Written by a female author with a clear disapproval of *zār*. She labels it as superstition, primarily adhered to by uneducated people in the country and artisans' wives in towns. She also notes the practice is certainly not nationwide. According to her, the ceremony itself is merely for fun or to enjoy presents from friends. She then goes on to describe a *zār* ceremony in some detail and is the first to mention jewellery items with spirit images. From her account, it does not become clear whether she describes an event to which she has been privy herself.

Kriss & Kriss-Heinrich 1962

Written by two male authors with the purpose of documenting folk beliefs and rituals in Egypt from an anthropological perspective. They had a *zār* organised for themselves in 1957, feigning illness that was most likely due to spirit possession. It is, however, unclear whether this event is to be regarded as representative for a *zār* during the 1950s: not only was the patient male, but also a foreigner, a Christian and wielding a considerable research budget. The publication includes a detailed account of jewellery used, published in 1962. This *zār* was held on the property of the family

---

60   Blackman 1927, p. 200.
61   Winkler 1936, p. 237 '*irgendein Schmuckstück*'- the spirit may want just about anything.
62   This was Dr Franz Taeschner. I have traced the manuscript of his wife to the collection of the Universitätsarchiv Munster, but under German law it could not be accessed until 1-1-2024: this book was finished before that date. The photographs are not with the manuscript and their current location is unknown. Personal communication via email Dr. Sabina Happ, January 24th 2019.

of the same 'Abd el-Rasoul who published the 1955 article. She was instrumental in organising the event: given her own opinion regarding *zār*, this makes the authenticity of this occurrence even more questionable.

Kennedy 1967

Written by a male author from the perspective of neuropsychiatry, this report is based on eye witness accounts of four informants in Nubia (Upper Egypt) and fieldwork carried out between 1963 and 1965. The general proceedings of *zār* are described, after which attention is focused on psychological afflictions for which *zār* offers relief. Even though this research is carried out from a more medical point of view, and jewellery is only mentioned in passing, the report does offer insight in *zār* practices in the 1960s in Upper Egypt.

Fakhoury 1968 and 1972

Written by a male author, the report from 1968 describes a weekly public *zār* at the shrine of Sheikh Mahfouz in Kafr el-Elow, followed by two cases of a private *zār*. The time of the events in relation to publication is unclear. Equally unclear is whether the observations are eye witness accounts or related by the *zār* specialist. The description of the public *zār* mentions the wearing of silver jewellery, but as specific for one particular spirit. The two cases of a private *zār* do include jewellery as necessary items in both cases, but in a different light. They relate the story of the mother of a possessed woman who consulted a male *zār* specialist, and that of a granddaughter of another woman. Both were advised to buy specific jewellery items for the respective patients. In this publication, *zār* jewellery is bought upon the advice of a *zār* specialist, but not used in a ceremony. The function of this jewellery was not to please spirits or fulfil their demands, but to keep them away. In this regard, the nature of these jewellery items comes closer to that of an amulet. The author does include the explanation given by the *zār* specialist in Kafr el-Elow of the, in his observation, declining popularity of *zār*.[63] In this respect the publication is useful for the change in use of jewellery in *zār* itself, and certainly for a glimpse of the way the practice is regarded.

These two instances are repeated in the 1972 publication, where *zār* is presented in the chapter on practices associated with Islam.[64] Here, the author discusses the general structure of both a public and private *zār*. Of jewellery, he notes that this may be part of the specific demands of each possessing spirit, alongside particular clothing, food and drink.[65]

El-Adly 1984

Written by a male author, this publication relates a *zār* the author attended seven years earlier in 1977. He presents general information about the proceedings, but in a more catalogue-style of reporting than describing a specific event. The author lists

---

63   This is the only clear reference in the publication, on p.55: 'the *zār* practitioner told the writer' Whether the two case studies are also relayed by the specialist or witnessed first-hand, is unclear. In the following publication Fakhouri 1972, p. 94-95, it becomes evident that the specialist shared the histories of the two case studies with the author.
64   Fakhouri 1972, pp. 92-95.
65   Fakhouri 1972, p. 94.

groups and families of *zār* spirits and presents a section called 'Amulets of the *zār*'. Alongside a short passage on men attending a *zār* to indulge in homosexual behaviour, this does seem to point to the presence of a certain bias. The jewellery items pictured and described in his work are much older than 1977. All of them are accompanied by a short description and where possible, an attempt to explain their meaning. In this publication, the transition from descriptive eye witness accounts of events where jewellery is actively used to cataloguing and explaining objects that are disappearing is visible.

A final and special mention has to made of Joseph McPherson, an Englishman living in Egypt from 1901 to his death in early 1946. A selection of the letters to his family were published in 1983 by a relative. McPherson had a keen interest in Egyptian popular beliefs and as such wanted to attend a *zār*. In 1920, an opportunity presented itself when he came across a *zār* in progress, which was greatly disturbed by his presence when he was caught watching the proceedings from an adjoining room. Eventually a compromise was reached, in which his presence was tolerated only if he sat with his back towards the company of ladies participating in the ritual. As curiosity got the better of him, he was able to describe glimpses of what went on, including one tantalizing sentence in which he observed how 'the women in their Bacchanalian frenzy were pulling from their bosoms, and holding carefully concealed in their hands as they danced, some little objects which I in vain tried to get an adequate glimpse of.'[66]

Since the 1980s publications concentrating on jewellery also include *zār* jewellery. The work of Bachinger & Schienerl, published in 1984, presents jewellery with spirit representations in the form of a catalogue. The article series by Weeks, published in *Cairo Today* in the 1980s, is a detailed exploration into what was offered as *zār* jewellery in the 1980s and as such a valuable source, even if not academic.[67] A more recent study is that of Darmody, who wrote her M.A.-thesis in 2001 on a collection of 200 pieces with spirit representations.[68] Jewellery with spirit representations also features in the book by Bonotto, published in 2010.[69] This book centres around jewellery and amulets in Egypt, and contains a chapter about *zār* jewellery with a short description of the ritual as it is carried out in Sudan, and a *zār* the author himself attended in Cairo in 1992.

1.3.3 Discussion

As this short introduction shows, not all sources can be used with an equal amount of credibility in all instances. Two publications stand out for their descriptive detail of jewellery: the work of Littman (1950) and Kriss & Kriss-Heinrich (1962). Of these, the publication of Kriss & Kriss-Heinrich is most often used as basis for identifying jewellery as connected to *zār*. The success and impact of this publication might be explained because it includes many other forms of popular beliefs in the Islamic world, illustrated with lots of photographs. Their work is an alluring account of folk beliefs

---

66   Carman & McPherson 1983, p. 245.
67   Weeks 1983-1986.
68   Darmody 2001.
69   Bonotto 2010.

encountered in places such as Turkey, Syria and Egypt and is still a very valuable source in terms of documentation of the materiality of informal rituals. Unfortunately, this source proves to be somewhat problematic when it comes to *zār*. Two foreign Christian men with a budget had a *zār* organised upon request, by someone who according to her own publication thought of the practice as superstitious tradition for the ignorant and a form of entertainment for, presumably, the better educated. As stated above, the authenticity of this event cannot be taken at face value.

The other source with a high degree of descriptive detail is Littmann. His publication is eclipsed by the work of Kriss & Kriss-Heinrich, even though it was published only 12 years earlier. Instead of an illustrated compendium of amulets and talismans, the publication of Littman is an annotated translation of two texts. The texts themselves stem from 1911 and 1930 respectively, and are therefore illustrative of two timeframes in the history of the Egyptian *zār*.

All the aforementioned publications offer insights in the proceedings of *zār* and the use of jewellery to varying extents, and can be used mindful of their authors' bias and temporal background.

1.4 STRUCTURE OF THIS THESIS

In search of understanding what *zār* jewellery is and does, this thesis will take us from storerooms in European museums and the *sūqs* of Cairo, and from the world of everyday spirit engagement in Egypt to Sudan, Ethiopia, Nigeria and further afield.

I start my exploration into the world of *zār* jewellery with an introduction of the background of *zār* itself: its origins, rapid popularity in Egypt, and the initial insights into the ritual provided by the examination of jewellery.

Chapter 3, 'Collected Objects', zooms in on the collection and publication history of *zār* jewellery. The assembly of objects forming the basis for this study is the result of collecting. The choice of objects to collect reflects, among other things, the preferences and economic limitations of the collector, the timeframe of collecting and the available knowledge at that time. This exploration into collected materiality is inherently a study in mediation. Before attempting to understand *zār* jewellery, this process needs to be unravelled first: how do we know what we think we know about these objects? How did various collectors identify *zār* jewellery throughout the decades of collecting, and how has that influenced our current perception? To unpick this puzzle, I will first trace the information with regard to *zār* jewellery that has been published over the course of the last century. Next, I will intertwine this with the collection history of these items: when did these appear on the market? This dual investigation aims to enhance our comprehension of how *zār* jewellery transformed into a decontextualised group of material culture.

Chapter 4, 'Living Objects', approaches the life of *zār* jewellery before it became the topic of publications and collections. Examining both the purpose-made jewellery and the use of bricolage, I contextualise *zār* withing the broader framework of African possession religions, and a way of dealing with spirits within the larger Egyptian landscape of spirit things. I propose a definition of *zār* jewellery and explore its various roles within the ritual. But there was more to jewellery in a woman's life than *zār*. There is an entire life of marriage negotiations, economic pitfalls and social dynamics where jewellery, in general, played a pivotal role. This inquiry extends to understanding how *zār* jewellery interconnects with the broader spectrum of a woman's life: how did *zār* jewellery fit in her world?

Chapter 5, 'Historic Objects', moves from the significance of *zār* jewellery on a personal level to its capacity as a historic source on a community level. As in many African possession cults, *zār* itself operates as a mechanism for collective memory, employing oral tradition and performance for its transmission. The way *zār* stores and transmits collective memory however is not to be confused with a form of permanent record-keeping: rather, it expresses a collective identity shaped by historic events. But only in Egypt does this collective memory assume material form in the jewellery with spirit images. Concentrating on these images, I will explore their potential to divulge views on Egyptian history and life in the early 20th century as experienced and expressed by women.

Chapter 6, 'The world of *zār*', paints a picture of the changing world these jewellery items belong to and traces the developments that led to their disappearance as well as their origin.

Chapter 7 presents the conclusions of this thesis, followed by an appendix of a case study in the cost of *zār*, a glossary of terms, and a bibliography.

Finally, the catalogue presents a selection of *zār* jewellery pieces from the sample collection. Where pieces from the sample collection are included in the catalogue, I refer to these as 'cat.no. in the catalogue'.

2

SPIRITS AND WOMEN IN EGYPT

2.1 ORIGINS AND DISSEMINATION OF *ZĀR*

The history of *zār* can with certainty be traced back almost a century and a half ago. This section introduces a short history of *zār* and clarifies how the framework of existing practices of spirit engagement, in combination with geopolitical developments, enabled its spread in Egypt.

2.1.1 An African phenomenon

Zār exists in a large geographical area, encompassing Ethiopia[70], Somalia[71], Djibouti[72], northern Sudan[73], Egypt[74], the Arab Peninsula[75], Kuwait and Israel[76], southern Iran[77] and Iraq[78]. Beyond this core region, it occurs possibly even in Pakistan[79] and the south of Algeria.[80] With more recent large-scale emigration to the West, *zār* has also established itself in the western world.[81] Significantly, it's not just the Muslim, but also the Christian and Jewish population who practice *zār*.[82] As there are no mentions of *zār*, or rituals and ceremonies that resemble *zār*, anywhere in the Middle East before 1839,[83] this points to a belief in possession that is not indigenous to any of the

---

70   Boddy 1989, p. 131; Mijanji 2015, p. 225; Hadidi 2016, p.4.
71   Boddy 1989, p. 13; Mijanji 2015, p. 225. Both authors mention that in Somalia, the phenomenon is called *sar*. el-Hadidi 2016, p.4.
72   Hadidi 2016, p. 4.
73   Boddy 1989, p. 131; Mijanji 2015, p. 225; Hadidi 2016, p. 4.
74   Boddy 1989, p. 131; Sengers 2003; Hadidi 2006.
75   Boddy 1989, p.131; el-Hadidi 2016, p. 5 mentions various locations in Yemen, as well as Mecca, as locations where the *zār* was reported.
76   Mianji 2015, p. 225; Edelstein 2002; Witztum 1996.
77   Boddy 1989, p. 131, Mijanji 2015, p. 225.
78   Hadidi 2016, p. 5.
79   Hadidi 2016, p. 5.
80   Boddy 1989, p. 132. It lies within reason that *zār* is also practised in countries like Libya and Afghanistan, due to their proximity to countries where *zār* is known to occur, but no firm evidence has come to my attention.
81   Boddy 1994.
82   Boddy 1989, p. 132-133; Edelstein 2002 adds that Ethiopian Jews who migrated to Israel hoped to be free of the influence of *zār* spirits in their new country. Loewenthal 2012 mentions the same expectation. Thompson 1913, p. 275 notes that she has been offered 'the opportunity to see something of this practice, both in Coptic and Moslem homes'.
83   Natvig 1987, p. 672, also Macdonald 1911, p. 330.

three monotheistic religions: it is originally an African cult.[84] In that respect, *zār* as it is practised in Egypt is one leaf on a complex family tree, a notion I will return to in chapter 4.

For the Egyptian *zār*, several indicators point to the origin of one of its main components in current-day Ethiopia. The word *zār* itself is one of these indicators, as it is generally accepted to be a Cushitic loanword in Amharic, one of the languages spoken in Ethiopia, meaning 'genius, evil spirit, demon'.[85] The Cushitic sky-god was called *jār*, a name that survived as a local word for 'god' and 'sky', and changed into a demon of sorts when Christianity became the main religion in Ethiopia.[86] But there is more than just linguistics to the origin of *zār*. *Zār* came to Egypt with the arrival of actual people. These people were enslaved women of colour, whose origin is mentioned as 'Abyssinians'.[87] Natvig pinpoints the origin of these enslaved women of colour more precisely to the Oromo.[88] Known as 'Galla' to the Western world and often shared under 'Abyssinians' as well,[89] the Oromo faced increasing occupation by the predominantly Christian Amhara during the 18th and 19th century, resulting in the conquest of their territories by Menelik II[90]. *Zār* in Egypt is shaped by this cultural background, and I will turn to this in chapters 4 and 5.

2.1.2 Taking the world by storm: the rapid spread of *zār*

The earliest description of a ritual that resembles a *zār*-ritual, believed to be an early version thereof, is a report by two missionaries who witnessed it in current-day Ethiopia in 1839.[91] Mentions of spirits called *zār*, so without the context of ritual, are even older, appearing in a travel journal from Tigray province, written in 1838[92], and possibly in 19th century prayer scrolls, again from current-day Ethiopia.[93] From there, *zār* spread through the Middle East, northward through the Nile Valley and southward over sea through Zanzibar, onwards to Oman and further east.[94]

Illustrating the northward spread through Egypt is the sequence of reports on *zār*. The earliest mention of *zār* in Egypt stems from 1869, when the terminally ill Lucie Duff Gordon writes from Aswan to her husband: 'Ask any learned pundit to explain to

---

84 As put forward in the works by Richard Natvig, also Kramer 1987; Lewis et al. 1991; Behrend & Luig 1999.
85 Nöldeke 1890, p. 701. The author is not certain about the origin of the word and suggests it may also be related to a word in Ge'ez, meaning 'to turn, to encompass'. Littman 1950, p. 46 also points to Amharic as the source language for the word *zār*.
86 See Natvig 1987 for a discussion and more elaborate sources on this interesting train of thought. The practice of an ancient deity living on in a new role is seen all over the world. Al-Masih 2008, p. 78 also presents the name of Cushitic god as the origin for the word *zār*. Megerssa & Kassam 2021 pp. 128-129 point out that this Christianisation came about through violence.
87 Le Brun 1902, p. 255, Macdonald 1911, p. 332, Winkler 1936, p. 237. See chapter 8.
88 Natvig 1987, p. 685-688.
89 Natvig 1987, p. 685; Megerssa & Kassam 2019, p. 22-25.
90 Natvig 1987, p. 687, Megerssa & Kassam 2019 p. 3, 9-10.
91 This consists of a certain event witnessed by two missionaries, who subsequently made mention of it in both their publications. It involved a woman who wanted 'to expel bad spirits which…would inflict her with sickness'. These spirits were called Sarotsh (pl), or Sar (sg). See Natvig 1987, p. 678-683 for the whole story.
92 Tubiana 1991, p. 19.
93 Natvig 1987, p. 676-677.
94 See Mijanji 2015, p. 228 for a description of the slave trade to Iran.

you the *Zar* – it is really curious'.⁹⁵ In 1878, the German quarantine doctor Klunzinger, based in Quseir on the Red Sea coast, observed that women, notably in Upper Egypt, had adopted a practice called *sār* which was introduced by Abyssinian female slaves.⁹⁶ These 19th-century accounts both originate from Upper Egypt; no later than 1902, the practice was known in Cairo, although the emphasis remained for at least a decade on the south of Egypt.⁹⁷

The rapid spread of *zār* has baffled earlier scholars, both contemporary and later. Macdonald, who wrote in 1911, observed for example that the practice had disseminated throughout the Muslim world 'in a comparatively short period of years, quite easily within thirty years, I should say' and that no mention of it was to be found with older travellers such as Lane and Burton⁹⁸ – apparently gaining momentum since the 1880s.⁹⁹ I propose two main factors for this swift dissemination in Egypt. First, *zār* in Egypt leveraged existing beliefs in spirit engagement. Second, the late 19th century witnessed significant geopolitical changes instigated by Muhammad Ali, resulting in an influx of people, and along with them, their customs and religions through Sudan from further south. I will introduce both factors next.

Spirit engagement in Egypt

Although *zār* was new to Egypt, the concept of spirit possession was not: this was firmly rooted in everyday life and had been for a considerable time. From a guideline banning possessed persons from attending a religious festival, it would appear that possession already occurred in ancient Egypt.¹⁰⁰ Ancient Egyptians regarded tombs and cemeteries as suitable locations to consult the spirits of the dead,¹⁰¹ and medical texts provide incantations to exorcise demons that cause certain illnesses.¹⁰² The notion of possession has long been unfamiliar to Western Egyptologists: it is quite possible that spirit possession is present in the many magical spells and incantations that survive from ancient Egypt, but has not been recognised as such.¹⁰³

In Late Antiquity, people would continue to visit shrines and tombs, but now those of Christian martyrs. The visitors hoped to experience spirit possession and, in

---

95   Duff Gordon 1902, Letters from Egypt p. 380. She would die the same year. Natvig 2010 renders the spelling in her letter as *Sar* and Waterfield 1937 as *Zarh*: I have chosen to use the spelling from the 1902 edition of her Letters from Egypt. Mörike 2021, p. 35 introduces a first mention for Egypt in 1886 by Emily Ruete Salma bint Said, referring to her memoirs: I have only been able to find the treatment of possession in Zanzibar (Ruete 1886, pp. 181-182).
96   Klunzinger 1878, p. 388, also related by Natvig 1987, p. 671 and again in Natvig 2010, p. 24-25.
97   Le Brun 1902. In 1911, Sidqi wrote that *zār* was taught to his interviewees by Copts from Upper Egypt, Littmann 1950, p. 1. Kahle stated that *zār* was more widespread the further south one traveled in Egypt, Kahle 1912, p. 6. Winkler 1936, p. 237 also mentions a southern origin for *zār*.
98   Macdonald 1911, p. 330.
99   Zwemer 1920, p. 240 writes that *zār* spread fast between 1870 and 1880 in Upper Egypt.
100 Sauneron 1960, p. 111-115.
101 Raven 2012, p. 127.
102 See for example Beck 2018, translating spells referring to an Asiatic illness-demon. In Borghouts 1978, spells 144, 66, 65, 54 may contain notions of spirit possession as well.
103 As argued by Derchain 2008. Derchain also suggests the *rh.t* or 'wise woman' known from ancient Egyptian texts might be comparable to the women in the Egyptian *zār* known today (p. 18), and that it is in this realm that the study of ancient Egypt might find more evidence of a practice known all over Africa. Many thanks go to dr. Rita Lucarelli of Berkeley University for taking the time to discuss this topic with me.

this manner, gather knowledge about the future and other hidden things.[104] Similar to later forms of spirit possession, these spirits were ambiguous and the practice existed on the fringes of formal religion.[105]

During the Middle Ages, the habit of visiting tombs continued.[106] People visited cemeteries to enter requests with the dead, for whom they left offerings and gifts. Women, in particular, visited tombs to pray for children.[107] This tradition persisted during the centuries of Ottoman rule.[108]

In the 19th century, Lane reports how belief in spirits permeated everyday life.[109] Blackman describes how the rural population ascribed diseases and mental afflictions, as well as phenomena such as nightmares and sleepwalking, to spirit possession.[110] Village 'magicians' relied upon the powers of the spirit that possessed them to cure ailments,[111] and at least three different ways of dealing with spirit possession existed side by side in the 1920s. I will revisit this later in this chapter and will now discuss the second factor in the fast spread of the *zār* in Egypt: the geopolitical changes set in motion by Muhammad Ali and continued by his successors.

A changing world

After the French army left Egypt in 1800, the Turkish sultan attempted to reclaim Egypt for the vast Ottoman Empire. For centuries Mamluks who nominally acknowledged the supremacy of the Ottoman sultan had ruled Egypt, resulting in an impoverished and depleted country. The sultan dispatched a young and ambitious officer, Muhammad Ali, to bring Egypt back into the imperial fold. Muhammad Ali embarked on a grand scale modernisation, based on European examples.[112] Instead of fully reintegrating into the Ottoman Empire, Egypt became Muhammad Ali's domain, and he successfully secured and expanded his control over this corner of the Empire.

Muhammad Ali modernized the army based on the French model, and significantly expanded it using forced conscription.[113] As a result, it quadrupled in size compared to its predecessors.[114] In 1822 he conquered Sudan, and then set out to add even more territory to Egypt. It is important to realise that precisely when *zār* was presumably taking the shape we would recognise today, Muhammad Ali effectively united

---

104 Frankfurter 2010, p. 31-33.
105 Frankfurter 2010, p. 36.
106 Shoshan 1993, p. 69 mentions that 'as early as 865, the prefect of Fustat forbade women to continue their custom of visiting graves' in the context of seeking intercession of the interred. The practice continued to be forbidden over and over again, but continued anyway (p. 69). As Shoshan writes on p. 68, medieval scholar Ibn Taymiyya (1263-1328) wrote a treatise 'On the Visitation of Graves', which condemned this practice. As late as 1979, the tombs of saints were 'some of the most significant elements that structure the feminine geography of Cairo', according to Madoeuf 2006, p. 476.
107 Shoshan 1993, p. 22, 68 and note 160.
108 Winter 1992, p. 98-102.
109 Lane 1842, p. 222.
110 Blackman 1927, p. 227-239.
111 Blackman 1927, p. 184-185.
112 Muhammad Ali restructured government, began draining the swampy parts of Cairo by digging canals, and rapidly expanded the cotton export. Descriptions of his endeavours can be found for example in Fahmy 2003 and İhsanoğlu 2012.
113 Cuno 2010, p. 81; Fahmy 2003, pp. 76-111 presents the expansion of the army and the consequences of forced conscription in detail.
114 Mitchell 1991, p. x.

Sudan and Egypt. This not only created a corridor, but also established the political circumstances for *zār* to spread northward.

The newly formed army played in important role in disseminating *zār*, as argued by Constantinides.[115] Muhammad Ali took control of the Nile slave trade in Sudan, redirecting it northward towards Aswan and from there further on into Egypt, instead of its previous route southwards towards the Funj sultanate.[116] From the 1860s onwards, during the development plans of the Khedive Ismail, there was a continuous demand for personnel with the growing elite in the main cities. The slave trade with Sudan was intense during the 1860s and formally lasted until 1877.[117] Servants and slaves from the south of Egypt and Sudan travelled northward in greater numbers and at a much higher pace than ever before, facilitated by the rapidly improving infrastructure connecting the capital with other cities. Additionally, also army contingents consisted of Nubians, traveling with their families to Egypt.[118]

Both existing belief in spirit possession and a rapidly changing world not only facilitated the spread of *zār*, but also had a profound formative effect on it. For example, the military presence in Egypt created by Muhammad Ali had a lasting impact: officers are the second largest group of spirits depicted on *zār* jewellery. Egyptian *zār* jewellery records more historic realities, which I will present in chapter 5. *Zār* also assimilated existing practices regarding spirit possession and spirit engagement. I will explore these and their influence on *zār* in the next section.

2.2 SPIRIT ENGAGEMENT AND THE WORLD OF WOMEN

Underlying the concept of spirit possession is the firm belief in the existence of jinn. We should discern between the attitude towards spirits in official and informal practices. Jinn, as these beings are called in the Qur'an, form part of creation akin to humans and angels.[119] While in official Islam their place and role in creation have been charted, studied and clarified, in informal practices their role is much more diffuse.[120] Throughout the period under study in this thesis, Egyptians accepted interaction between the visible and invisible world widely as a fact of life.[121]

Associated with this interaction is a diverse array of amulets, which may also take the form of jewellery. These jewellery items are also present and identified as *zār* in the sample collection, alongside pieces with spirit images, which have been purpose-made for *zār*. I believe this presence is not the result of faulty identification of jewellery by their collectors and curators; there are simply too many, and they share similar characteristics.[122] What all of them have in common, is that they are worn by women

---

115 Discussed in Kenyon 2012, p. 5.
116 Kenyon 2012, p. 29-31.
117 Cuno 2010, p. 104.
118 In the Baedeker travel guide from 1902, the presence of slaves is still presented as normal, although the guide mentions it would likely be abolished soon. On pages XLIII and XLIV the various ethnic groups in Egypt at that time are presented, including the army contingents of Nubians.
119 McDonald et al, Djinn in Encyclopaedia of Islam, accessed February 23, 2023.
120 McDonald et al, Djinn in Encyclopaedia of Islam, accessed February 23, 2023.
121 Drieskens 2008, wonderfully titled 'Living with Djinns', presents an overview of recent belief in jinn, Blackman 1927 presents the same for the first decades of the 20th century, and Lane 1842 for the beginning of the period under study.
122 Kriss & Kriss-Heinrich 1962 mention specific jewellery associated with other traditions in *zār* as well.

and served to protect them from spirits. In that respect they function as amulets. This protection is achieved by selecting materials, shapes, colours, decoration and texts believed to advance this purpose.

The use of the colours red and blue, as well as small globular dangles (*jalājil*) is abundant, as is the use of pendants with the name of God or verses of the Qur'an. A specific choice of material is iron, worn as anklets to ward off the Qarina or one's own *qarin*.[123] But who are these spirits? Why are there so many amulets in the sample collection? And what is it that women in particular needed protection from – and how does that relate to *zār*?

To understand the inclusion of amulets in the sample collection, I will broaden the scope beyond spirit possession to examine spirit engagement in general. Following this exploration of the dynamics of dealing with the invisible, I will then introduce the key traditional beliefs for women associated with these jewellery items.

2.2.1 Understanding the spirit world

Central to our understanding of the spirit world must be the concept of *multiplicity of approaches*.[124] This entails that multiple, sometimes even mutually exclusive versions of a phenomenon can be simultaneously valid. Multiplicity of approaches is rooted in context-related interpretations and is therefore contrary to absolute and final coherency. For example, I can be described truthfully both as close friend and as complete stranger: even when these concepts are contradictory at first glance, they are valid in the specific context the narrator has encountered me in. Although the concept of multiplicity of approaches was developed in relation to the religion of ancient Egypt, its emphasis on context-related interpretation is superbly applicable to the spirit world in modern Egypt as well. Here, tales of spirit encounters are numerous and vary considerably. As Drieskens has shown, a single incident with a spirit encounter may be described differently when told on different occasions. The variation in the story depends on the context of participants as well as the purpose of telling this particular story at that particular moment: these changing approaches and contexts of a spirit encounter are not a case of bad memory, but serve to construct meaning in everyday life.[125]

Egyptian popular tradition throughout the study period is replete with additional beliefs concerning jinn. Egyptians believe them to dwell in unclean places such as ruins and toilets, in liminal spaces such as under doorsteps or on crossroads, under the earth (hence they also call them *taḥtaniyyīn*, the people below) and in places such as wells, rivers, caves and the desert.[126] Spirits are assumed to have the power of transformation and can appear in the form of cats, dogs, snakes and other animals, but also as human beings.[127] As spirits are either invisible or disguised as something or someone else, this

---

123 Iron is known to ward off *jinn*, see for example Wickett 2010, p. 70, where iron was used to protect against *kabsa*. Lane 1842, p. 338 on jinn and iron, Blackman 1926, p. 168 and Kriss & Kriss-Heinrich 1962, p. 149 on the use of iron anklets.
124 Frankfort 1948, p. 4 and 18.
125 Drieskens 2008.
126 Lane 1842, p. 337, Blackman 1927, p. 227-228, Drieskens 2008, pp. 216-218. See also Sengers 2003, p. 38.
127 Lane 1842, p. 336 and 339-341, Drieskens 2008, p. 97, 172; also McDonald et al, Djinn in Encyclopaedia of Islam, accessed February 23, 2023.

poses somewhat of a problem for humans: you never know for sure if you are in the presence of a spirit. Add to that that spirits are easily offended, and disaster is just waiting to happen. This has led to a myriad of ways to avoid offending a spirit. It is for example customary to utter a formal greeting even when entering an empty room and activities like walking through dark alleys or entering bathrooms or toilets require speaking protective formulas to protect oneself from possibly present spirits.[128]

This continuous awareness of the possible but uncertain presence of spirits permeates everyday life of both men and women. This can be positive, but also negative: both can marry them and have children with them, but also be harmed or possessed by them.[129] For women in particular, spirits constitute a serious threat: they may afflict their possibilities to get married or have children.

2.2.2 Spirit influence in the world of women: fertility, marriage, and childbirth

Having children, and notably boys, is of the utmost importance. The existence of a son to pray for his parents after their death is essential.[130] Obviously, impotence on the part of the man can be equally to blame if a marriage remains childless, but this possibility is only looked into after the woman has explored all available options to get pregnant.[131] Fertility is such a central theme in a woman's life that it even features prominently in funerary laments for women.[132] Being a mother cements a woman's social position and ensures her the respect a mother is due.[133] Infertility, on the other hand, could lead to divorce, with all its social and financial consequences.[134] It is in this context of fertility and reproduction that we should understand the interaction with spirits in the female domain and its accompanying material culture in the form of jewellery.

Spirits are an important factor in traditions and rituals surrounding fertility, marriage, childbirth and motherhood, in short, during all major life transitions. In all of these cases, the goal is averting spirit engagement as much as possible, or reversing unwanted situations caused by spirits. A jealous, love-struck or hurt spirit may harm chances at finding a husband or becoming a mother, careless behaviour on the part of the woman may lead to possession or obstruction of her ability to conceive. Women will, therefore, go through great lengths to assure a pregnancy, involving remedies thought to be helpful (both medical and supernatural[135]) and avoiding situations that could lead to infertility or miscarriage.

---

128 Lane 1842, p. 337; Blackman 1927, p. 229; Drieskens 2008, p. 89; also my own experience in Egypt.
129 Blackman 1927, p. 177 writes 'It is a well-known belief that a man can marry and have children by an 'afrīta' – an afrīt is a spirit. Drieskens 2008, p. 170-173 recounts a case of human-jinn marriage as well as possession cases.
130 Hansen 2006, p. 140.
131 Hansen 2006, p. 142. In these cases, magic is often suspected to cause impotence. See Blackman 1927, p. 233 for a husband in distress because his wife could not conceive, also Sengers 2003, p. 197 for blaming the wife in case a marriage remains childless.
132 Wickett 2010, p. 85-86.
133 Lane 1842, p. 74; Blackman 1927, p. 45; Sengers 2003, p. 197.
134 Blackman 1927, p. 97; Morsy 1978, p. 605 sums it up by stating succinctly 'Childless women are considered "useless" '. See also Van der Most van Spijk, Fahmy & Zimmerman 1982, p. 14, 77; Van der Most van Spijk 1982, p. 21, 67.
135 See Early 1993, p. 82-83 for an example that combines the two.

Spirits in general can cause physical obstructions leading to infertility.[136] Because spirits are attracted to unclean substances, death and blood, menstruating women will avoid places where spirits are present, such as cemeteries, to prevent a spirit from touching them and thereby causing infertility.[137] If infertility is caused by a possessing spirit, attending a *zār* may lift it.[138] Visiting tombs of specific saints or sheikhs is also thought helpful in case of infertility, as they may either intercede with God or revert spirit influence themselves.[139]

Another persistent belief in relation to fertility and conceiving is *mushāhara* or *kabsa*. This is infertility with a very specific cause. Bleeding women (after the main crisis-events of circumcision, defloration, childbirth or miscarriage) are considered ritually vulnerable.[140] These ritually vulnerable women may be rendered infertile by the presence of certain polluting materials or people that have been in contact with these.[141] The period during which the potential for *kabsa* is high is limited to a month after the crisis-event or, in another variation, until the first new moon after the crisis-event.[142] In the south of Egypt, spirits are also thought to bring about *kabsa*, while this is less common in Lower Egypt.[143]

Women who have passed through one of these crisis-events are secluded for the duration of the *kabsa*-period to prevent pollution and keep spirits from entering the body.[144] This prevention is arrived at through great lengths: materials and goods that bear even the slightest association with blood or death are kept away from the vulnerable woman, as are people who may have been in contact with these materials. Both may transfer their pollution onto her.[145] Because these practices associated with fertility are so deeply intertwined with everyday life, up to the point that they even regulate social contact and interaction, they are of greater importance to *zār* than at first glance might be assumed. I return to this in chapter 4.

When a woman has succeeded in becoming pregnant, another adversary may show up: the Qarina, a female jinn causing miscarriages or stillbirths. This spirit is also intent on harming or killing babies and young children. While the Qarina is a specific spirit, she is closely related to a type of jinn that is often seen in Egyptian popular

---

136 Haverhals-Werkman 1996, p. 15.
137 Haverhals-Werkman 1996, p. 17. Lane 1842, pp. 393-394 however mentions visiting the location where convicts are decapitated to prevent barrenness.
138 Van der Most-Van Spijk 1982, p. 46-47; Haverhals-Werkman 1996, p. 16.
139 De Jong 1976, p. 32 describes how the shrine of Abu Su'ud is visited by women who request intervention of the saint to become pregnant. Lane 1842, p. 363 mentions also men visiting shrines of saints to make a vow to the saint to obtain a son.
140 Van der Most van Spijk 1982, p. 44, 67; Early 1993, p. 89-89; Kennedy 2005, p. 125-150.
141 Inhorn, p. 115. Substances to be kept at distance from vulnerable women include blood, blood-related products, bodily fluids and anything related to death, but also eggplants, lemons and gold.
142 Inhorn, p. 121. Weddings are if at all possible scheduled closely to the date of new moon, so the *kabsa*-risk period after defloration will be short.
143 Inhorn, p. 118-119.
144 Kennedy 1978, p. 128.
145 Haverhals-Werkman 1996, p. 18-19.

tradition,[146] the *qarin*.[147] The Qur'an mentions the *qarin* as a companion to humans.[148] The *qarin* is born together with every human and is, like other jinn, thought to live beneath the earth.[149] Various approaches towards its gender exist: there are those who believe the *qarin* is of the same sex as the human, and others believe it is the opposite.[150] The relationship between a human and his/her *qarin* is, as with all spirits, manifold and ranges from jealous behaviour to protection.[151] Women believe the *qarin* to exert influence over important issues like fertility and childbirth, and often assume the *qarin* to be jealous of a pregnant woman and planning to kill her child.[152] The presence of the *qarin* is similar to that of *zār* spirits in its permanence and inseparability.

2.2.3 Spirit possession

Spirit possession occurs frequently and can be treated in various ways. Here as well, sources from the beginning and the end of the period under study present similar ways of dealing with spirit possession for both men and women. In the 1920s, Winifred Blackman described several ways of treating spirit possession that do not differ much from recent accounts. These can be divided in two types: exorcisms and pacification.

In the case of an exorcism, the goal is to make the spirit leave the human host. Blackman describes a case where possession was a consequence of a human mistake, in which the human had accidentally disturbed or harmed a spirit.[153] Following a back-and-forth on how to leave the body, the spirit eventually left through a toe, and the possessed person returned to normal.[154] Writing some eighty years later, Drieskens describes a similar procedure and observes that these exorcisms usually end with a small incision in a toe or finger for the spirit to exit through.[155]

In the case of pacification, the spirit does not leave the human host. A second case described by Blackman involved a possessed woman, where the diagnosis of spirit possession was already established. The possessed woman was troubled by her spirit, so a female magician was called in to advise on the matter. The spirit asked for a pair of gold earrings and a new yellow *gallābīya* to be worn by the woman. Upon a later visit, the woman was still possessed, although less miserable, and the spirit seemed to have made additional demands.[156] Although in this case the spirit was asked what it wanted, this treatment was not the same as a *zār*.

---

146 Sengers 2003, p. 37-39; Wickett 2010, p. 69.
147 As with all spirit matters, several variations exist regarding the relation between the Qarina and a female *qarin*. Blackman 1926, p. 165-166, explains that the Qarina is indeed the female *qarin* of a woman, but other authors emphasise that the Qarina must not be confused with a female *qarin*.
148 Though not necessarily in a positive way. See Q4:38, Q37:51, Q43:36, Q50:23. See also Ishaq 2016 for an interesting insight in how modern Muslims experience their *qarin* as a force determined to lead them astray.
149 Blackman 1926, p. 163-164 clarifies that the *qarin* is not the same as the *ukht* (sister) underground, and that the underground spirits are not the same as the equally subterranean folk of the *aqran* (plural of *qarin*) At least in 1926 this distinction was made by Blackman, but she discusses variations as well on pp 167-168.
150 Zwemer 1920, p. 107 describes that men have a female qarina and vice versa. Nalder 1926, p. 82 states that this is new to him, and that he only knew of same-sex doubles. See also Drieskens 2008, p. 179-181.
151 Drieskens 2008, p. 183.
152 Blackman 1926; see also Drieskens 2008, p. 180-186 for the complicated relation of women and their *qarin*.
153 The same transgressions were named in Drieskens 2008, p. 171. See also Ejibadze 2011, p. 138.
154 Blackman 1927, p. 231-232.
155 Drieskens 2008, p. 163; also observed by Sengers 2003, p. 173-174.
156 Blackman 1927, p. 187.

A third case is *zār* itself. Blackman remarks that in the case of spirit possession, 'sometimes it is necessary to have a ceremony called a *zār* – in fact, most people who are troubled with a sheikh either have such a performance at home or attend one which is being held in another person's house.'[157] According to Blackman, a week after a *zār*, having a *ṣulḥ* or reconciliation was an option.[158] During this event, the human host and the possessing spirit reached an agreement. This follows the structure of a traditional method of settling disputes that has existed in the Arab world for centuries and was used to reconcile a human with his or her *qarin* as well.[159] Notably, Blackman states that *zār* is not necessarily followed by a *ṣulḥ*. Apparently, *zār* in her experience consisted only of the diagnosis, arrived at through drumming, trance, and songs. Morsy makes the same differentiation between *zār* and *ṣulḥ* in 1978[160], while Nabhan mentions *ṣulḥ* as a term to indicate the animal sacrifice in relation to the agreement with the spirit.[161] Most authors include the *ṣulḥ* as integral part of the *zār* and do not mention it as a separate occasion. I will present the relevance of this observation for *zār* jewellery in chapter 4.

So, what does all this have to do with *zār*? The general apotropaic jewellery in the sample collection attracted my attention and led me to look at other forms of spirit engagement in Egypt. After all, *zār* is not an isolated phenomenon but is part of the larger landscape of Egyptian traditions concerning spirit engagement. The presence of apotropaic jewellery seems to indicate something else: the need to protect oneself during a *zār*. This observation, in turn, tells us that there is a parallel approach to spirits occurring in *zār*: the possessing spirit needs to be pacified, but apparently attention for other spirits is required as well. With this duality in mind, I will now turn to the ritual itself.

2.3 *ZĀR*

At first glance, *zār* appears to be the opposite of the ordinary attitude towards spirits as introduced in the previous chapter: where people generally avoid contact with spirits, *zār* actively invites such contact. As I introduced in chapter 1, the sample collection of jewellery does contain both purpose-made jewellery and general amulets, which seems to indicate a more nuanced view of this apparent paradox. Combining the practices of spirit engagement in the female world as presented in the previous chapter with the main structural elements of *zār*, this chapter explores the multiple approaches to interaction with spirits that occur simultaneously within the same ritual.

---

157 Blackman 1927, p. 198. A sheikh is a possessing spirit.
158 Blackman 1926, p. 198-199
159 See Pely 2011 and Lang 2002 for a general layout of a human *ṣulḥ*; Drieskens 2006b for an example of a *ṣulḥ* between humans from Cairo.
160 Morsy 1978, p. 601.
161 Nabhan 1994, p. 211.

2.3.1 The ritual specialist

The ritual specialist in charge of *zār* is called a *shaykha* or a *kōdiya*.[162] Most of the contemporary literature on the Egyptian *zār* uses the latter term, and it is also prevalent for Sudan.[163] The word most likely stems from the Hausa language, meaning 'horse', in a referral to the spirit mounting the medium like a horse.[164] A less frequently used epithet is '*arīfat as-sikka*, which literally translates as 'she who knows the way'.[165] Adly and Kahle interpret 'way' to mean 'method'[166], affirming her role as leader of the ritual, knowledgeable about the successful execution of the ceremony. However, it could also be interpreted more literally, referring to a woman who, from personal experience, knows the way in, through and more importantly, out of the trance state. This explanation aligns with the special talents required to become a ritual specialist in the first place: being able to function as medium and channel the *zār* spirits herself, without being possessed by them.[167] Having travelled the way in, through and out of the trance state herself many times, the ritual specialist serves not only as the leader of the ceremony but also as the guide of both humans and spirits attending the event. From the beginning of the available written records, the ritual specialist is described as a woman of colour, preferably from the south of Egypt.[168] Her role is often hereditary, passed down from mother to daughter,[169] but it can also be acquired in apprenticeship[170].

2.3.2 General configuration of *zār*

What does a *zār* look like? As Hadidi points out, the world of *zār* is infinitely multifaceted and always changing.[171] There are however several common factors that are usually present in *zār*. I will introduce these below to create a framework

---

162 Littman 1950 p. 49 discusses the two words and proposes that *shaykha* is pertinent to Egyptian *zār* leaders and *kōdiya* is used for non-Egyptian, *zār* leaders of colour. According to el-Hadidi, there is a difference in role between the two: only the *kōdiya* can also officiate in a *zār* involving the spirit known as *Sitt el-Kebira*, the Grand Lady, whilst a *shaykha* can officiate in any *zār* but this one. This distinction is not made in other literature, but a reality of her extensive field research. See el-Hadidi 2016, p. 103-104. Nelson 1971, p. 198 discerns between *shaykha* and *kōdiya* in terms of actorship; according to her, both can be present at the same time.

163 For example Boddy 1989, *passim*.

164 Hadidi 2016, p. 104. Al-Masih 2008, p. 77 explains the origins of the word as Arabic for 'beggar', referring to a group called Kudia 'known for their cunning and cleverness in obtaining money from others'. She surmises that some members of this group took up the *zār* as profession. The riding of the patient like a horse by the *zār* spirit is also mentioned by Kriss & Kriss-Heinrich 1962, p. 142. Nünlist 2011, p. 155 points to the possible relation with the image of *jinn* using animals and humans as actual mount, citing the example from Upper Egypt described by Winkler.

165 Kahle 1912, p. 8; El-Adly 1984, p. 656.

166 El-Adly and Kahle translate the term as 'she who knows the method'.

167 Pielow 1997, p. 357, also Kriss & Kriss-Heinrich 1962, p. 143.

168 Macdonald 1911, p. 332 states 'carried out under the direction and personal control of Negro women'. In 1957 this was still a requirement, as mentioned by Kriss & Kriss-Heinrich 1962, p. 143: 'the kūdya always has to be dark-skinned'. Klunzinger in 1878 says the leader of the ceremony is a slave woman: as most slaves were dark-skinned, this is in conformity with the other observations. The ritual specialist being dark-skinned is still a requirement, see for example Nelson 1971, p. 198.

169 Littmann 1950, p. 16; Kriss & Kriss-Heinrich 1962, p. 143; Fakhouri 1972, p. 95 mentioning hereditary knowledge for a male specialist.

170 Personal communication dr. Hadidi, Nov. 11th, 2020; also Nabhan 1994, p. 69-71.

171 Hadidi 2016, p. 51, calling it 'modular'.

of understanding, and I will refer back to this section when discussing individual descriptions of *zār* ceremonies later on. *Zār* is divided into two separate ceremonies: the personal ceremony designed for a specific patient and the public, weekly *zār*.[172] The first ceremony is elaborate, designed to communicate with the spirit or spirits that have taken possession of a woman and to honour their wishes. After having had a personal ceremony, the possessed woman can join the weekly *zār*. As a result of the tight social networks, the distinction between them is blurred: a personal *zār* usually is quite public as well.[173] Both public and personal *zār* are never held in the holy month of Ramadan.[174]

Diagnosis

When a woman is suffering from symptoms that cannot be cured by a regular doctor, she will turn to a ritual specialist to see if possession by a *zār* spirit or spirits could be the cause of her symptoms. Symptoms of possession often include excessive yawning, tiredness, headaches, but also hallucinations, apathy, seizures and infertility[175] as well as lack of appetite and weight loss.[176] Possession is not limited to just one spirit: a single person can be possessed by several *zār* spirits. Two or three are not uncommon, but the number can amount to five or even eight.[177]

To learn if her patient is indeed possessed by a spirit or spirits and if so, which one(s), the ritual specialist will first take a piece of cloth and a coin from the patient. The cloth can be a handkerchief, a piece of clothing or any other textile that can be associated with the person.[178] This practice is also known from non-*zār* possession cases.[179] The coin preferably is a pillar dollar.[180] These were Spanish coins: the depiction of the Pillars of Hercules on the coin was misread as a depiction of cannons, and the preference for this coin in amulets in general can be explained through this misinterpretation. As guns were made of iron, a material which was considered very powerful against jinn, the depiction of iron objects carried the same power against malevolent jinn. The pillar dollar features regularly in amuletic jewellery, and so it is unsurprising to see it preferred in *zār*, too: its power would hold jinn at bay that could thwart the ritual specialist's attempts at diagnosing the identity of the spirit

---

172 Nabhan 1994, p. 164-181 describes four different ceremonies. In addition to the private *zār* and the public *zār*, she also has witnessed the *zār gabalāwī*, which is carried out in a cemetery, and the *zār bahrī* which is held at the banks of the Nile and on a boat on the river. As these types of ritual have not been mentioned by researchers of the first half of the 20th century, they may be a relatively new form, or alternatively have never been witnessed before.
173 Drieskens 2008, p. 55.
174 Kriss & Kriss-Heinrich 1962, p. 143; Fakhouri 1972, p. 92.
175 Fakhouri 1968, p. 50.
176 Littmann 1950, p. 1. Over the past decades, attention has been given to the medical and psychological background of these symptoms in for example Kennedy 1967, Coker 2009 and Mianji 2015.
177 Littmann 1950, p. 51. Le Brun 1902, p. 258 mentions when interviewing candidates for a housekeeping position, all of them admitted to having one, two or three spirits, some had five, and a few even seven or eight. Blackman 1927, p. 198 states that a person may be possessed by several spirits of both sexes.
178 Littmann 1950, p. 1, Thompson 1013, p. 276. Granzow 2008. p. 14 mentions also personal elements such as hair or nail clippings.
179 Blackman 1928, p. 231 (the same incident is described earlier in Blackman 1924, p. 179). In Blackman 1924, p. 181, she describes another possession situation where a piece of cloth was needed to identify the nature of the ailment.
180 Littman 1950, p. 1-2 (manuscript from 1911); Kriss & Kriss-Heinrich 1962, p. 161.

possessing her client.[181] Their association with *zār* was so strong that later authors claimed imitation coins were produced especially for *zār*.[182] After receiving the piece of cloth and the coin, the ritual specialist will sleep with the objects under her pillow.[183] In her dreams the nature of the spirit or spirits possessing the client will be revealed to her, as well as its demands. Another method of diagnosis is to visit a weekly public *zār*, where various beats associated with spirits are drummed, to see if the patient reacts to a specific beat.[184]

Agreement

The next step is to contact the spirit and to negotiate a contract: in return for fulfilling the demands of the spirit, it will stop harming the client. This is the ultimate outcome and goal of the *zār* ceremony: to ensure the patient is no longer harmed by her *zār*-spirit. In this agreement, the *zār* differs from an exorcism: the spirit does not leave the human host.[185]

To reach this agreement, a personal *zār* ceremony is held. The preferred location for a personal *zār* is the house of the patient, if she can spare the room.[186] If it is not possible to have the ceremony at home, the ritual specialist will arrange for a suitable space. In the room, she and her assistants set up an altar or *kursī*, loaded with candles, drinks, foodstuff and other objects that the spirit desires, including jewellery. The money to acquire all of this comes from the patient. Incense is burnt aplenty, and after reciting the opening verse of the Qu'ran the drumming and chanting of *zār* songs for the spirits begin. The patient, dressed in white[187], reaches a trance-state, reacting to the beat of the spirit that possesses her. The agreement with the spirit is eventually sealed by the slaughter of sacrificial animals. The ritual specialist uses their blood to daub onto the patient[188] and pours it over the jewellery lying in a bowl[189]. In addition, in some cases, the contract also has a material form: the patient has to wear the coin used by the specialist during diagnosis, after retrieving it from the blood.[190]

After the agreement, the ceremony concludes with more dancing and a festive meal. The length of the ceremony varied according to the wealth of the afflicted: people who could afford to, had *zār* ceremonies that lasted from three days up to a

---

181 See for more on the pillar dollar as amulet Schienerl 1980a, p. 504-505.
182 Kriss & Kriss-Heinrich 1962, p. 161; Schienerl 1976, p. 127-128. In chapter 4 I will discuss this entanglement further.
183 Littmann 1950, p. 1 and Kriss & Kriss-Heinrich 1962, p. 161 both specify that this takes three nights, repeated by Hadidi 2006 p. 61 and Granzow 2008 p. 14.
184 Granzow 2008, p. 14 mentions this method can be used when the dream method has been unsuccessful, Battain 1993 lists the two methods as equal.
185 Endrawes et al 2007, p. 182 however mix their description of the *zār* with that of an exorcism.
186 Thompson & Franke 1913; Zwemer 1920 p. 229. Kriss & Kriss-Heinrich 1962, p. 141 describe how a private property was used, both the house and garden; Fakhouri 1972, p. 94.
187 Already in Thompson 1913, the woman was dressed in white; also found with Nabhan 1994, p. 193.
188 Granzow 2008, p. 16; Nabhan 1994 p. 203-209. The degree in which blood is administered, varies: in some reports blood is poured over the patient, in others the patient even drinks blood (Thompson & Franke 1913, p.279 and 283-284), in others the specialist prints bloody handprints on the *gallābīya* of the patient.
189 Hadidi 2016, with photograph.
190 Kriss & Kriss-Heinrich 1962, p.179; Nabhan 1994.

week.[191] In some varieties, the patient spends time in seclusion after the sealing of the agreement before the final festivities.[192]

Maintenance

When the ceremony concludes, the afflicted woman will remain in the constant presence of her *zār* spirit or spirits without being possessed all the time. If the terms of the agreement remain upheld, the *zār* spirit will manifest itself only in ritual context when his or her beat is drummed.[193] This manifestation is facilitated by the weekly *zār*, also overseen by a ritual specialist. This is also called *hadra*, 'visiting day'.[194] The name stems from the particular days the shrines of saints and other important figures were visited.[195]

Here, we see an existing particular Egyptian practice of spirit engagement adopted in *zār*. In Egypt, shrines, tombs and cemeteries continue to be locations for public gatherings and supernatural encounters. As I introduced above, this practice is rooted deep in popular culture, and the same locations also present a venue for the public *zār*. This is different from Sudan, where *zārs* are held in the courtyard of a private home, either of a *zār* leader or the patient.[196] In both countries the locations are liminal spaces that fit the character of *zār* (the courtyard of the house is in between the inner home and the outside world, the shrines are in between the world of the living and the dead), but the choice of location aligns with a tradition particular to each country.

In 1912, Paul Kahle described how the weekly *zār* was held at various Cairo shrines on their respective *hadra* and had been so since 1885.[197] The *hadra* allows women who have had a personal *zār* to communicate with their individual *zār* spirits. The musicians play the rhythms associated with various spirits, either on demand or in a set order; when the beat of her personal spirit or spirits is drummed, the spirit will manifest itself and the possessed woman will get up and dance. Instead of the lengthy personal ceremony, these weekly gatherings take up no more than a few hours.[198] Nowadays, these gatherings are held at a space the ritual specialist provides or in a private home; the liminal aspects of the location have become less important.[199] Participants pay the musicians per song, and the assistants of the ritual specialist per censing.

---

191 Kahle 1912, p. 9; Zwemer 1920, p. 240; Kriss & Kriss-Heinrich 1962, p. 141 mention theirs took two days.
192 See for example Kennedy 1967, p. 189.
193 Natvig 2010, p. 22. Reaffirmation of the agreement through another personal *zār* in some cases is necessary.
194 Also called *ziyâra*. See De Jong 1976, 28-29, who discerns between the two: a *ziyāra* is a visiting day, while the *hadra* takes places on such a visiting day and is an event consisting of communal reading, a *dhikr*, and prayers. He notes that *hadra* and *dhikr* are used interchangeably in everyday language (p. 29) and that on a *hadra*, drums and flutes may also be used (p. 30): as *dhikr* is also a form of trance-inducing prayer and *hadra* is its synonym, transferring this name to another form of trance-inducing ritual makes sense.
195 A practice already mentioned by Lane 1842, p. 363 and dating back to the Middle Ages according to Shoshan 1993, p. 21-22.
196 Boddy 1989 and Kenyon 2012.
197 Kahle 1912, p. 4 quotes an article from 1885 by Yacoub Artin Pasha in which the sanctuary of Sheik Bidak was used by 'freed negro slave women' to hold a *zār* until it was renovated. The author himself had witnessed a *zār* at the sanctuary of 'Sheik Abu Se'ûd al Gârihî', which, according to the sheikh's visiting day, was on a Tuesday evening. Zwemer 1920, p. 239 also describes the use of sanctuaries for a *zār*. In 2008, Drieskens describes a public *zār* held near the tomb of 'Abu Suud' at the edge of Cairo's City of the Dead (p. 230-234).
198 Kahle 1912, p. 9.
199 Personal communication dr. el-Hadidi, Nov. 11, 2020.

2.3.3 Elements of *zār*

Zār contains several elements that help to understand the nature of the proceedings and thus aid in placing the jewellery of *zār* in a more specific context. I will introduce these elements below.

Wedding and *ṣulḥ*

The structure of a personal *zār* ceremony is said to resemble that of a wedding.[200] The patient is called *'arūsa* or bride, and in the more elaborate *zār* ceremonies, elements of a wedding are used such as the henna night, the *zaffa* or festive procession, the festive meal, and even the period of seclusion in some *zār* varieties. This resemblance is an important aspect for the understanding of the role of jewellery in the ritual, as jewellery forms an important part of both ceremonies. Despite these similarities, the goal of a *zār* is to reconcile with a spirit, not to marry one.[201] That becomes visible in the inverted direction of jewellery transfer: the regular bride receives, but the *zār* bride gives. Whereas at a wedding the bride <u>receives</u> jewellery from the person she enters into an alliance with (her husband and his family), during the *zār*, she <u>presents</u> jewellery to the spirit with whom she reaches an agreement. Klunzinger describes the aim of this gift-giving already concisely in 1878: to pacify the possessing spirit.[202] Writing in 1913, Anna Thompson remarks that the material things observed were 'intended to make peace between the patient and the *Asyad* (demons)'.[203] As I mentioned above, Blackman also mentions pacifying in 1926, when she identifies this part of the proceedings as the *ṣulḥ*. In general, a *ṣulḥ* is held to pacify a spirit, either a *zār*-spirit, the *qarin* or another possessing spirit, by giving it what it demands. This, in turn, is relevant for our understanding of *zār* jewellery, and I will return to this in more detail in chapter 4.

Music and songs

In both personal and public *zār*, music and songs are key elements. The beat of the music corresponds to the preferred beat of the spirit invited. Each spirit has its own beat and descends when this is drummed. The lyrics of the accompanying songs also serve to welcome and please the spirit. However, not all songs pertain to the visiting spirits: there are also songs that evoke God, the Prophet and/or various saints. These songs, generally called *madīh* songs, can be identical to songs performed at *mawālid*, the festivals in honour of the birthday of the Prophet or saints. These songs, in turn, are sometimes well-known songs from popular culture, fitted with new lyrics to become a *madīh* song. Natvig has convincingly argued that these particular songs are originally not meant to add a more acceptable Islamic cosmetic layer to *zār*, but that they are consciously included in the ritual to create a

---

200 Boddy 1989, p. 310-336; Nelson 1971, p. 199 states the ceremony is even called *farah*, literally 'happiness', as does Sengers 2003, p. 98. Kahle 1912, p. 14 is the earliest mention of the *zār* 'bride', followed by Franke 1913, p. 282.
201 Drieskens 2008, p. 224, for example refers to zār as 'rituals of reconciliation'. Boddy 1989, p. 311 states explicitly that the patient does not marry the spirit, but that a wedding is used as metaphor for the contractual character of both relations. In general, the aim of *zār* is perfectly clear.
202 Klunzinger 1878, p. 388-389.
203 Thompson & Franke 1913, p. 277.

protective framework surrounding the core of *zār*, where humans interact directly with spirits.[204] Noteworthy is that these particular songs already occur in 1911 and, therefore, are not a more recent invention.[205]

Colours

Spirits are often identified by colours. The importance of colours to spirits is attested by the earliest reports of *zār*. For example, in 1902, a spirit did not like to see black[206], or in 1913, blue and white beads were associated with a Sudanese spirit.[207]. The candles used on the altar have to be of a specific colour, as does the clothing for each spirit. The use of colours for individual spirits is still a main element in *zār* today.[208] The beaded jewellery in the sample collection is colourful *par excellence* and may, in this context, be seen as associated with the predilection of the spirits.

Incense

Many accounts of *zār* mention incense. The use of incense fulfils a distinctly dual role. The ritual specialist and her assistants provide incensing for the space, the attendees and the spirits. In everyday life, incense is burnt to keep jinn at a distance: these prefer dirt and uncleanliness, and general belief has it that agreeable scents drive them away. The *zār* spirits, on the other hand, can be quite specific about the type of incense they want to see burned to welcome them; in Sudan, this link is even so strong that a *zār* spirit will descend when it smells its personal incense.[209]

2.3.4 Inviting and averting: a dual approach to dealing with spirits in *zār*

What does all this mean? The ordinary attitude towards spirits is to avoid their attention. Given the importance of avoiding spirits in relation to fertility and childbirth, these fears are especially present in a context where inviting spirits is the main goal. These two stances appear to be incompatible. Upon closer inspection, however, the interaction with spirits in *zār* accommodates both positions. Table 2.1 illustrates that point.

The goal of *zār* is to alleviate the suffering of the patient. In order for the ritual to be successful, therefore, not only an understanding with the possessing *zār* spirit must be reached to its satisfaction, but also the possibility of the patient being harmed by other spirits must be prevented. The presence of invited spirits is needed for the negotiations and reaching of an agreement; uninvited and potentially dangerous spirits need to be kept out. The duality of *zār* is visible in its jewellery, and upon closer inspection is also reflected in incensing and songs. Although the distinction between preferred scents to please *zār* spirits and its general use to ward off jinn is certainly not always clear or even consciously made, the copious use of incense functions as both inviting and averting at the same time. In the songs, the same dual occurrence of inviting and averting is present, although the latter is not formulated explicitly

---

204 Natvig 2014, p. 319, treating the interpretation of these songs by Littmann on p. 317, and Natvig 2018, p. 89.
205 Littmann 1950, p. 1, manuscript of Sidqi 1911.
206 Le Brun 1902.
207 Thompson & Franke 1913, p. 276.
208 The use of colours for specific spirits is for example described by Hadidi 2006; also Fakhouri 1972, p. 94.
209 Kenyon 2012, p. 12.

Inviting *zār* spirits	Averting other spirits
Zār spirit songs	Prophet and saint songs
Specific incense	General incense
Jewellery with specific colours and colour combinations	Jewellery with dangles and protective formulas
Jewellery requested by the spirit	Jewellery feared by spirits

Table 2.1. Elements in *zār* pointing to a dual approach of both inviting and averting spirits.

but wrapped up in the use of certain songs. These songs call upon the Prophet and various saints; their function is to protect the participants. Where the specific *zār* songs actively seek out the presence of *zār* spirits, the non-*zār* songs comply with the general attitude towards jinn, namely to protect oneself from their possibly malevolent intentions. Even the location of choice for the public *zār*, near a tomb or shrine of a saint, in this light assists in this protection: Egyptians consider these to be blessed spaces filled with *baraka*.[210]

Starting from an initial observation of the sample collection and proceeding with an exploration of a broader spiritual landscape based on that observation, it has become clear that *zār* considers spirits simultaneously from two different viewpoints. In general studies on *zār*, the interaction with invited spirits and the effects of that interaction on the patient have been the focal point of attention. Its duality in also actively keeping unwanted spirits out has not been fully recognised.

What else may we be missing? Our current understanding of *zār* jewellery is based in collected objects: unpicking how collecting has shaped our view is a necessary first step. How do we know what we think we know?

---

[210] Drieskens 2008, p. 218-220.

3

COLLECTED OBJECTS

3.1 THE CURIOUS CASE OF THE MISSING JEWELLERY: PUBLISHED OBJECTS

Jewellery with spirit images is the most recognizable category to be attributed to *zār*. In fact, the largest group of objects in the sample collection consists of these, and they bear hallmarks from 1913 onwards. Yet, intriguingly, none of the descriptions of *zār* mention this particular jewellery up until 1955, when 'Abd er-Rasoul gives a very brief description of engraved plates with designs of human figures. These become widely known only in 1962, when Kriss & Kriss-Heinrich include the now well-known objects with spirit images in their book on folk belief. Apparently, the main body of *zār* jewellery and the only category to be attributed with certainty to *zār*, managed to stay out of sight for nearly half a century. In this section, I explore the history of research and publishing.

3.1.1 A century of publications

From the moment *zār* appeared in Egypt, people began writing about it. Initially, this was in letters home or travel reports, and later in linguistic and anthropological studies. As is common in research, authors frequently refer back to earlier works, include or exclude previous publications and incorporate other sources. So, our current understanding of *zār* jewellery is based on a century of publications. I have traced the primary chain of information that has led us to where we are today.

For every publication as introduced in chapter 1, I have asserted whether the authors' main focus was on ritual or on material culture (particularly jewellery). I have also traced how these publications build upon one another (or not) by analysing their references. This presents an interesting watershed in the period 1960-1980. The earlier publications mainly focus on the ritual itself, and are cited up until Littmann 1950, Kriss & Kriss Heinrich 1962 and el-Adly 1984. Later publications dealing with jewellery rarely cite these earlier works, but refer to Kriss & Kriss-Heinrich 1962. I will explore this in more detail next.

3.1.2 19th century – 1950s: first publications

The first publications firmly focused on *zār* itself. These emphasised the proceedings of the ritual themselves and, if jewellery was mentioned at all, this was more as a side observation. These early works comprised travel reports, notes for Christian mission periodicals and linguistic studies: the authors described their observations or analysed texts they considered relevant. Littman's 1950 publication *Arabische Geisterbeschwörungen in Ägypten* lists a variety of jewellery, but this is part of an annotated translation of two separate manuscripts by the Egyptian author Sidqi. In his own annotations and comments, Littmann barely touched upon jewellery: his focus was on the ritual itself and on linguistic aspects of *zār* songs. Notably, none of these early authors were collectors themselves.

In contrast, Blackman, who compiled an anthropological study, *The Fellahin of Upper Egypt*, had assembled a large collection of objects. She used these to illustrate her book on the everyday life of the Egyptian fellahin. We will see more of her collection in the next chapter. Interestingly, although her 1927 publication is in English as well as written for a general audience, which makes it more accessible to non-academic readers, it seems to have had limited impact on subsequent publications about *zār* jewellery: very few later authors refer to it.[211]

'Abd er-Rasoul, writing in 1955, presents an overview of *zār* in general as a description of the ritual itself, and mentions the use of jewellery with spirit images.[212]

3.1.3 1960s: a changing perspective

This focus on ritual shifts to material culture in 1962, with the publication of Kriss & Kriss-Heinrich, *Volksglaube im Bereich der Islam*. The second volume of this book, *Amulette, Zauberformeln und Beschwörungen*, centred around all sorts of amulets, for which the authors provided explanations and background information. After having attended a few *zārs*, the two men had a private *zār* organised in order to observe the jewellery items they collected in context and as a means of collecting a few more: their starting point was collected material culture.[213]

This publication by Kriss & Kriss-Heinrich marked the start of the separation of jewellery from ritual in the available literature, a transition that was completed in the 1980s. A new genre emerged: catalogues of *zār* jewellery. In 1981, Khoury published an article focusing on the iconography of the hoopoe on a single *zār* pendant.[214] In 1984, Adly concluded his work *The Zar* with a catalogue. He first discussed the ritual itself, drawing on various older publications and his personal experience in 1977, and concluded with an illustrated catalogue of *zār* jewellery items, frequently referring back to Kriss & Kriss-Heinrich. The same year saw the publication of *Silberschmuck aus Ägypten* by Bachinger and Schienerl, where *zār* jewellery was one of the entries in an exhibition catalogue of Egyptian jewellery. This was a publication for a larger audience and, as the first widely accessible publication with both photographs of *zār* pendants as well as information and captions in both German and English, is still highly sought after by current-day collectors. It serves as a reference book for both collectors and

---

211 Stevenson 2013, p. 145 notes that Blackman's work was well-received upon publication, but as the fields of both Egyptology and anthropology continued to develop and drifted more and more apart, her work fit in neither.
212 'Abd er-Rasoul 1955, p. 83.
213 De Jong 1976, p. 32, note 23 notes that 'they have not too carefully scrutinized the material collected by them' when discussing the *hadra* of Abu al-Sū'ūd.
214 Khoury 1981.

museums. The emphasis of *zār* jewellery in this book is on silver jewellery with spirit images; the accompanying text is brief and limited to iconographical descriptions.

3.1.4 1980s: from academia to the wider public

In 1980 Schienerl published an article about *zār* jewellery in U.S.-based *Ornament Magazine*. Not only is the article based on material culture, it is also published in a medium devoted to personal adornment in the widest context possible, rather than anthropology or ritual. Importantly, it is in English, whereas German prevailed in earlier works. *Ornament Magazine* is a non-academic medium celebrating the world of jewellery, and so is read in other, and notably wider, circles. This divide between academic publications and media for larger audiences is also reflected in changing citations and references. Where Kriss & Kriss-Heinrich referred to many earlier sources (Klunzinger 1878, Kahle 1912, Thompson & Franke 1913 and Littmann 1950, but not Blackman 1927), most publications after 1962 refer mainly to Kriss & Kriss-Heinrich 1962 and not earlier sources. Adly's work did refer to earlier sources, but unfortunately, it has not gained wide reach. This divide between language and medium is evident in Schienerl's work. His work in English, published in popular mediums such as *Ornament Magazine*, has become the standard for *zār* jewellery, whereas his earlier work in German, published in academic circles, is rarely cited.

From the 1980s onwards, anthropological studies on the Egyptian *zār* increased. These contained eye witness accounts of multiple *zār*s as well as interviews with attendees and patients. However, in these studies, jewellery is either presented briefly or completely absent. When jewellery is discussed, references are to Kriss & Kriss-Heinrich 1962 and/or Bachinger & Schienerl 1984. Jewellery references in both publications and museum registration files frequently rely on these two sources as well.

3.1.5 1990s: information circulation in social networks

The interest in *zār* jewellery has been expanding since the 1980s, notably among jewellery collectors. Expats in Egypt, as in other Middle Eastern countries, started collecting jewellery as a pastime and hobby. For many, collecting formed a social network in foreign surroundings: sharing stories, showing and comparing new acquisitions and even 'hunting' for jewellery together provided an opportunity to make new friends through a shared interest.[215] The series of articles by Susan Weeks in the magazine *Cairo Today* during the 1980s is an example of this interest of foreigners in jewellery: she collected traditional Egyptian jewellery and published about it in a magazine with expats as its target audience.[216] *Zār* jewellery was, and still is, a firm favourite because of its intriguing story and recognizable appearance. These social networks became also the main conduit for sharing and obtaining information, rather than perusing books. A major anchor for collectors, and often their starting point for finding out more, is the information that sellers provide. I will briefly explore that

---

215 See for the social aspect of collecting Ter Keurs 2021, p. 118.
216 In her article on *zār* jewellery from 1984, she writes 'Many other zar amulets, including ones of beads and shells can be seen at the Folklore Institute and Ethnography Museum in Cairo, but it is more fun to search the small shops of the *Sagha* for an interesting new design.'

information, starting with sources within Egypt, and will then expand to the Internet both in and outside Egypt.

In Egypt itself, collectors look for jewellery in Cairo's Khan el-Khalili. Here, Alaa Abdou is a well-known and trusted vendor that many expats visit. He owns a copy of Bachinger & Schienerl 1984, which has become a shopping list of sorts for *zār* jewellery for many of his clients and is their main source of information.[217] Another place expats visit in search of old jewellery is Nomad Gallery in Cairo. Its main branch on Zamalek offers artisanal products as well as a selection of jewellery.

Egyptian vendors also use the Internet to sell *zār* jewellery both within Egypt and beyond. A popular reference is this text:

> 'Zar is an Egyptian cult possession that's little known outside of Egypt. Zar means the practices or rites, which are performed in order to conciliate the Zar-Spirit, whom [sic] seized possession of a person, causing physical and/or physiological illness. These rites consist of ecstatic dancing, rousing music and drum beating, singing, and burning of aromatic substances and sometimes animal sacrifice, usually lasting for a few days. In the course of the ceremony, the patient wears numerous amulets and jewelry depending on the Zar-Spirit taken hold of that person. The Zar-Spirit is represented on this amulet, which is usually hung on the headdress.'

This text is based on the paragraph 'The Egyptian Zar' in Bachinger & Schienerl 1984.[218] The same sentences are repeated by two online sources: Hussein Gouda and Nomad Gallery in Cairo. Hussein Gouda has been using this particular text on Ebay since 2002. Although it is not a direct quote, he adds 'P.W. Schienerl' to these lines as citation.[219] The same wording again is found with Nomad Gallery in Cairo, who used it in 2021 to describe *zār* jewellery on offer.[220]

Jewellery is also sold by non-Egyptians on the Internet. They also provide information on *zār* jewellery on offer, but sparingly. Most vendors do not include a reference with their information about *zār* jewellery. Where they do, Fahmy 2015 is the most popular resource.[221] This is the second edition of the book about traditional Egyptian jewellery by famed Egyptian designer Azza Fahmy.

But not all information provided with *zār* jewellery is valid: some vendors embellish their descriptions with unreferenced factoids. An example is a heavily decorated *zār* pendant offered on Etsy in May 2023.[222] Its dangles have been embellished with coloured beads and fish pendants. The description of this piece also includes the supposed

---

217 Personal communication Sylvia Walters-Jennette (Feb 2nd, 2018) Noel Adorno (November 11th, 2020), also personal observation.
218 Bachinger & Schienerl 1984, p. 18-19 for the English version.
219 For example https://www.ebay.com/itm/402826329001?hash=item5dca51fba9:g:j-0AAOSweoxdsBI2, accessed March 31st, 2023.
220 https://www.nomadgallery.net, accessed April 20th, 2021.
221 Rita O'Krent collection refers to Fahmy 2015 and DesertSilver.com (sic); AfganBazar on Etsy refers to Fahmy 2015 and Desert Silver (2010); Siwa Gallery on Etsy refers to Fahmy 2015, p. 181. Vendor Silverethnicjewels refers to Fahmy 2015, p. 173. Other vendors do include information on zār, but without references.
222 https://www.etsy.com/nl/listing/606436690/rituele-hanger-zar-bedouin-alexandrie?, accessed March 30, 2023.

apotropaic qualities of the beads and the fish pendants, again unreferenced. Both the embellishments themselves and the description have most likely been added to entice prospective buyers, although not necessarily by the same person: the (European) vendor may well have purchased this piece in its current form in Egypt.

3.1.6 2000s: the Siwa-effect

Current-day private collectors often get their information mainly from vendors and the Internet. Notably that latter invention has played a major role in the dissemination of information about *zār* in a non-academic context: the Internet is home to digital social networks of collectors and vendors. On Facebook, they share photos of pieces on various digital platforms, with the purpose of selling pieces as well as providing or asking information about a particular piece. References usually consist of comparing results found on Google or Pinterest, often without checking correct attributions. Here, Schienerl and Kriss & Kriss-Heinrich are notably absent: both books are out of print, near impossible to obtain and do not exist in digital form. References (if any) are made to more recent publications. For *zār* jewellery, platform members refer to RAWI Magazine 2013 (3), Fahmy 2015 (2), Hadidi 2016 (once).[223] Only once Boddy 1989 is cited, but also qualified as 'extremely dry anthropological and academic reading'.[224]

It is hardly surprising collectors and vendors alike do not refer to academic sources. First, that is not the main goal of a social network: collectors wish to show, share, and appreciate jewellery. The social platforms on which they convene are, for many, a place where their passion for both jewellery and collecting is recognised and celebrated, instead of frowned upon.[225] Academic sources do not play into that passion. Secondly, these sources are unavailable for most, as they are either locked behind paywalls or difficult and costly to obtain. The growing number of open access academic publications is not always on the radar of collectors. Additionally, the high percentage of academic studies written in other languages than English, notably German, adds to their inaccessibility for many collectors. Instead, online resources and accessibly written books that can easily be ordered online serve as main source. These are focused on jewellery only, and mention the world, or, in the case of *zār* the ritual it belongs to, only in passing.[226] The result is that little pieces of information are repeated and circulated time and again, while the major background studies remain unknown, and no new knowledge is generated – while that knowledge does exist, as for example the article series of Susan Weeks as I mentioned above, shows. Furthermore, the information available to collectors becomes increasingly convoluted through the mixing in of other bits and pieces: Nubian jewellery in particular is often offered for sale as *zār*, without sound references or background information.

---

223 In all posts containing *zār* on Facebook groups Ethnic Jewels Community and Ethnic Jewellery Discussion Forum, accessed on April 24th, 2020.
224 Comment on a post on Facebook-group Ethnic Jewels Community of March 2, 2016. (https://www.facebook.com/photo?fbid=10153976676363659&set=gm.1060951223926298, accessed March 22, 2023)
225 Ter Keurs 2021, p. 118, points out how collectors often are 'Einzelgangers'. My personal experience on collectors' digital platforms is that members feel that they indeed are in everyday life, but that this, much to their relief and joy, is a space where they are not.
226 The exception is the study by Hadidi.

Another interesting development in recent years is the attribution of *zār* jewellery to Siwa oasis. Increasingly, vendors of *zār* jewellery list the provenance of their pieces as coming from Siwa oasis. This idea has taken hold, as several collectors now believe their *zār* jewellery is from Siwa.[227] The attribution to this remote oasis in the northwest of Egypt, close to the border with Libya, is interesting. The material record contains no reference to Siwa, as several major collections of Siwa jewellery and other objects do not include *zār* jewellery. The extensive collection of Bettina Leopoldo, collected in the 1980s and housed in the Weltmuseum in Vienna, contains many amulets, of which only three are similar to *zār* pendants. Two of these carry text only, one has spirit images, and all three are catalogued as 'Schriftamulett'.[228] The part of her collection now in the Musée d'Ethnographie in Geneva does not hold any *zār* jewellery at all.[229] The Schienerl-collection contains many items from Siwa as well, but among these are no *zār* pieces. Given the Schienerls' avid collecting of *zār* jewellery items, their absence supports the impression that *zār* was not practised in Siwa.[230] This evidence from the material record is supported by Bliss and Vale.[231] Both from the material record and literature, it would appear that *zār* was not practised in Siwa, but jewellery with spirit images is attributed to this oasis nonetheless. This attribution to Siwa, in my opinion, reflects two things. First, it illustrates how the already scant factual knowledge about *zār* jewellery continues to water down further. Second, it shows that vendors will look for a story that 'sells': conjuring up a provenance in a remote oasis that few collectors have been to is apparently believed to add to their chances of selling an object.[232]

3.1.7 A timeline of publishing

In this section, we have seen that jewellery with spirit images managed to escape the attention of cultural outsiders for half a century. Most publications between 1880 and 1962 are academic in nature, focusing on the ritual itself and treating jewellery only in passing.

From the 1960s onwards, jewellery with spirit representations starts to appear in publications which are aimed at a larger audience and centring around jewellery. The availability of publications aimed at a wider audience introduced *zār* jewellery to the world on a larger scale, and sparked the assembling of collections. In the next section, I will explore the history of collecting, after which I will go into the matter of availability to cultural outsiders.

---

227 As seen in several posts on Facebook-group Ethnic Jewels Community, such as a post on July 6th, 2017 'A small zar amulet from Siwa oasis' (https://www.facebook.com/groups/1033803409974413/permalink/1486108318077251/ accessed March 22, 2023), a post on November 27th, 2017 'Siwa zar pendant' (https://www.facebook.com/groups/1033803409974413/permalink/1622887251066023/, accessed March 22, 2023).

228 I have studied this collection during my study visit to the Weltmuseum in May 2019.

229 Internet consultation of the collection of the Musée d'Ethnographie in Geneva (http://www.ville-ge.ch/meg/sql/en/musinfo00.php?what=siwa&dpt=ETHAF&debut=0&bool=AND, accessed March 22, 2023).

230 *Zār* jewellery is not mentioned in Schienerl 1980c, an article focusing on female jewellery from Siwa.

231 Winkler 1936, p. 237 notes that *zār* is not practised in Kharga oasis. Bliss states that *zār* is not practised in the western oases (p. 314 and 326); Vale 2016 does not mention *zār* in her elaborate account of life in Siwa. Haggman (pers. comm. via email on March 30th, 2020) confirmed from personal experience that *zār* is not practised in Siwa.

232 One vendor even attributed a *zār* pendant to India, although it carried an Egyptian hallmark. The pendant came to my attention because the prospective buyer asked for my opinion.

3.2 TO HAVE AND TO HOLD: COLLECTED OBJECTS

The *zār* jewellery we know today comes to us as collected objects in museum and private collections. The sample collection shows a periodisation in collecting: the oldest collections contain the highest number of old pendants. Of all jewellery hallmarked between 1913-1916, 70% is found in collections gathered in the 1970s and early 1980s. Jewellery hallmarked in 1978 is mainly found in collections assembled from the 1990s onwards. In this section, I will go over the collections that form the sample collection to see when these were put together and why: what motivated collectors and sellers?

3.2.1 Buying: museum collections from 1960 onwards

Zār jewellery is present in several museum collections. Collections that are labelled *zār* are invariably assembled after the 1960s, when the jewellery with spirit images first started to be published. I start my exploration into museum collections here and address older collections in the next section. Aside from the massive collection assembled by the Schienerl couple, which ended up in three different museums, several museums hold smaller amounts of *zār* jewellery and related items.

The collection of Peter and Jutta Schienerl

The largest collection of *zār* jewellery has been assembled by Peter and Jutta Schienerl between the early 1970s and the late 1980s. Peter Schienerl, an art historian, ethnologist, and collector, lived in Cairo from 1967 to 1986. Both his research interests and his collecting focus were Egyptian amulets and jewellery. He obtained his PhD on Egyptian traditional jewellery in Vienna in 1980 and had started collecting in the early 1970s, first for the museum in Vienna and the Ethnographical Museum of the Geographic Society, and soon also privately. These collections do not only consist of jewellery, but include a wide variety of objects including utensils and even tourist souvenirs. According to Gerber, who devoted her PhD to the Schienerl Collections, the motifs for his private collecting are difficult to trace but seem to have been related to a desire to fill the gap of ethnographic research in a country that attracted mostly the attention of archaeologists.[233] However commendable the goal, his methods of collecting and documenting pose a few challenges. The majority of the objects was bought in Cairo: Schienerl preferably bought from vendors in the capital.[234] These are also his main source of information; Gerber notes that Schienerl rarely conducted field research.[235] As he was a man, it would, of course, have been difficult for him to actually attend a *zār*, but most of his collecting, in general, took place in the *sūqs*. She notices that Schienerl collected first and interpreted later, both selectively to sustain his many theories.[236] This *modus operandi* has contributed to our current limited understanding of the function of *zār* jewellery. The collection holds mainly silver and beaded jewellery items, all labelled *zār*, and is now present in Museum für Völkerkunde in Dresden, the Landesmuseum Oldenburg and the Weltmuseum in Vienna.

---

233   Gerber 2008, p. 96, 97.
234   Gerber 2008, p. 96; Mörike 2021, p. 29; also apparent from the *Einkaufsbücher* or ledgers held in Dresden, where mainly Cairene vendors are listed as source, and in a few occasions Aswani dealers.
235   Gerber 2008, p. 96; Mörike 2021, p. 29.
236   Gerber 2008, p. 97.

Indiana University Museum of Archaeology and Anthropology, USA
The Indiana University Museum of Archaeology and Anthropology in Indianapolis, USA, holds 142 pieces labelled as *zār* in the collection of Dee Birnbaum.[237] These are part of a donation of 2,300 pieces to the museum, hailing from Turkey, Syria and Egypt. Mrs. Birnbaum travelled to Egypt every year since 1987, and collected *zār* jewellery using the book by Bachinger & Schienerl 1984.

Medelhavsmuseet, Sweden
Although the collection of the Medelhavsmuseet in Stockholm holds only two *zār* pendants, their context is of interest.[238] They were acquired in 1978 as part of the inventory of an *aṭṭar*-shop (a herbalist) by Carl Axel Silow. Silow was not an ethnographer, but an ethno-entomologist with Uppsala University. He neither spoke nor understood Arabic. As curator for the Ethnographic Museum in Göteborg, he spent three weeks in the area of Cairo and collected everything he came across; a barber shop tool kit, dresses, tools – and the aforementioned content of an *aṭṭar* shop, which sold both herbs and magical amulets.

National Museum of World Cultures, the Netherlands
The National Museum of World Cultures (the Netherlands) is an umbrella organisation spanning four ethnographic museums.[239] Three of these hold *zār* jewellery: the World Museum in Rotterdam, the World Museum in Leiden and the World Museum in Amsterdam. The fourteen pieces of the World Museum in Rotterdam were collected in Cairo 1971 by curator Fred Ros. The collection of the World Museum in Amsterdam consists of seven pieces. Four of these were acquired in 1997 in an antiques' shop in Cairo by Mirjam Shatanawi, who later became curator at the museum. Three pieces were a donation to the museum by Johan Weststeijn, whose great-aunt had acquired them while living in Upper Egypt in the 1970s: no further information about their acquisition is known.[240] Interestingly, the World Museum in Leiden holds two *zār* pendants that have been collected before the 1960s, and that brings me to early collections featuring *zār* jewellery.

3.2.2 Buying: museum collections before 1960
Zār jewellery with spirit images started to be photographed and described from the 1960s onwards – before that, these pieces were invisible. Invisible and unknown though they might have been, they did exist. Therefore, it occurred to me that jewellery that we would recognise as *zār* today might be present in other museum collections but not labelled as such. To see whether this was the case, I have contacted ethnographic museums in Europe to ask about their Egyptian jewellery from between ca 1880 – 1960, and perused

---

237 This section is based on personal communication via email with dr. Emily Bryant, October 23, 2020.
238 This section is based on information received from Dr. Häggman, curator of the Medelhavsmuseet in Stockholm, March 30th, 2020 and April 2nd, 2020.
239 At the time of writing, the Africa Museum in Berg en Dal was also part of the National Museum of World Cultures. However, their collection does not hold *zār* jewellery.
240 Personal communication via email with J. Weststeijn on October 9th 2020, and J. Voorhoeve (nephew) on October 12th, 2020.

collections that have been placed online. Besides the World Museum in Leiden, two other museums hold *zār* jewellery with spirit depictions collected well before 1960.

Haus der Kulturen, Basel

The oldest piece that bears spirit images was collected in 1889.[241] It was acquired by Paul and Fritz Sarasin, two grand-cousins whose collection forms the foundation of the ethnographic collection of the *Haus der Kulturen* in Basel. The collectors travelled in Egypt from January to March 1889 and collected with the objective of finding original Egyptian pieces that were in daily use and 'free from European influences'. To reach this goal, they used the 5th edition of the work by Edward Lane, *An Account of the Manners and Customs of the modern Egyptians*, published in 1871. They considered this to be an authoritative and complete work, and so the search for ethnographical objects was focused on the pieces described and depicted here, to make sure they only acquired 'real' Egyptian material. They found help in this endeavour with a Swiss jeweller, mr. Bangerter, who knew his away around the *sūqs* in Cairo and spoke Arabic. This piece is described as a forehead-ornament and shows two human-headed fish. It is identical to later *zār*-pendants with human-headed fish in its design.

The collection of Winifred Blackman

Winifred Blackman, an anthropologist from Oxford, worked as assistant-curator at the Pitt-Rivers Museum.[242] During her studies and subsequent position at the museum, she developed a strong interest in ethnography, particularly in jewellery. She first visited Egypt in 1921 and returned many times afterwards for anthropological research and ethnographic collecting. These collections also did not focus exclusively on jewellery, but included utensils as well. For every object she acquired, either as gift or as a purchase, she took notes to describe its function and meaning.

She collected throughout Egypt, in Cairo as well as in Middle and Upper Egypt. Her main sources of information were both the people she acquired objects from, including 'wise women'[243], village women, and vendors in markets. She also relied on her own observations of informal ritual events she attended. Additionally, Egyptian friends sent her objects with elaborate descriptions. She collected both for herself and for various institutions.

The ornaments she collected are now housed in the Pitt-Rivers Museum in Oxford (almost 4,000 pieces, most of them amulets and medicine), the British Museum (128 pieces, most of them utensils) and the Garstang Museum of Archaeology of the University of Liverpool. The collection in the Pitt-Rivers Museum contains one silver *zār* pendant showing a mermaid, and one silver temple pendant that in later collections is identified as *zār*. Neither are explicitly labelled *zār*: the information documented for the mermaid-pendant is that it helps, oddly enough, against stomach ache. It was

---

241 This section is based on personal communication via email with curator Franziska Jenni, who kindly included excerpts from the *Jahresbericht* 1894 describing this collection, November 2, 2020.
242 This section is based on Stevenson 2013, Del Vesco 1915 and personal communication with the Garstang Museum of Archeology, University of Liverpool, April 24th, 2019.
243 Stevenson 2013, p. 143.

labelled as hailing from India in the museum registration: not by Winifred herself, but a later registrar mistakenly added this attribution into the database.[244]

Two beaded necklaces are also present: again, not labelled *zār*, but identical to the beaded *zār*-jewellery illustrated and labelled as such in the caption in Blackman 1927. The collection also holds a cloth wrapped around several coins and dipped in blood, said to have been used in a *ṣulḥ*: in the previous section we have seen this to be a part a ritual to deal with spirit possession. Apart from jewellery that we would recognise as *zār* jewellery today, the collection holds dozens of pebbles, pieces of bone, incense and a few glass beads that are labelled as amulets in various cases of spirit possession.

The collection of the World Museum Leiden, the Netherlands

The two pieces in the World Museum in Leiden (The Netherlands) form part of the collection originally assembled by the Oosters Instituut (Oriental Foundation). The museum received them on permanent loan in 1958 as part of the larger collection of the foundation: the two amulets have been acquired before that date. Although the collection in its entirety was labelled as coming from the Arab Peninsula, subsequent research has shown that it holds objects from several countries. At the moment of transfer from the Oosters Instituut to the World Museum, information about its geographical provenance was already missing.

3.2.3 Buying: private collections

Where museum collections have been assembled by people that can mostly no longer be asked directly about their objectives and criteria, this is different for current private collections. I have interviewed collectors about their motivations for collecting this type of jewellery in particular.

From this round of inquiries, one main factor emerges: the majority of collectors of *zār* jewellery have a personal connection with Egypt. They are either Egyptians themselves or have lived and worked in Egypt as (partner of) long-term expats or archaeologists. In the case of foreigners, they learned of *zār* jewellery through other expats or encountered *zār* items when searching for traditional silver jewellery in the *sūq*. Every foreign collector finds the background story in a possession ritual intriguing, but none have actually attended a *zār*.[245] This interest reflects an outsider's point of view: possession, for Western collectors, is an alien concept and more of a curiosity, whereas for the original wearers, possession was a fact of life. For Egyptian collectors, the perspective is different. Dr. el-Hadidi is a *zār* specialist as well as collector and academic researcher. Other Egyptian collectors may regard *zār* as folk belief, but as they accept jinn to be existing creatures, this is still different from Western collectors who do not share a similar belief at all. The jewellery items collected by both groups are mainly the pendants and bracelets with spirit images. These are the most recognizable, and the variation in spirits is attractive.

What about collectors of traditional jewellery of the Middle East who do <u>not</u> collect *zār* jewellery? I have asked two major collectors why their collections, that

---

244 Confirmed via email by Faye Belsey, November 10th, 2020. The attribution as amulet against stomach pain comes from Blackman herself.
245 Some have attended the performances by the musical group *Asyad al-Zar* in Makan theatre in Cairo.

otherwise do include Egyptian jewellery, lack *zār* jewellery.[246] First, neither has a personal connection with Egypt. Availability was the main other factor for Joost Daalder (Adelaide)[247]: he never came across Egyptian *zār* jewellery, but assured me that even if he had, he would not have bought any due to aesthetic reasons. René van der Star (The Netherlands) also gave aesthetic reasons for his decision not to acquire this type of jewellery. These aesthetic considerations towards *zār* jewellery, in my opinion, align with the general way traditional jewellery has been collected and regarded since the 1960s: the aesthetic aspects of jewellery take precedence over other contexts, as also argued by Unger[248] and Alsop[249].

3.2.4 Selling: vendors

On the other end of the buying spectrum are, of course, the sellers. I have enquired with three vendors in Egypt, all of whom share similar experiences with jewellery availability over the past few decades.

Alaa Abdou (Cairo)[250] began his business in 1990 after having worked in the gold *sūq*. He recalls how he started looking for old silver jewellery when tourists expressed an interest, initially sourcing his jewellery from silver ore dealers. These dealers supplied silversmiths with raw materials by melting down silver jewellery, a practice also witnessed by Azza Fahmy, who obtained both raw silver for her designs as well as pieces of old silver jewellery.[251] Alaa is well known among expats, including for *zār* jewellery, as we have seen above.

Usama Dawood (Cairo)[252] started his business in antiques and jewellery in 1987, and has since sold most of his *zār* jewellery collection to foreigners. He confirms that *zār* jewellery is now hard to find: he collects pendants with spirit representations by visiting the old Friday market in Cairo and finds approximately one piece per month. Alternatively, his friends and other sources in the rest of the country let him know if they come across a good piece, and if the price is right, he will take it.

Hussein Gouda (Cairo)[253] accidentally ended up in the trade of old silver jewellery. He was selling newly made silver jewellery when he came across old jewellery with silver suppliers, much like Alaa told me earlier. These suppliers obtained their goods from local village vendors: the Cairene wholesale vendors were well-known throughout the country, and local vendors would travel to the capital to sell jewellery they had collected from women in the village. Hussein recounts how many of these items were available as they were not popular in Egypt and were mainly bought by foreigners. These days, traditional silver jewellery is hard to find: it is no longer available in the same quantities and what does remain, has mostly been acquired by tourists (as one-time souvenir) and collectors. Regarding *zār* jewellery, he notes that mass produced designs

---

246 René van der Star (Amsterdam) and Joost Daalder (Adelaide). Both have built up important collections of traditional jewellery.
247 Personal communication, September 18, 2020.
248 Unger 2019, p. 175.
249 Alsop 1982, p. 89.
250 Personal communication on September 19, 2020.
251 Fahmy 2007, p. 10-11.
252 Personal communication on March 19 and 20, 2019.
253 Personal communication on October 1, 2020.

can still be found but only in a few shops, while the rarer designs are very hard to come by at all. I will return to this differentiation in rare and mass-produced items in the next part of this thesis, when we will look at the jewellery itself.

If these vendors, who began their business in the late 1980s and early 1990s, found their stock at wholesale dealers, where did the Schienerls get their jewellery a decade earlier? Their yearly ledgers provide a record of what they bought, where, and at what price.[254] From these records, it appears that they acquired silver jewellery, including their collection of pendants with spirit images, from wholesale dealers as well. An example is a set of eight jewellery pieces, bought in 1983 from a certain Atef at 50 piaster per gram, including a text amulet, two *zār* pendants, a headdress pendant, an amulet container, two pillar dollars (or imitations thereof) and a Yemeni amulet container. An interesting feature emerging from the ledgers is that they obtained beaded *zār* jewellery from an unspecified '*zar-händler*'; a vendor of *zār* supplies. In 1974, for instance, they listed seven beaded items from a *zār* supplier, followed by a crescent moon necklace acquired from Mekkawy, the most famous wholesale dealer according to Fahmy[255]. At this point, the Schienerls seem to have found silver *zār* jewellery with wholesale sellers, while there were also designated vendors of *zār* supplies active.

3.2.5 Life as collected object

The majority of the collected *zār* jewellery became part of a museum collection. It is spending its life unseen, stored in drawers. It is only taken out when needed for an exhibition, but rarely becomes part of the permanent display: I have seen this only in the Medelhavsmuseet in Stockholm. Those exhibitions often rely on private collections as well. For instance, the exhibition on jewellery from the Arab world held in the National Museum of Antiquities in Leiden in 2010 featured *zār* jewellery from three private collections, including my own.[256] The exhibition Healing Power, held in the World Museum in Leiden in 2019, showed *zār* pendants as objects of ritual.

Private collectors engage more actively with their jewellery. Since their primary goal is acquiring the object itself, these pieces take on new meanings. Collectors wear one or several pendants on a necklace, or take their jewellery out to show to others, either in real life or by sharing photos online. In both cases, the pendants (as these are the main item collected) are shown with their spirit-side outward and the Throne Verse inward. An example is a necklace designed by Reem Maguid Amin (Figure 3.1), including sample coll. 801 and 802.

Here, the spirit side is worn outward, and the two pendants now function as spacer elements for a multi-strand necklace. Numerous such creations exist and are proudly worn by their owners. The images of spirits carry more meaning than the Throne Verse: many collectors cannot read Arabic, and the visual variety is what makes these pendants so attractive.

As we shall see, this is the exact opposite of how they were worn in their previous life. Not only have these jewellery objects entered a social context entirely different

---

254 I have studied these during my stay in Dresden, where they form part of the collection of the Museum für Völkerkunde.
255 Fahmy 2007, p. 10.
256 Exhibition 'Charming' in the National Museum of Antiquities, Leiden, from November 2010 – March 2011.

Figure 3.1. Necklace showing two pendants with spirit images, reused as spacer elements. Design by Reem Maguid Amin. Photo Sigrid van Roode.

from their previous life, the value attached to them has also changed: they have changed from profoundly private to proudly public objects.

3.2.6 A timeline of collecting

Based on the collection history outlined above, it appears that before the 1960s at the earliest, *zār* jewellery was not widely collected, and access to it by Western collectors was likely limited. Only a few silver jewellery items that we would recognise as *zār* today, found their way to museum collections at this point. This started to change in the late 1950s/early 1960s, when Kriss and Kriss-Heinrich acquired several silver pendants which they identified as *zār*. In the 1970s older pendants became available with wholesale silver dealers in Cairo, serving as raw material for silversmiths. By the mid-1980s, owners of silver shops began offering individual pieces for sale, attracting a growing clientele of private collectors, fuelled by the publications by Schienerl. From the mid-1990s, the availability of *zār* jewellery started to decline. Nowadays, in the early 2020s, *zār* jewellery is hard to find in Egypt. In the 1960s-1970s, silver *zār* jewellery, which had been hallmarked 50 years earlier, became available – the *zār* jewellery of the first generation of users. From that point onward, *zār* jewellery continued to enter the market, where cultural outsiders could purchase it to their heart's content. In the next section, I will explore what the jewellery in the sample collection reveals about its life before it was collected, and after its wearers did let go of it.

3.3 DISASSOCIATION FROM THE PRIMARY LIFE

How did these items become separated from their original role as jewellery associated with *zār*? What transpired in between their appearance on the market and their use by the possessed? The sample collection of jewellery items provides clues about another life – sometimes lived very briefly, sometimes for a considerable amount of time – before they became the collected objects they are today, forming the starting point of this study. Traces of alterations, adaptations and reuse provide glimpses of their transition beyond *zār*. These traces are prominently visible in one category of jewellery: the jewellery pieces uniquely produced for *zār*, recognizable by their spirit images. This section presents other occasions in which *zār* jewellery was used in Egypt and beyond before the objects moved to the collections they are in now, and explores a possible indicator of disassociation from *zār*.

3.3.1 Reuse within *zār*

Six pendants have their representation altered or overwritten completely.[257] Four of these pendants form as such palimpsests, while two have an added text only.[258]

Figure 3.2 shows an example of a reworked pendant. Originally, this seems to have been a pendant with text on both sides: the faint remnants of three dividing lines can be discerned on the reverse. These are similar to the division on the obverse. The original text is also still visible. At some point, the reverse was changed from text to spirit representation. Over the text, a female standing figure was engraved. The contours of her face have been filled in with extremely fine lines, possibly to make her stand out from the original text. Her dress is also filled in with deep zigzag lines. Remarkably, in this case as well the outer border decoration has been renewed.

Another form of refashioning within a *zār* context is adding (semi)precious stones or glass to the pendant at a later stage in honour of the spirit possessing the wearer, making the piece even more personal.[259] Sample coll. 846[260] has a red glass inset placed between two spirits and may well be an example of this practice. All of these pendants apparently remained in use within a *zār*-context, retaining their status as singular object.[261]

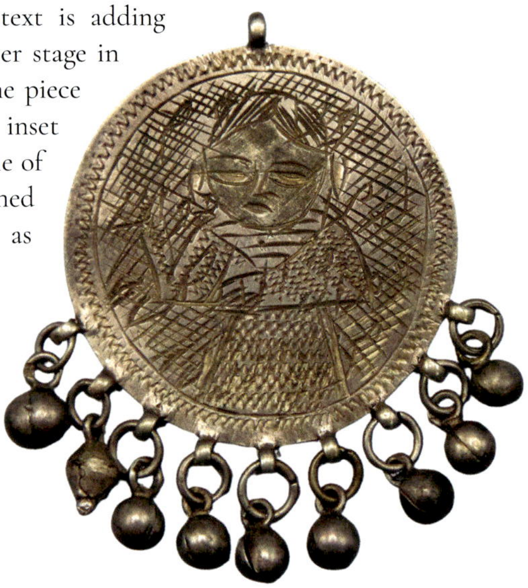

Figure 3.2. A pendant which has been redecorated completely (sample coll. 321). Not to scale. Collection and photo S. van Roode.

3.3.2 Reuse beyond *zār*

Jewellery with spirit images has been used as source material for other jewellery items, indicating their use beyond the *zār* itself and as such their transition into a commodity.

---

257 The redecoration of sample coll. 125 was already noted by Schienerl, who made a note of it in his *Einkaufsbuch* 1981-1982 under entry 520. He describes the original decoration as *Sultan mit Tarbush*.
258 The four palimpsest pendants are sample coll. 45, 125, 161, (all Landesmuseum Oldenburg) and 321 (my own collection); sample coll. 71 and 91 (both Landesmuseum Oldenburg) have added text.
259 This practice was shared with me by dr el-Hadidi on November 10, 2020. She described to me how she added a piece of emerald to her pendant in honour of her spirit.
260 Weltmuseum Vienna, inv. no. 161704.
261 Sample coll. 125, Landesmuseum Oldenburg, no inventory number, might be refashioned in the context of the 1919 revolution: see chapter 5.

Figure 3.3. Two *zār*-pendants reworked into earrings or headdress ornaments (sample coll. 360 & 361). Not to scale. Collection and photo S. van Roode.

Alterations

Re-cutting *zār* jewellery into new shapes is telling of this process. In total, 25 pendants have been recut.

Figure 3.3 is an example. It shows sample coll. 360 and 361, both from my own collection. These were both originally a pendant in the shape of a writing board, depicting a male and female spirit with a fish in between. They have been turned into a rectangular amulet by removing the upper part of the original pendant. In doing so, the image was cut in half. On the reverse, the new rectangular surface has been used to apply a zigzag-border enclosing the Bismillah-formula. The secondary engraving is in a much cruder hand than the original engraving on the front side. They may have been used as headdress ornaments. The orientation of the suspension loop for the bells may even indicate a third refashioning. They indicate these pendants are meant to be worn with the spirit representation outward. This is unusual for headdress ornaments, where one would see the text side worn outward: given that this is a pair, they may be refurbished into earrings for the tourist trade. Similar reworking of pendants into earrings are in the collection of the Landesmuseum Oldenburg.[262]

Beyond the sample collection for this study, refashioned *zār* pendants appear in other collections as well. The collection of Jordanian-Iraqi fashion designer Hana Sadiq contains another two *zār* pendants which have been refashioned into earrings, one with a representation of a male and female spirit and one with a camel carrying the *maḥmal*. She describes them as 'silver earrings with magical symbols' from Egypt.[263] Her collection includes another pair of earrings crafted from two

---

[262] Sample coll. 143/inventory number Sch1121 in the Landesmuseum Oldenburg is a pair of triangular earrings, cut out of two originally round *zār* pendants. Both have a different year-stamp and a different original engraving: they have been worked into a pair of earrings at a later stage. At this point, the silversmith added new dangles and added a Star of David-decoration over the existing the spirit representations on the original amulets. The texts on the other side have not been adapted, and as a result the earrings show only fragments of the original text. On both sides, a new border decoration has been engraved.

[263] Sadiq 2014, p. 218, image number E2.

refashioned Egyptian pendants, this time with calligraphy: she attributes this pair to Syria.²⁶⁴ Among her jewellery is also a silver necklace, composed of several 'pendants with magical inscriptions' attributed to Egypt, Syria and Iraq, including several Egyptian *zār* pendants.²⁶⁵

The sample collection also shows other signs of adaptation for sale to collectors. These are minor alterations, primarily aimed at making the piece more appealing for purchase: missing bells have been restored, broken bails have been repaired. This is standard practice with all silver vendors in Egypt: they keep a stash of spare parts to restore jewellery pieces, and are happy to assist in adding a new bail or additional decoration.²⁶⁶ Examples in the catalogue that show these smaller adaptations are cat. nos. 035, 041 and 045.

In sixteen cases, beads have been added, such as shown in Figure 3.4. Two original dangles are missing altogether, leaving only the remnants of their bails to hint at their previous existence, while the rest has been embellished with beads. I suspect that, in most cases, this serves to heighten the piece's appeal to potential buyers, as touched upon in 3.1.5, rather than serving the purpose of honouring the spirit possessing the wearer. I base this assumption on the visibility of the piece when worn: as I have

Figure 3.4. Pendant with added beads (sample coll. 701). Not to scale. Collection and photo R. Cappers.

asserted in 3.1, the pendants with spirit depictions remained out of sight. Adding a conspicuous set of beads and other embellishments makes that goal considerably more difficult. I return to the delicate balance between visibility and invisibility in the next chapter.

Adaptations for textile

Another indicator for renewed use is the presence of a hole pierced directly into the pendant itself. This occurs in fifteen cases. The presence of a perforation indicates the piece has been worn sewn onto a textile backing, such as a veil or a dress, as illustrated in this detail of a coin sewn onto a Sinai face veil in my personal collection (Figure 3.5).

This method ensures the ornament is securely affixed to the textile and less likely to get lost. In these cases, the wear on the hole provides insight into how the pendant was sewn onto the piece. Since it was pierced from one side, the other side of the hole will exhibit serrated edges. To avoid damaging the fabric underneath, a pierced piece is sewn on with the 'exit'-side of the hole upward, away from the fabric. Judging by the wear on the hole, it appears pendants with spirit images were sewn on with the Throne

---

264 Sadiq 2014, p. 231, image number E17.
265 Sadiq 2014, p. 135, image number C158. I have included this necklace here, instead of in the section of collectors' designs, as in this case the pendants have not been recognised as *zār*.
266 Added decorations are also the topic of much debate concerning the price: beads make the piece heavier, which translates into a higher price as the weight is usually the starting point to calculate a price.

Figure 3.5. Detail of a coin sewn on a veil, showing the construction. Similar holes are present in pendants with spirit engravings in the study collection. Collection and photo S.van Roode.

Verse outward and the spirit representations inward: the text would be on the visible side of the ornament. Figure 3.6 shows an example in the sample collection.

Similar alterations indicating the use on textile are visible on sample coll. 137 and 138.[267]

These alterations and adaptations of *zār* jewellery items prompted me to look outside of the sample collection for jewellery items that have not been collected as single items, but may remain on textiles or composite pieces of jewellery. In the next section, I discuss my findings.

Figure 3.6. Zār pendant with several pierced holes (sample coll. 1027, see also cat. no. 053 in the catalogue). Not to scale. Collection and photo S. van Roode.

---

[267] Landesmuseum Oldenburg, no inventory number. Both are triangular pieces cut out of an originally round *zār* pendant, and have five holes pierced in one corner and one in the middle of the opposite border. Here as well, the direction in which the holes have been drilled indicates wear with the Throne Verse outward.

3.3.3 Zār jewellery on the fringes of Egypt

If *zār* jewellery items were remade into general pendants or sewn on textile, they might be present but unrecognised in collections of veils, garments and jewellery. To see if this is the case, I have examined the collection of Egyptian and Palestinian veils of Wearable Heritage/Jolanda Bos (Zandvoort, the Netherlands). As *zār* jewellery seems to have travelled beyond Egypt after its disassociation from its primary life, I have also used publications of parts of the Tiraz collection in Amman, Jordan[268], the publication of the collection of Hana Sadiq in Jordan[269] and the publication of Angela Fisher featuring the Rashayda[270]. The aim of this excursus was to increase my understanding of the use of *zār* jewellery outside *zār*.

Bedouin of Sinai and Palestine

One pendant with spirit images in the collection of Widad Kawar is published in Volger 1987, together with a pendant carrying the Throne Verse on both sides.[271] In this publication, the pendants are called by the general name *higāb* or *maskeh*, both meaning 'amulet.' Both pieces eventually made their way to Gaza, where the pendant with texts underwent alterations. The original disc was embellished with six Ottoman coins and one stylised hand. In addition, two beads, a red and a blue one, were added to the dangles. The pendant with spirit images has not been recognised as belonging to the Egyptian *zār*, and the author notes that the appearance of human figures on this pendant is highly unusual.[272] Rahm-Mottl published another *zār* pendant in the Widad Kawar collection[273], as well as an amulet necklace of various beads with one *zār* pendant[274]. These necklaces were worn by the Bedouin of southern Palestine and Sinai. According to Rahm-Mottl, the pendants carry meaning for the Bedouin due to the Throne Verse inscribed on them; their origin in *zār* carries no meaning.[275]

It's not impossible for elements like these to end up on face veils as well; these were heavily decorated with coins, metal discs, beads and an array of other objects.[276] However, I have not found complete *zār* pendants attached on Bedouin headdresses or face veils; they seem to have been used as element in necklaces only.

One example, found on a face veil in the collection of Wearable Heritage/Jolanda Bos (Figure 3.7), might be a reused *zār* pendant, judging by its decoration on the one side and the presence of text on the other. It has been cut into a lozenge. Lozenge-shaped embellishments are frequently added to Bedouin face veils, and, in this case, the pendant has been repurposed as source material to create such a lozenge from.

---

268   The information in this section comes from Volger 1987 and Biasio 1998. I have not been able to travel to Amman myself, and Tiraz Centre was unable to verify if these are the only examples in the vast collections, or that there may be more.
269   Sadiq 2014.
270   Fisher 1996.
271   Collection Widad Kawar, published in Volger 1987, p. 348 (text) and 349 (photograph). Catalogue nrs 308 and 309. Tiraz inventory numbers TRX5J and TRX6J.
272   Volger 1987, p. 348.
273   Biasio 1998, p. 243, Tiraz inventory number 22165b.
274   Biasio 1998, p. 251, Tiraz inventory number 22106.
275   Biasio 1998, p. 243-244.
276   Vogelsang-Eastwood 1996, p. 57; Bos 2016, pp. 136-142.

Figure 3.7. Recut *zār* pendant on face veil. Collection Wearable Heritage/Jolanda Bos. Photo S. van Roode.

The Bedouin of Sinai and Palestine do not practice *zār*: as in the western oases, *zār* pendants are used as decorative element, as raw material for new forms of adornments or as amulet because of the text inscribed on the obverse.

Rashayda

The Rashayda tribes of the Red Sea coast wear elaborate face veils. The heavy textiles, decorated with silver thread, are embellished further by sewing ornaments on the outside. Rashayda face veils feature ornaments from Yemen, Nubia and the Nile Valley, with the most distant piece being a *salhāt* pendant from Siwa or even Libya. Among these ornaments, *zār* pendants also appear.[277] The choice of an ornament does not seem to be based on a specific meaning attributed to them but rather on availability. Here, the use of *zār* jewellery is the opposite of that in Sinai and Palestine: the pendants are worn on the face veil but never in necklaces. The Rashayda, like the Bedouin, do not practice *zār*.[278]

This brief exploration into the use of *zār* jewellery outside the ritual itself demonstrates how *zār* jewellery with spirit images on the fringes of Egypt already functioned as a commodity rather than a singularity in the sense put forward by Kopytoff: *zār* jewellery served as source material for other forms of adornment. The material record further illustrates that the popularity of *zār* as ritual was concentrated

---

277 See Fisher 1996, p. 276 for a photograph.
278 Personal communication Martina Dempf on November 15th, 2018 and Ingrid Langerak on January 25th, 2019. Dempf has worked intensively with the Rashayda, Langerak has lived in Ethiopia for over 30 years and used to trade with the Rashayda. I have asked both about their experiences with the Rashayda. Winkler 1936, p. 237, notes that the Azaiza, a semi-sedentary tribe living more northern in the Eastern Desert, in the vicinity of Qift, do not practice *zār* either.

in the Nile Valley itself, and reflects the direction of material culture of *zār* moving eastward rather than westward: in the Western oases, *zār* jewellery with spirit images is absent, in the east jewellery is reused as general embellishment. Costume and dress specialists do not always recognise the nature of embellishments sewn onto their textiles, and scholars well versed in jewellery varieties from, for example, Palestine do not necessarily identify 'strange' ornaments correctly. There may be more *zār* jewellery items hiding in plain sight – an interesting avenue for future research.

3.3.4 Telling damages

The previous sections have focused on the reuse of *zār* jewellery before and up until their availability on the market for cultural outsiders. One last form of treatment visible in the sample collection may point to the step before that, when the disassociation from their primary life took place: intentional damage. In this final section of this chapter, I will approach the threshold between primary and secondary lives from the point of view of collected objects. In the next chapter, I will explore the other side of this disassociation process from the point of view of living objects.

Returning to the topic of damage, this could of course occur during the jewellery's lifetime, as it was worn close to the body for many years. Damage certainly also occurred after their primary life, when they were thrown in bags and boxes with other jewellery items. Given that some of the pieces even are almost a century old, some wear and tear is be expected.

Damage occurs in the form of bending (fifteen pieces) when pendants are bent double lengthwise, along the axis of eye to dangles. While most examples have been flattened again, the fold always remains visible. Six pieces show deep cuts, as if someone tried to cut them in half or initiated a refashioning process only to stop after the first attempt. Both are, in my opinion, forms of 'regular' damage to pieces that have become a commodity. However, the type of damaging I would like to address here consistently occurs in nearly 10% of the pendants with spirit representations and, in my view, reflects its singularity instead.

Of the 681 pendants with spirit representations, 66 bear a pattern of diagonal scratches on the surface, in almost all cases through the depiction of the spirit or spirits. Shown here in figure 3.8 is sample coll. 325 with visible scratch marks on the pendant. It is almost as if the images have been struck through with a sharp, multi-toothed instrument. On the other side, no damage is visible.

The majority of the pieces treated this way (49 pieces) date from before 1950: seven are hallmarked in 1953-1959, and another ten are not hallmarked but can stylistically be placed in the first half of the 20th century as well. All of them are hand engraved pendants: this type of damaging does not occur in the later, machine-tooled pieces. None of the literature on *zār* jewellery mentions this: it only becomes apparent as a factor of significance now, when jewellery is studied in larger numbers. I feel that this scratching occurs too consistently to be attributed to later mishandling or refashioning attempts. I interpret these damages as intentional and consider them to be material

Figure 3.8. Pendant with diagonal scratches (sample coll. 325). Not to scale. Collection and photo S. van Roode.

remains of a commodification process, whereby the object transited from a personal, singular object to a general commodity, along the lines put forward by Kopytoff and applied by Garcia Probert for the Tawfiq Canaan collection of Palestinian amulets.[279] This latter collection is very similar to regular amulets as they were used in Egypt, as a comparison with the collection of Winifred Blackman or the publication by Kriss & Kriss-Heinrich shows. Garcia Probert discusses the commodification process of amulets in great detail, both for the circulation within Palestine as well as for the moment they are taken out of circulation and end up in the collection of Canaan himself.[280] Damaging, however, is not asserted as practice of commodification for objects in this collection, and is usually not encountered on comparable Egyptian amulets either. Why did part of the wearers of pendants with spirit representations feel the need to damage these before letting go of them? I feel this practice prompts a reconsideration of the nature of *zār* jewellery – and of *zār* itself. I will explore this in the next chapter.

---

279 Garcia Probert 2021, p. 140.
280 Garcia Probert 2021, chapter 2.

4

LIVING OBJECTS

4.1 CHALLENGES WITH INTERPRETING DECONTEXTUALISED OBJECTS

What is zār jewellery? We know the jewellery with spirit images was produced for zār, but other than that, how do we distinguish between regular and zār-jewellery? Scholars and collectors have been struggling with this very question since the 1960s. As zār jewellery has become a decontextualised group of material culture, that struggle becomes even more challenging. In this chapter, I will take a closer look at the sample collection, as well as the written sources, to trace what jewellery has been described as used in zār, and if we may learn anything about that use. This exploration will show that distinguishing zār jewellery from regular jewellery based on visual characteristics is nearly impossible. However, this exploration has not been entirely fruitless: while it may reveal that this has been the wrong approach, it also paves the way for a better understanding of what zār jewellery is.

4.1.1 Jewellery in written sources pre-dating the collection phase

I turn first to the written sources that pre-date the collection phase. As these describe bits and pieces of the events witnessed, at this point I would like to refer back to chapter 2 for the general framework of the ritual. With this framework in mind, I will look at what picture written sources, pre-dating the collecting phase, paint. And what did its authors believe the jewellery was used for?

Klunzinger

In 1878, Klunzinger mentions a thick silver ring without a stone, and occasionally bracelets and anklets as the only jewellery used in zār.[281] They are used to satisfy the spirit: as an example, Klunzinger related that the possessed are shown a silver ring, henna paste or *busa* (a form of beer), which they will snatch from the hands of the offeror after which they will calm down, a sign that the spirit has indeed been satisfied. It is unclear whether the patient keeps the silver ring, or returns it to whoever showed it to her once the spirit had calmed down. The chosen moment of offering jewellery is when the patient apparently already is possessed by her spirit: one could argue that the spirit, rather than the patient, is the intended recipient. And while the exact title is

---

281 Klunzinger 1878, pp. 388-389.

not specified, it lies within reason to assume that the individual offering the jewellery to the spirit possessing the patient is the ritual specialist.

Le Brun

In 1902, Le Brun attended a *zār* in Cairo and noted of the women as they were coming into the venue these were wearing 'clanking jewellery of bizarre forms, outfitted with dangles and light sequins suspended from their headdresses, shimmering in the dim light.'[282] While describing as much of the ritual as she could see, Le Brun notes that after the sacrificial animal had been led away and slaughtered out of her sight, the possessed returned into the room preceded by the ritual specialist who carried a platter filled with jewellery, 'bathing in blood'.[283] The purpose of this jewellery remains undiscussed, although her explanation of the success of the ritual specialist with their clients may shed light on her perception of this aspect. Regarding this success, she says that *kōdiyas* are able to convince people that their suffering is caused by spirit possession, and can be cured by means of a *zār*, incense and 'consecrated jewellery'.[284] A second *zār* she attended stretched for multiple days and is different in that it was a gathering of ritual specialists in the house of a colleague.[285] Here, all elements of the previous *zār* occur, but Le Brun only briefly mentions jewellery at the beginning of her observation, before the incensing starts. She describes how the jewellery worn by the ritual specialists present at this point glinted when it caught the sunlight, and mentions in particular necklaces from fine shells and coral beads, that hung down to their waist.[286]

Sidqi

In 1911, Mahmud Sidqi describes a *zār* as it was carried out for normal and rich people. In the section about regular people, he describes the *zār* 'bride as wearing white clothing.[287] The ritual specialist is also wearing white.[288] She wears silver rings on her thumbs, on the index finger and middle finger of her right hand and on the ring finger and little finger of the left hand. Around her neck she wears several amulets in silver, among which round ones that carry the Throne Verse, and another silver rounded amulet that sports bells all around it. These may very well be what was visible of *zār* pendants with spirit images as we know them today – but whether they actually sported such images is not mentioned. In addition, she wears a 'heart' amulet, consisting of a deep red carnelian set in silver, sometimes in the shape of an egg and sometimes round, with bells, and an amulet depicting the mermaid Sitt Safina. As I have noted earlier, none of the literature mentions the now familiar pendants with engraved spirit representations. So, how does Sidqi's description fit in with that statement? The mere fact that this particular amulet was described, means that it must have been visible. This, in turn, indicates the type of jewellery worn:

---

282 Le Brun 1902, p. 268.
283 Le Brun 1902, p. 273.
284 Le Brun 1902, p. 293.
285 Le Brun 1902, p. 283.
286 Le Brun 1902, p. 278.
287 Littmann 1950, p. 2, translating a manuscript by Sidqi from 1911.
288 Littmann 1950, p. 2, translating a manuscript by Sidqi from 1911.

pendants with mermaids worn around 1911 looked different. They are often embossed, like the example shown in Figure 4.1, and so are meant to be seen from one side only. I will return to these amulets in the final part of this thesis.

The outfit is described in the paragraph preceding the detailed description of the actual ceremony, leading me to conclude that the ritual specialist wore all this from the start of the events. Upon the slaughter of the animals, only the thaler used earlier to diagnose the patient is put into the blood.[289] After the week of seclusion, the patient puts the thaler on her neck, hanging on her chest, 'for ever and ever'.[290] This wearing of the thaler is described as the 'binding' or the contract between spirit and patient. The thaler is used before the ceremony, during diagnosis, and at the end of the ceremony, serving as the material part of the contract between patient and spirit.

For the rich, the same manuscript lists a variety of jewellery. First, Sidqi mentions how the ritual specialist discusses the necessary offerings, clothing, and amulets for the patient. Following this, he describes the clothing and jewellery in two separate paragraphs. Based on this sequence, and the statements in the jewellery paragraph, it appears that this description pertains to the patient's jewellery rather than that of the ritual specialist.[291] The jewellery is usually made of silver, but the very rich can order some of these in pure gold. Sidqi describes the following items:

Figure 4.1. Embossed pendant with mermaid, hallmarked before 1916 (sample coll. 970). Not to scale. Collection Qilada Foundation – Eric and Marion Crince Le Roy. Photo S. van Roode.

- A heart amulet;
- A head amulet;
- A small band of silver or gold, decorated with small bells, worn on the upper arms and called 'shinshillu';
- Silver rings with bezels in a round and flat shape, or in the shape of baklava (trapezoid). Sidqi explicitly notes that these bezels are made in this shape instead of inlaid stones;
- Rings without bezels;
- Anklets with small bells;
- *Zu'ra*, a round piece in gold or silver with small and delicate plaquettes hanging from it. These are used for pregnant patients;
- Earrings worn in the earlobe;
- Small rings without bezels with delicate round plaquettes, worn in the upper ear;
- A side-amulet: a long plaquette, with holes on the upper side, worn on a thin silver chain around the neck and below the left armpit.

---

289 Littmann 1950, p. 3, translating a manuscript by Sidqi from 1911.
290 Littmann 1950, p. 4, translating a manuscript by Sidqi from 1911.
291 Littmann 1950, p. 4-5, paragraphs 5, 6 and 7, translating a manuscript by Sidqi from 1911.

Upon the slaughter of the animals, all jewellery is put into the blood. The patient is daubed with the blood and stays in seclusion for a week. The manuscript does not mention when the jewellery is taken from the blood and worn, and it remains wholly unclear whether the patient continues to wear all jewellery or just a few items.

Kahle

In 1912, Paul Kahle describes the *zār* 'bride' being dressed in precious clothing, adorned with jewellery,[292] but makes little mention of jewellery in his paper, although he touches upon all other aspects such as the slaughter of animals and the trances.[293] In the translation of the Arabic text he presents, however, the *zār* bride is described as being dressed in white and wearing amulets called '*dandara*'.[294] In the annotation, Kahle refers to 'roughly triangular amulets in silver or gold, with texts such as Ya Hafez and Ya Amin, surrounded by small coins, as in Lane III 208 and Plate 62'.[295] He states that these jewellery items have been created for this purpose.[296] The reference to Lane is interesting, albeit confusing: Kahle does not clarify which edition of Lane's work he refers to and Lane's *Manners and Customs of the Modern Egyptians* is typically published in two volumes, not three. The only plate showing jewellery with the texts *Ya Hafez* and *Ya Amin* is in the section on female ornaments: here these are called *kamarah*,[297] rather than *dandara* as Kahle writes. Lane does not mention *zār* at all, and this absence is one of the main anchors for establishing the time of appearance of *zār* in Egypt. However, the jewellery items mentioned by Kahle <u>are</u> depicted in his book, and described by Kahle as 'purpose-made'. This discrepancy is significant and I will return to it later in this chapter.

Thompson & Franke

Writing in 1913, Anna Thompson relates how she and a few other missionaries attended a ceremony in a house where she and her companions often read the Bible to its inhabitants. She describes how, after the setting of the altar, 'the woman began to dress for the performance which casts out Sudanese spirits.' It is not clear who 'the woman' is. Thompson then describes how 'she and others were wearing blue and white Sudan charms, silver chains, anklets, bracelets etc., which had cowries or shells that rattled.'[298] In this case, the spirit was Christian, and the possessed woman wore a silver cross and crucifix. Thompson notes that this is to keep the spirit happy: if she would take these items off, she would suffer. In addition, she wore 'a silver medallion with bells on it, and silver rings on each finger, one having a cross on it.'[299] The threat of suffering if she were to remove these items indicates that these are supposed to be worn permanently. The silver medallion with bells on it may have been a *zār* pendant

---

292 Kahle 1912, p. 5.
293 Kahle 1912, p. 25 mentions a *zar*-song with a Sudanese beat including amulets from blue beads and an apron decorated with gold coins to be worn for Abu Danfa, and on p. 28 the song for Sitt Safīna mentions rings.
294 Kahle 1912, p. 31.
295 Kahle 1912, p. 31, note 2.
296 Kahle 1912, p. 31 note 2.
297 Lane 1842, p. 402; Lane 1860, p. 563-564.
298 Thompson & Franke, p. 276.
299 Ibid.

as we recognise it today, similar to the description in Sidqi 1911. She left before the animal sacrifice was made.

In the same publication, Elisabet Franke describes what she calls 'charms', consisting of 'silver ornaments and coins, worn on the breast beneath the dress, a ring with special inscriptions, or some other article'. These are given to the *zār* bride during the performances.[300] She also notes: 'The charms which are given to the Zar bride during the performances must never be removed, or the spirit will return at once.'[301] The generic description of 'ornaments' and 'articles' is not very precise, although she continues to describe amulets with Christian symbols such as the cross and the Virgin Mary engraved upon them, carrying the Throne Verse on the reverse side.[302]

Zwemer

In 1920, Zwemer noted the following items in his own collection which had been worn 'at the time of exorcism by the sheikh: First, a head-dress made of beads and cowrie shells with a fringe six inches wide, and a three-fold tassel. It is called a *takiet kharz*. A belt of the same beadwork, green and white beads mounted on a red girdle with border of cowrie shells. In addition to these, two small amulets are worn of the same material: one square and containing Koran passages and the other circular of the same character with other potent material against demons.'[303]

Sidqi

In 1930, the same Mahmud Sidqi wrote another manuscript on *zār*. Here, the description of jewellery follows only after the description of the ceremony and its songs, is much shorter and does not clarify who is wearing what. The items listed are[304]:

- An amulet for the head in silver or gold with little bells all around it;
- A heart amulet, carried on the chest;
- An amulet for the joints[305];
- Anklets;
- A head amulet, worn on the head;
- A bracelet with small bells, worn on the upper arm;
- A silver belt, worn on the body;
- Gold and silver rings, stuck on the fingers;
- Diamond earrings with gold and silver, made upon special request by the spirits, etc.
- The ominous 'etc' hints at more jewellery items used, but not listed.

---

300 Thompson & Franke, p. 284.
301 Thompson & Franke p. 284.
302 Zwemer 1920, p. 230, referring to this same article by Thompson & Franke, mentions having seen these in the bazaar in Cairo.
303 Zwemer 1920, p. 236.
304 Littmann 1950, p. 37, translating a manuscript by Mahmud Sidqi from 1930.
305 In German 'Gelenke'.

'Abd er-Rasoul

In 1955, 'Abd er-Rasoul published in article on *zār* in which she lists the jewellery items used. This is the first time jewellery with spirit images is mentioned. She identifies these as *'hegab'*, 'amulets', and describes them as 'square, oval, rectangular or round 'plates', with rattles or stones attached. Some of them have certain words in Arabic or designs engraved. These designs may be humans, fish, swords, stars or a crescent'.[306] She indicates that these may have different names depending on where they are worn on the body, such as heart amulets worn on the heart and head amulets worn on the forehead. The possessed person may also wear thumb rings, and/or bracelets and anklets.[307] She further notes that these amulets must be worn by the patient throughout their life.

Discussion

The identifications of '*zār* jewellery' diverge significantly in all these publications: the jewellery items listed differ from *zār* to *zār*. However, a few common features appear with regard to their agency and function within the ritual. Le Brun is the first to mention that jewellery is put in blood. Based on her description of 'consecrated' jewellery, this appears to be a central point of the proceedings. Blood is also mentioned by Sidqi 1911, but solely for the thaler that was used during the diagnosis stage, and once again in 1930 when he describes all jewellery being immersed in blood. Thompson and Franke both mention that the jewellery may not be parted with, lest the spirit becomes angry – a notion also present with Sidqi 1911 for the thaler, which must be worn forever. Beaded jewellery appears in the accounts of both Thompson and Zwemer. Two other points that stand out are the existence of jewellery made upon special request by the spirit, and the use of amulets for pregnant women. Jewellery made upon request for the spirit is mentioned for Egypt by Blackman as well, in the possession case addressed in chapter 2, where the spirit requested gold earrings and a new yellow garment.[308] The specific use of amulets for pregnant women aligns with the presence of numerous amulets in the sample collection, reflecting fear of uninvited spirits, as I have introduced in chapter 2. In the next section, I will go over the sample collection itself, to see what its collectors identified as *zār* jewellery.

4.1.2 Purpose-made *zār* jewellery in the sample collection

Three types of jewellery are undoubtedly purpose-made for *zār*: jewellery with spirit images, jewellery with written mentions of spirits, and beaded jewellery. The last type, beaded jewellery, may require a brief introduction as it is commonly worn in Egypt, with each region having its own distinctive style. Beaded jewellery used in *zār*, however, stands out: it forms a recognizable category of its own. None of the jewellery labelled as *zār* in the sample collection bears any resemblance to regional styles of jewellery. Considering that they were obtained from *zār*-dealers, and are included in the description by Blackman, I believe these to be purpose-made as well. In this section, I will go over all three types of purpose-made jewellery.

---

306 'Abd er-Rasoul 1955, p. 7.
307 'Abd er-Rasoul 1955, p. 7.
308 Blackman 1927, p. 187.

Jewellery with spirit images: pendants

The largest group of jewellery in the sample collection consists of the pendants with spirit images (n = 681). The spirit images are enclosed in a zigzag border design. The pendants are in the shape of disc, pear, triangle, rectangle, a writing board, or crescent. Five of these pendants still bear the remains of dried blood. Most of these pendants are either to be worn on a necklace, or (in the case of rectangular pendants) suspended from a headdress by a hook connected to a small chain attached on both upper corners. Following the terminology used by every author, starting with Blackman, these are generally referred to as 'zār amulets'. Whether they are, in fact, to be labelled as <u>amulets</u> remains to be determined.

Jewellery with spirit images: other items

A few other items carry spirit images (n = 20). These are upper arm bracelets, and necklaces called *kirdan*. The upper arm bracelets and necklaces belong to a type commonly worn in the south of Egypt, but the pieces with spirit images seem to have been specifically created for *zār*.

The nine upper arm bracelets are of a type generally worn on the southern Red Sea coast, and across the Red Sea in Saudi-Arabia as well.[309] They feature a rectangular silver plaquette, usually decorated with geometrical designs, on a narrow silver band: see an example in cat. no. 100 in the catalogue. This common type of upper

Figure 4.2. Upper arm bracelet in *zār* variety (sample coll. 315). Not to scale. Collection and photo S. van Roode.

---

309 Weeks 1984.

Figure 4.3. Silver necklace with an imitation pillar dollar (sample coll. 369), not exclusively made for *zār*. Not to scale. Collection and photo S. van Roode.

arm bracelet also exists in a designated *zār* variety. Here, the plaquette features a representation of one or more spirits, usually accompanied by text of some sort. An example is shown in Figure 4.2. The existence of these bracelets in a *zār* variety has spilled over into their regular occurrence: collectors increasingly identify common upper arm bracelets as *zār*.

Another ten pieces with spirit images form part of necklaces usually called *kirdan*[310], commonly worn in the southern Nile Valley. These necklaces feature an elaborate pendant as a central piece, consisting of a crescent with tips pointing downwards, above a central coin or decorated pendant (Figure 4.3). The necklace itself is constructed of small silver bars, connected with loops. Both bars and loops feature one or more dangles. The ten necklaces and necklace elements in the sample collection have their crescent and/or central pendant decorated with *zār* spirits. In three of these cases, it is unclear whether the central *zār* pendant is even original to the necklace, as it does not match the decoration on the crescent element. It is not improbable that an incomplete, common *kirdan* was finished with an old *zār* pendant lying around in the workshop, to be sold as a complete

---

310 Meaning 'necklace' in general, and not referring to a particular type.

Figure 4.4. Pair of rings inscribed for a general pair of *zār* spirits indicated by 'Sultan' and 'Sister of the Sultan' (sample coll. 0372 and 0373). Not to scale. Collection and photo S. van Roode.

piece to cultural outsiders. In this case, too, it would seem that regular *kirdan* necklaces are not exclusively intended for *zār*. These necklaces are addressed below again for their regular variety.

Finally, one ring labelled as *zār* (sample coll. 832)[311] carries an image of a male bust with a *tarbush*. This image is shown *en profil* however, rather than *en face* like spirits are invariably shown on the jewellery, and the zigzag border around the image is missing. Therefore, I suspect that this is an attempt at mimicking a coin, rather than a piece of *zār* jewellery.

Jewellery with written mentions of spirits

Seventeen other rings appear to have a direct relation with *zār* because of their text inscriptions. These refer to *zār* spirits, recognizable by their prefix 'Sultan'. An example is shown in Figure 4.4.

Beaded jewellery

The beaded jewellery items in the sample collection (n = 52) vary from simple bracelets and single-strand necklaces to elaborate copies of known types of silver jewellery. Additionally, the sample collection includes headdresses and a beaded apron. The beaded copies of regular jewellery show amulet necklaces with square and cylindrical amulet containers, necklaces with beaded forms of *zār* pendants such as shown in Figure 4.5, solid anklets, and even the upper arm bracelets with the rectangular plaque described in the previous paragraph. All of these items are constructed around a core of tightly folded textile sewn into the desired shape. An intricate netting of beads has been threaded around it, obscuring the core from sight.[312]

Where the silver originals would have carried silver bells, their beaded counterparts are decorated with cowrie shells. According to the ledger kept by

---

311 Weltmuseum Vienna, inventory number 165754.
312 I have been able to observe the construction on two beaded items in Dresden that were damaged. Using a microscope, I have been able to identify the construction of the core. I have not been able to inspect the core for further contents and so cannot verify Zwemer's claim that they hold Qur'an verses or 'other potent material against demons'.

Schienerl, these beaded items were available as recently as the first decade of the 21st century. Their attribution to *zār* is already apparent in the work by Zwemer, as we have seen above. Blackman depicts a set of beaded jewellery in her *Fellahin of Upper Egypt*,[313] and the collection of the Pitt-Rivers Museum in Oxford holds two similar beaded necklaces in blue and white.[314] Schienerl acquired this type of beaded jewellery from a specialised *zār* dealer. These are present in the collections currently in Vienna and Dresden.

4.1.3 Other jewellery ascribed to *zār* in the sample collection

Apart from purpose-made jewellery, the sample collection contains a large variety in other pieces that are sometimes ascribed to *zār*, but also function outside of *zār*. These include necklaces, bracelets, anklets, rings and other jewellery items.

Necklaces

Necklaces in the sample collection labelled as *zār* (n = 35, including the pieces with spirit images) are either *kirdans* in the fashion of southern Egypt, or a long necklace with amulet boxes. I will discuss both types here.

Figure 4.5. Beaded pendant. Not to scale. Collection Museum fur Völkerkunde, Dresden (inv. no. 86878), photo S. van Roode.

Southern Egyptian kirdans

These necklaces are among the regular jewellery types of southern Egypt. As mentioned above, the sample collection holds ten of these with spirit images. And as with the upper arm bracelets, here, too, there seems to be confusion about whether the regular variety also can be ascribed to *zār*. Over the past decades, they have increasingly been labelled as *zār*. Schienerl, however, does not identify these as *zār* necklaces, either in his acquisition ledgers or in his articles dealing with *zār* jewellery. In his book from 1984, the *kirdans* are presented as regular necklaces from Nubia, while the book also presents several pages of *zār* items.[315] Azza Fahmy on the other hand presents them as *zār* necklaces in her 2007 book, and does not include them in the section on Nubian jewellery.[316] In private collections and online, these are now invariably presented as *zār* jewellery. The sample collection holds 25 of them: see cat. nos 110 and 111 in the catalogue for an example.

---

313 Blackman 1927, p. 200.
314 Inv. nos. 1985.54.1652 and 1985.54.1612, both collected in 1928.
315 Bachinger & Schienerl 1984, p. 68-69. The only doubt seems to be their ascription to Nubia.
316 Fahmy 2007, p. 171.

Necklaces with amulet boxes

Among the private collections, ten necklaces with triangular or square amulet boxes that can be opened have been labelled as *zār*. Two of the necklaces have been embellished with facetted carnelian beads. The amulet boxes are usually executed in repoussé and show floral or geometrical decoration, or in some cases the word Allah. An example is shown in Figure 4.6 and cat. no. 112 in the catalogue. From the amulet boxes usually several silver bells or (imitation) coins are suspended. The association of these necklaces with *zār* however is unclear: they have been collected as such only by later collectors, are not included as *zār* in the Schienerl collection[317] or mentioned in earlier literature. These amulet boxes are of a general type found in the Ottoman realm of the eastern Mediterranean: comparable boxes are also worn in southern Palestine, Jordan, and Syria, without association to *zār*.[318] These are also the ornaments depicted in Lane[319] and referred to by Kahle as purpose-made *zār* jewellery, as discussed above in 4.1.1. I will present a possible explanation for this claim in chapter 5.

Figure 4.6. Amulet boxes of a type often associated with *zār*. Collection Qilada Foundation – Eric and Marion Crince Le Roy. Photo S. van Roode.

Bracelets and anklets

Bracelets and anklets are equally difficult to identify with certainty as *zār* jewellery. There appear to be no clear commonalities underpinning their identification as such, other than the presence of silver bells. Kriss & Kriss-Heinrich list silver bracelets with small silver protrusions on the outside, as well as silver anklets with bells.[320] These silver anklets, consisting of a small silver band with large bells, are of a widespread type of children's anklets throughout Egypt and further afield in Saudi-Arabia.[321] Anklets as worn by the ritual specialist in the ceremony for Kriss & Kriss-Heinrich, featuring red beads and silver bells, are present in the sample collection and identified as *zār* by their collectors and curators (see cat. no. 102 in the catalogue), but in other museum collections, they are listed simply as anklets.[322] Conversely, a type of anklets mentioned in relation to *zār* in earlier literature but notably absent from the sample collection are anklets made of iron, as have been presented in chapter 2. These will be discussed in more detail at the end of this chapter.

---

317   Schienerl 1976b, p. 311 illustrates these and makes no mention of *zār* in the description on p. 318; Bachinger & Schienerl 1984, p. 70-72 list these as amulet containers only.

318   See for example Volger 1989, p. 335 PL 262, inv. no. TR IX 4 J from the region of Jaffa; Kalter 1992, p. 98-99 for Syria. A comparable embossed amulet box is in the Victoria & Albert Museum, London (inv. no. 1102-1869, acquired in 1869 in Cairo, without association to *zār*).

319   Lane 1842, p. 411.

320   Kriss & Kriss-Heinrich 1962, p. 149 and Fig 113 2-3.

321   An example is inv. no. 1113-1869 of the Victoria & Albert Museum, London, which was acquired in 1869 in Cairo without association to *zār*. The type is illustrated in Weeks 1983a and discussed in Weeks 1984b, where they are said to protect children from the *Qarina*. For Saudi-Arabia, see Colyer Ross 1981, p. 100.

322   Bachinger & Schienerl 1984, p. 58 list a comparable anklet simply as anklet.

Figure 4.7. Ring associated with *zār*. Not to scale. Collection and photo S. van Roode.

Figure 4.8. Rings with polyhedral terminals and with bells (sample coll. 0376 and 0377). Not to scale. Collection and photo S. van Roode.

Rings

Rings are plentiful in the sample collection (n = 70), but their association to *zār* is again troublesome except for the seventeen pieces presented above.[323] Even in the collection assembled by Schienerl, some rings are labelled *zār*, while identical examples in the same collection are not.

A particular type of ring featured in the sample collection as *zār* ring (n = 13) is a solid silver ring with flower-like protrusions underneath a solid silver, usually undecorated, round, oval or square bezel. These exist in both very large and heavy as well as regular and even small varieties: a regular piece is shown in Figure 4.7. These rings are also present in the collection of Winifred Blackman, but not as *zār* jewellery: she lists one as 'worn by women to cure pain in the arm'[324] and one as 'to appease the evil spirits'.[325]

Rings with bells (n = 4) and polyhedral terminals (n = 2), both as pictured in Kriss & Kriss-Heinrich Fig 113, are also in the sample collection (Figure 4.8), but the ring with coral or red glass that Kriss & Kriss-Heinrich describe, worn 'in honour of the sister of sultan', is not. The Schienerl collection presents various other rings as *zār* rings, but it is impossible to determine what Schienerl based his identification on. Several examples of rings associated with *zār* are shown in cat. nos.104-110 in the catalogue.

Coin pendants

A selection of coin pendants (n = 26) is also present in the sample collection. Twelve of them are part of a *kirdan*, as mentioned above, while another twelve are individual pendants, and two are fashioned onto a ring. Their association with *zār* is also problematic. Using coins in jewellery is a common practice throughout the Middle

---

323 This is also visible in publications. Compare for example Fahmy 2007, p. 169 and Mayer 2021, p. 62-63. Both show a set of rings, among which several identical pieces. Fahmy lists them as *zār*, Mayer as Nubian jewellery in general (but does specify these have a high symbolic function).
324 Pitt-Rivers Museum inv. no. 1985.54.9, collection year not listed.
325 Liverpool inv. No 285, collected in 1920. A third example is in the British Museum, bought on a local market in Shantur, Upper Egypt, inventory number Af1981,14.61. The description on the website does not match the depicted ring however. J. Hudson of The British Museum has kindly verified that the original description of Blackman for this particular ring is missing or never existed (email, July 20th, 2018).

East. Coins in jewellery show value and often indicate the financial position of the wearer. The coin most often encountered in the sample collection is the Spanish pillar dollar or imitations thereof. As introduced in chapter 2, the pillar dollar also plays a role in *zār*: the ritual specialist uses it to determine which spirit is ailing her client. However, as this particular coin holds its own amuletic value, it is frequently used in regular jewellery and in my view does not necessarily imply a connection to *zār* – the presence of the pillar dollar itself is not enough to definitively identify a piece of jewellery as *zār*. Other coins also appear: the Maria Theresia Thaler or imitations thereof, coins depicting King Farouk, and commemorative coins from Sudan. A few examples are included in cat. nos. 95-99 in the catalogue. I will go into the role of coins later in this chapter.

Other jewellery pieces

The collection holds also a variety of other jewellery items. A silver belt and silver diadem in a private collection (sample coll. 286 and 287) were both acquired as *zār* jewellery. An applique in the shape of a mermaid, in a private collection, (sample coll. 132) was also listed as *zār* jewellery. A final piece worth mentioning is a silver wand with dangles (sample coll. 1136)[326] in the collection of the Indiana University Museum of Archaeology and Anthropology. Although technically not a piece of jewellery, it was included in the jewellery section by its collector. In some cases, the attribution to *zār* changes over time: the Museum für Völkerkunde in Vienna holds a segment of a Rashayda jewellery piece, recognizable by its characteristic dangles, that has not been labelled as *zār* by its collector Schienerl, but its inventory card has additional information scribbled onto it identifying it as *zār*.[327]

Amulets

Finally, the sample collection holds a large group of amulets (n = 383) in varying materials and forms that were ascribed to *zār* by its collectors, but whose use is widely attested outside *zār* as well. Among these are many text amulets that share the same shape (disc, pear, triangle, the shape of a writing board or rectangular), size and zigzag border on both sides as the pendants with spirit images. However, instead of images of *zār* spirits, these pieces display verses from the Quran, the five- or six-pointed star, or general formulas. Rectangular pendants in filigree are often ascribed to *zār*, but are also widely used headdress adornments of a general Ottoman type.[328] Other amulets associated with *zār* in the sample collection include cylindrical amulet containers of a general type, pendants in the shape of fish, banded agate known as *sumlūk*, and a selection of Christian crosses. The pendants in the shape of fish are a popular necklace design in general in the south of Egypt, according to Weeks, who also recounts one instance of such a pendant having been used for *zār*.[329] Banded agate, also known as 'Sulemani', is considered a powerful amulet throughout the Islamic world, referencing

---

326   Indiana University Museum of Archaeology and Anthropology inventory number DB-2149.
327   Inventory number 86526.
328   See for example the two pendants in the Victoria & Albert Museum, London (inv. no. 303&A01901, acquired in 1901 in Cairo, without association to *zār*); Schienerl 1976b, p. 310 (figs 17-19) and p. 316, where he identifies these as temple pendants (hung from the headdress at the level of the temples).
329   Weeks 1983b.

King Solomon.[330] The Christian crosses are shown in Schienerl 1976b, along with a pendant in the shape of the Qur'an: he identifies these as regular amulets for Christian people, just as the Qur'an is for Muslims.[331] See the catalogue for several examples of regular amulets identified as *zār* by their collectors.

Discussion

This overview illustrates that the sample collection, too, is ambiguous in what *zār* jewellery is. Like in the written sources predating the collection phase, a wide variety in jewellery is present. Of course, this variety may be due to the fact that the sample collection was largely assembled by cultural outsiders buying from a secondary or even third source. Most of it was purchased from vendors, either in or outside Egypt, and the selection is based in publications where jewellery was already dislodged from the ritual itself. However, since earlier sources also lack unanimity, I believe this this variety to be significant in itself. It appears that, beyond the well-known purpose-made *zār* items, all other jewellery exhibits varying degrees of bricolage. This concept, coined by Lévi Strauss, proposes the use of changing and varying objects to deal with a matter at hand instead of working with a pre-organised set of items.[332] When we consider the fluid world of spirit interactions, governed by multiplicity of approaches as I have introduced in chapter 2, bricolage is a far more fitting approach for its material culture than a rigid classification. An exploration of the amulet collection of Winifred Blackman will illustrate this point.

4.1.4 The spirit world in Egypt: the Blackman collection of amulets

Zār is not the only method of dealing with spirit possession in Egypt, as I have introduced in chapter 2: *zār* is part of a much larger landscape of traditions in spirit engagement. In this light, the collection of Winifred Blackman, introduced in chapter 3, is particularly relevant. She collected all sorts of objects related to informal ritual, including possession.[333]

Only a few of the objects connected to spirit possession in her collection meet the description of jewellery used in a *zār* context as other authors have mentioned: a silver ring with a red stone[334] or a red glass amulet in a silver setting[335]. Blackman however does not list these as *zār*, but as objects to be used with spirit possession in general. From her notes with each object, it appears these are not even exclusive to possession remedies. An iron ring of identical shape and stone is listed as 'worn by men only to bring happiness to the wearer'[336], and an identical red glass amulet is listed as 'effective against pain in the temples'[337].

---

330 Weeks 1986, p. 22 writes glass beads called *sumluk*, can be found widely in the Muski: the beads were imported from India.
331 Schienerl 1976b, p. 311 (figs 26 and 27), p. 306 and p. 317-318 for his identification.
332 Lévi Strauss 1962, p. 11.
333 I have used the online database of both the British Museum and the Pitt-Rivers Museum, as well as a preliminary unpublished inventory of the Liverpool collection.
334 Pitt-Rivers Museum inv. no. 1985.54.2687, collected in 1930.
335 Pitt-Rivers Museum inv. no. 1985.54.1750, collected in 1929.
336 Pitt-Rivers Museum inv. no. 1985.54.1739.
337 Pitt-Rivers Museum inv. no. 1985.54.397.

Iron anklets, mentioned in the chapter on *zār* by Kriss & Kriss-Heinrich as being worn by the ritual specialist during a *zār*, are present in the Blackman collection, but their use appears to be varied and not directly tied to spirit possession. Several pairs of iron anklets in the Blackman collection are labelled as keeping the Qarina away[338] – a stance we have seen in chapter 2. Another pair of iron anklets must be worn by a pregnant woman if she is visited by a menstruating woman, to avoid *kabsa* (see chapter 2).[339] The collection however also holds identical iron anklets for other causes entirely: to cure pain, swelling and tumours in the ankle[340] or to enable a boy to walk[341]. It appears that a given object is not exclusively tied to one purpose.

When we look at the type of objects related to spirit possession in the Blackman collection, this notion of bricolage only grows stronger. The largest number of objects related to spirit possession are not jewellery, but pebbles, animal teeth, pieces of incense, wood, bone, glass or early plastics. I present a few examples from her collection here, with the descriptions she provided with these. She has included a brown polished stone, 'to be used by a possessed woman'[342], another brown smooth stone 'to be used by a woman who has been possessed by two sheikhs'[343], a piece of amber 'used by young girls that have a spirit'[344], or a black stone 'used by possessed men and women'[345]. The fascinating thing is that her collection holds hundreds of such pebbles, bones etcetera. And these are not exclusive to spirit possession, but are used for an astounding variety of ailments: pebbles, bones, pieces of incense, that cannot be visually distinguished from the pieces used for spirit possession, are listed as helping against infertility and with cramps in the right or left leg, headaches, muscle problems, fever, neck pain, toothaches, eye diseases and more. It would seem any given object could be useful for or against just about anything.

The Blackman collection shows how dealing with spirits and spirit possession may involve an endless variety of material culture. There is not one single purpose for a single type of object. Rather, her collection reflects the dynamics of dealing with the invisible. Instead of absolute and final coherency, the bricolage in material culture used in spirit engagement demonstrates a multiplicity of approaches, that permeates every interaction with the spirit world.

Based on the brief comparison with the Blackman collection, the wide variety of jewellery in the sample collection other than purpose-made jewellery in my view is indeed indicative of bricolage. Before discussing how this observation affects our understanding of *zār* jewellery, there is one last point I would like to address: where did this acknowledgement of bricolage in *zār* disappear, and how did people start wanting to make lists, classifications and attributions of individual jewellery pieces?

---

338   Pitt-Rivers Museum inv. no. 1985.54.1775 and 1985.54.1780, collected in 1929.
339   Liverpool inv. no 148, collected in 1929.
340   Pitt-Rivers Museum inv. no. 1985.54.419, collected in 1929.
341   Pitt-Rivers Museum inv. no. 1985.54.1737, collected in 1929.
342   Pitt-Rivers Museum inv. no. 1985.54.2405, collected in 1931.
343   Pitt-Rivers Museum inv. no. 1985.54.1414, collected in 1933. A sheikh is a possessing spirit.
344   Pitt-Rivers Museum inv. no. 1985.54.2342, collected in 1931.
345   Pitt-Rivers Museum inv. no. 1985.54.2046, collection year unknown.

4.1.5 From generic to specific

To see where this critically different way of thinking originated, I return to the collection and publication phase once again. The work by Kriss & Kriss-Heinrich is the first publication to attribute specific jewellery to individual spirits. I will now turn to their account in more detail to illustrate how their publication and its reception by later authors on the one hand, and the transition from publications on ritual to publications on jewellery on the other, have shaped our thinking about *zār* jewellery.

Jewellery in Kriss & Kriss-Heinrich 1962

Although this is a lengthy chapter in their book on amulets, it is not always that clear. It remains occasionally vague whether jewellery is described as *zār* jewellery or as general amulet,[346] or how the various jewellery items were used and by whom.

The ritual specialist wore rings without stones on her thumb, shaped like miniature anklets: plain bands with polyhedral knobs on both ends.[347] On her ring finger, a ring with a round cabochon of coral or red glass was worn. These are of a simple design, and refer to the female spirit accompanying the male spirit.[348] Together with the coral ring, a silver ring with a round plaque was worn. On the round plaque, the word 'sultan' is inscribed, a reference to the male spirit.[349] Rings with banded agate are also used, but unclear is how and by whom.[350]

The ritual specialist wore amulets in abundance on her head. Here, Kriss & Kriss-Heinrich describe the pendants with spirit representations. An important distinction they make is that pendants with the Throne Verse on both sides can be used in *zār*, but <u>also</u> as regular amulets.[351] They identify the spirits depicted generally as Sīd (male) and Sitt (female): this identification is found in numerous later publications and has become the standard description of pendants bearing representations of spirits. Very significant is that they also state that the most famous spirits are represented individually in just a few occasions. Next, the authors list a range of amulets. Unclear is whether these still fall under the description of amulets worn by the ritual specialist on her head, as the original description started out with, or if general amulets used in *zār* are meant. They list [352]

- pear-shaped amulets;
- rectangular amulets;
- amulets depicting a fish (identified by the authors with Sultān al Bahrī or Sitt al Bahrīya) or a mermaid (identified with Sitt Safīna);
- amulets in the shape of a fish to honour Sitt al Bahrīya;
- amulets in the shape of a crescent;
- amulets in the shape of a writing board.

---

346 An example is the discussion of iron anklets as protection against the Qarina in Kriss & Kriss-Heinrich 1962, p. 149-150. They are presented in the chapter on *zār*, but were these used specifically in *zār*?
347 Kriss & Kriss-Heinrich 1962, p. 151 and Fig. 113, 4.
348 Kriss & Kriss-Heinrich 1962, p. 151.
349 Kriss & Kriss-Heinrich 1962, p. 151 and Fig 113, 4-10.
350 Kriss & Kriss-Heinrich 1962, p. 151 and Fig 113, 4-10.
351 Kriss & Kriss-Heinrich 1962, p. 151.
352 Kriss & Kriss-Heinrich 1962, p. 152-153.

A distinct amulet is a rectangular amulet made of silver filigree and mentioned as being worn for the spirits called Hawanim al-Habash, the Abyssinian Ladies, although sometimes also for as-Saʿīdī.[353] The authors continue their list of amulets with silver amulets called *zu'ra*. These are generally worn by new-borns and their mothers, but can also be used in *zār* and in general by pregnant women.[354] A small cucumber-shaped amulet container that can be opened is described as being used for as-Saʿīdī.[355] Another important type of amulet mentioned by the authors is made of banded agate. These are used for Sitt as-Sūdānīya, but also for other *zār* spirits.[356] Silver crosses are worn for a Coptic spirit[357], and a group of iron amulets were used by the ritual specialist in those cases where infertility or child mortality were specific causes to have a *zār*.[358]

Kriss & Kriss-Heinrich in later publications

The publication by Kriss & Kriss-Heinrich features detailed descriptions and attributions of individual jewellery pieces for the first time. Their work marks the start of the separation of jewellery and ritual, not just because it is an external account instead of an emic lived experience, but because it has been misinterpreted itself as well.

Important nuances Kriss & Kriss-Heinrich were aware of and have written down, have been omitted from later publications. One example is how they write that some ornaments can be used for other *zār* spirits besides the one they list.[359] Further, their fundamental observation that only in a few occasions individual spirits are depicted for example, is not picked up: later authors often present identities for the spirits depicted, such as all military officers being presented as Yawri Bey.

While the jewellery pieces described in the account of Kriss & Kriss-Heinrich may definitely have been of use in those particular circumstances of possession and have been selected at the discretion and with the knowledge of the ritual specialist, subsequent publications and collections seem to have taken their account as a rational and universal truth. Instead of a unique, individual account of a personal *zār* tailored to the needs of a specific patient, their work has been interpreted as a definitive list of items belonging to 'the' *zār* in general.

From ritual to jewellery studies

Where Weeks' article in 1984 shows keen awareness of the multi-faceted nature of *zār* images[360], the popular publication by Bachinger & Schienerl in the same year does not: from that point on, *zār* jewellery is presented and described based on stylistic capacities only: if it looks like this, it is meant for that spirit.

---

353 Kriss & Kriss-Heinrich 1962, p. 153.
354 See Van Roode 2016 for their use as amulets for children.
355 Kriss & Kriss-Heinrich 1962, p. 154 and Fig 114, 3.
356 Kriss & Kriss-Heinrich 1962, p. 154 and Fig 123, 5-7.
357 Kriss & Kriss-Heinrich 1962, p. 155.
358 Kriss & Kriss-Heinrich 1962, p. 155.
359 Kriss & Kriss-Heinrich 1962, p. 154, speaking of the *sumlūk* pendants. They count these among the 'zār amulets'.
360 She mentions how the male-female spirit pair is also called 'Faruk and his wife' in Abydos, and 'King and Queen' in Qurna. These local differences are incredibly important, but have rarely been included in descriptions by foreigners.

I attribute these gradual omissions and simplifications to the transition of the study of *zār* jewellery to the field of jewellery and adornment. Jewellery studies are largely conducted from an iconographic perspective without much consideration for context, a point jewellery historian Unger devoted her PhD-thesis to.[361] Much like jewellery historians determine whether a piece of jewellery is Georgian or Victorian, ancient, antique or modern based on the way it looks, visual characteristics became the first factor to determine whether or not a piece of jewellery is *zār* jewellery. This iconographic approach however is incompatible with the nature of *zār* jewellery. And with that, I return to the significance of bricolage.

The wide variety in the available accounts, the sample collection and the Blackman collection clearly shows it is not so much the visible capacities of the object itself, be it its material, colour or shape, that constitute its relevance. A pebble can be used for anything from spirit possession to throat aches, a piece of jewellery can be worn as amulet for a number of reasons. Sengers has demonstrated how *zār* itself draws upon bricolage[362], and I would like to expand that notion to include the jewellery as well. So, instead of searching for iconographic parameters to establish what is, and what is not, *zār* jewellery, I will now turn once again to the ritual this jewellery belongs to in order to trace the meaning it may have carried.

4.2 HUMANS, SPIRITS, AND OBJECTS

4.2.1 *Zārs* ancestors: possession cults in Africa

When writing about *zār* in Egypt, scholars often emphasise that *zār* is not Islamic. It is described as a form of popular Islam, or even as a relic of ancient Egyptian traditions.[363] In recent decades increasing attention has been drawn to the fact that *zār* has its roots in African cults.[364] Looking at *zār* through the lens of its African ancestors and their way of interacting with objects may result in a shift in our understanding of and terminology for the jewellery items used. As I wrote in chapter 1, *zār* as it is practised in Egypt is one leaf on a complex family tree. It has certain elements that are unique to Egypt, such as the weekly public *zār*, but the version of *zār* as it was brought to Egypt through the slave trade was itself already an amalgam of East African and West African cults, which had flowed together in Sudan.[365] This amalgam is generally called *zār-bori* after its two main components. *Zār* stems from East Africa, notably Ethiopia, while *bori* has its roots in West Africa, mainly in Nigeria and Niger.[366] Both *zār* and *bori* are in turn umbrella terms for a variety of possession cults. Constantinides describes for Sudan the existence of *zār-tumbura* and *zār-bori* as the main branches, with additional mentions of a *zār* particular to Suakin and a *zār-Habashi*, referring to Ethiopia.[367] This Ethiopian *zār* in turn is pluriform as well: Natvig has argued that

---

361 Unger 2019.
362 Sengers 2003, p. 172-175; Hadidi 2016, p. 51 writes how *zār* is infinitely malleable.
363 Naguib 1993 includes the *zār* in a treatise on ancient Egyptian echoes; Nabhan 1994 speaks of pre-Islamic symbols (p. 66), expressly mentioning ancient Egyptian symbols on p. 68.
364 For example in the works by Richard Natvig, also Kramer 1987; Lewis et al. 1991; Behrend & Luig 1999.
365 For an overview, see Lewis 1991.
366 Lewis 1991, p. 2.
367 Constantinides 1991, p. 94.

zār as it was eventually exported northward to Egypt may have originated from the violent cultural encounter between the Oromo and the Amhara in Ethiopia.[368] East African and West African possession cults share many elements, that are also present in *zār*, such as the interaction with the spirit during a trance, the manifestation of the spirit through dress and adornment, the music and drumming, and the sacrifice of animals.

There is, however, a significant difference that is of consequence here: the presence of particular objects that stretches beyond the ritual itself into everyday life. West African possession cults employ these, while East African cults do not. Observing how objects interact with humans in West African possession cults provides a framework to re-evaluate *zār* jewellery. In the next section, I will use candomblé as experimental case-study to explore that relation, because both cults share a similar history: both are possession cults, transported via forcibly displaced people into another country with a monotheistic religion.

4.2.2 *Zār*s cousin: candomblé

Candomblé is an Afro-Brazilian cult, rooted in the cults of several African ethnic groups, notably the Yoruba from Nigeria and Benin, but also the Fon and Bantu[369], mixed with Catholic elements. Candomblé is an umbrella term for the varieties of this cult, such as Xangó, Batuque and Tambor de Mina.[370] Just as *zār* devotees are faithful Muslims, candomblé devotees operate in the realm of Catholicism. Central to the cult are deities called *orixás*, which are often equated to Catholic saints.[371] These can possess devotees, who are guided in their contact with their *orixá* by a ritual specialist. While all varieties of candomblé have their own characteristics, they also share common basics. These are in turn quite similar to the elements of *zār* as outlined in chapter 2. As in *zār*, the possessed person is reconciled with its possessing deity during an initiation, called *assentamento*.[372] Here as well an altar is set up, from which the ceremony derives its name, which displays objects the deity wants presented to him/her. These objects are 'powerful objects' or 'cultic objects' and necklaces called *conta fina*.[373] As part of the initiation, an animal is slaughtered and its blood poured over the objects on the altar as well as over the initiate, who may also drink from the blood.[374] The use of blood is central to all candomblé gatherings, not only to initiations. In the following, I will go over the characteristics of each element.

Transferring life through blood

The use of blood is a central feature of many African possession cults, both Eastern and Western, as blood literally transfers life and identity from one being to another.[375] Most possession cults use the sacrifice of animals as the culmination of the ritual, the

---

368 Natvig 1991, p. 181.
369 Motta 2019.
370 Motta 2019.
371 Halloy 2013, p. 136; Motta 2019.
372 Halloy 2013, p. 136.
373 Halloy 2013, p. 143.
374 Halloy 2013, p. 143.
375 Colleyn 1999, p. 73; Motta 2005, p. 297

moment where possessed and possessor become one. As Motta describes in the context of candomblé: 'saints and humans eat, communicate, commingle and assimilate one another'.[376] In West-African possession cults, this transfer of life and identity includes a third party: the powerful object. Halloy describes the importance of the sacrificial blood for the bond between deity and possessed in Xangô.[377] Pouring blood over both the powerful objects and the possessed person is treating all three equally: deity, person and object are equals and become one.[378] Blood itself holds the power of life and can transfer life and identity to inanimate objects as well. So, what are these powerful objects?

Powerful objects

Many West African diaspora cults make use of an intermediate object between human host and possessing entity: a powerful object. As Halloy presents for Xangô, these objects are a mediator between humans and their personal deity.[379] During the *assentamento*, particular objects are consecrated, connecting the possessed and their deity. When these objects are discarded, misfortune befalls the possessed.[380] The change in nature of the object during the ritual is crucial: after the sacrificial blood has touched it, it does not simply symbolise the deity, but *is* the deity itself.[381] The *orixá* can manifest itself in both the human host and in the object: object, deity and human body are interwoven. These powerful objects in turn take two forms: location-based objects of stone or iron (called *otás* or *ferramentas*), and wearable objects. The location-based objects remain on the altar to the *orixá*, while the wearable objects are permanently with the human. These are the *conta fina*, beaded necklaces, worn under the clothes by Xangô cult initiates. Halloy describes these necklaces as providing 'material continuity, outside the ritual sphere, of a spiritual relation established through ritual action between the initiate, his/her *orixás* and the initiators'.[382] The wearing of these necklaces is present in all candomblé affiliations, the colours and materials of the beads vary per *orixá*.

Manifestation objects

Both Eastern and Western African cults employ a range of other pieces of dress and adornment for the possessed during the ritual. Different headdresses, sashes, sticks, staves and other attributes are used for different possessing entities. These are not be understood as mere props or costumes to dress up as a possessing deity. As Rasmussen put it, these objects are used by the spirits 'to manifest themselves into being'[383]: spirits embody themselves in humans through objects.

---

376   Motta 2019, see also Motta 1998, Motta 2005 for a variant: 'Gods and men eat, communicate, commingle, assimilate and identify with one another'.
377   Halloy 2013, p. 143-144.
378   Halloy 2013, p. 145.
379   Halloy 2013.
380   Halloy 2013, p. 137.
381   Halloy 2013, p. 137-140.
382   Halloy 2013, p. 142.
383   As expressed by Rune Rasmussen in his talk at EASR Resilient Religion on Sept. 2nd, 2021.

4.2.3 Purpose-made jewellery in *zār*: an interpretation of its role

After this brief exploration into candomblé, let us now turn to *zār* again. Here, I would like to address the consistent use of the term 'amulets' for all jewellery, which presupposes a particular agency, usually of protection and prevention.[384] The purpose-made jewellery items however come into play <u>after</u> the diagnosis of spirit possession: protection from a *zār* spirit when the spirit is already present, so 'after the fact', makes little sense. Also, the spirit representations are unique to *zār* jewellery and do not occur on general amulets.[385] They are in my view not to be understood as amulets, but as powerful objects as West African possession religions employ. Although the contemporary descriptions of *zār* and its use of jewellery are imprecise and vague, a few recurring observations stand out. These are that jewellery is put in blood, some of it must be worn continuously and none of it can be parted with.

Powerful Objects

I now turn to the most particular jewellery in the *zār*: pendants with spirit representations. In keeping with the parallel in candomblé, I propose the agency of these is that of a powerful object. I arrive at this proposal based on three arguments, following the use cycle of the pendants.

First, these jewellery items are put in blood. This is not only evident from written descriptions, but also from jewellery pieces in the sample collection that still show traces of blood. Although these are very few, they indicate that these pieces have indeed been subjected to this process. The pouring of blood during the *zār* is the culmination of the ritual. At this point the three parties (spirit, possessed and power object) become symbiotically linked through the force of blood.[386]

Here, I should reflect briefly on the use of blood. This is also attested in non-*zār* possession cases when an animal sacrifice has to be made to appease the possessing spirit, or in non-possession cases dealing with the invisible. For example, animals are slaughtered when a new home is occupied or a new well dug to appease spirits that may be living in that spot.[387] It is in *zār* however the specific physical appearance of the objects (carrying spirit images), combined with the following two points, that lead me to believe that in this case the use of blood is more analogous with its role in African possession cults.

Second, acts by humans pertaining to the jewellery have a direct effect on the symbiosis of spirit, possessed and object reached during the *zār*. Treating the jewellery in a particular way is akin to treating the spirit itself in the same manner. The additional decorating of the pendants such as presented above serves to honour the spirit: embellishing the object is embellishing the spirit. Reversely, parting with

---

384 The term 'amulet' has a wide range of definitions. See for example Garcia Probert & Sijpesteijn 2022, p. 1-12 for a discussion of definitions.

385 See van Roode 2016, pp 110-152 for a general introduction into shapes and forms of amulets and Probert Garcia for a collection of Palestinian amulets. Pielow 1997, p. 367, notes this discrepancy in imagery in her article on protection from demons, but as she considers the *zār* to be ultimately an act of magic, she defines these objects as amulets.

386 Hadidi 2016, p. 50 writes 'The blood of the sacrificial animals anointing the body of the possessed initiand binds her to her zars. For the rest of her life, the initiate wears the *zar* amuletic jewelry that has been anointed by the sacrificial blood'.

387 Blackman 1929, p. 236.

jewellery objects also has a direct effect on this symbiosis, and one the spirit does not take kindly to. Several authors stress how nothing used in connection to *zār* could be sold or given away until the owner died, while others assert that some jewellery pieces must be worn every day after the ritual.[388]

Expanding on this idea, I would thirdly like to recall how the pendants have sometimes been intentionally damaged. When the need arises to intentionally disfigure an object, apparently that object carries power that needs to be annulled at some point, possibly after the wearer had died. Inflicting damage on the pendant may be another way of treating object and human as equals: as the human had lost their life, so the object should as well.

Manifestation objects

The spirits need objects to manifest themselves with in *zār* as well. Like in candomblé, these are items of dress and paraphernalia such as staves and sticks. The *zār* items of dress are regular pieces of clothing, in an adaptation for the spirits: tarbushes carry additional symbols in sequins, and colour is of great importance. I propose the beaded jewellery pieces are part of this set and are to be understood as manifestation objects.

4.2.4 Roles of jewellery in and beyond *zār*

With this capacity of material culture in mind, I will now present my suggestion for a comprehensive overview of jewellery in the Egyptian *zār*: what did these living objects do? I propose five roles for jewellery used in *zār*. These range from *zār*-specific to general, as outlined in Figure 4.9. I will elaborate on these roles below, with an emphasis on the most *zār*-specific objects: the jewellery items with spirit images.

Role 1: Powerful objects

The first role is that of the powerful objects. These are the purpose-made and *zār*-specific pieces with spirit images, which continue to be active outside the ritual as well. They are not merely jewellery with meaningful decoration, but powerful objects themselves. They exist in symbiosis with human and spirit and have become living entities of their own.

Spirit images

In the use of images, Egyptian *zār* powerful objects are unique: images of spirits do not occur in other countries where *zār* is practised.[389] In the symbiosis of possessed, spirit and object I suggest these images provide us with an extraordinary point of view, and that is how the spirits are imagined to experience their encounter with the possessed. To my knowledge these are the only objects used in possession religions that show us the perceived spirits' outlook on events. How do they do that?

The spirits look directly at us and interact with us from their side of the powerful object. Half of the anthropomorphic spirits have one arm raised up

---

388 Darmody 2001, pp. 34-35; Bonotto 2010, p. 87.
389 Some Iranian amulets labeled as 'zār' show depictions of spirits, however, I have not been able to establish whether these are in fact *zār* jewellery, or ascribed to *zār* based on their visual analogy with Egyptian pendants.

(317 of 649 anthropomorphic spirits). Some of these spirits raise their hand in a gesture of greeting (n = 57) as shown in Figure 4.10.

The remainder is holding something up (n = 260), with the vast majority holding plants or flowers (n = 189). Another ten spirits hold plants or flowers with both hands. I suggest this interaction reveals a fundamental aspect of the expected reciprocity between humans and spirits in *zār*. I base this on the significance that the acts of

1 POWERFUL OBJECT
- SPIRIT REPRESENTATIONS/MENTION
- WORN BY POSSESSED AND RITUAL PRACTITIONER

2 MANIFESTATION OBJECT
- BEADED JEWELLERY
- WORN BY EMBODIED SPIRIT DURING ZAR

Purpose-made zar-jewellery

3 CONTRACT
- COIN JEWELLERY
- WORN BY POSSESSED

4 AMULET
- ANY AND ALL AMULETS
- WORN BY ALL ATTENDEES

5 REQUESTED JEWELLERY
- ALL TYPES OF JEWELLERY
- WORN BY POSSESSED

General jewellery also used in zar

Figure 4.9. Schematic overview of the various roles jewellery can have in *zār*, with indicative reference images of the type of jewellery.

waving palm branches and offering flowers carry in the human world. Palm branches are used on happy occasions, as decoration of a house or in festive processions. In 1867, Lucy Duff Gordon wrote in a letter to her mother how one morning she woke up to find her house covered in palm branches and lemon blossom in celebration of the arrival of a much-anticipated visitor later that day.[390] According to the introduction to the book in which her letters were published, branches were also thrown on her path by villagers when she passed by, as they were happy to see her.[391] Palm branches are believed to convey that happiness to the dead as well: according to Blackman, palm branches were carried in funeral processions and placed on graves to bring happiness and blessings to the deceased.[392] On the *zār* powerful objects, these roles are reversed: it is the spirits holding these and waving. As such, I believe the powerful objects show the desired outcome of the ritual: happy and content spirits. This may even work along the lines of analogous magic, where depicting an event is believed to manifest it in reality.[393]

When half of the anthropomorphic spirits interacts with humans, what does the other half do? These look at humans as well, but do not engage. In some cases that is because it is anatomically impossible: several of the mermaids do not have limbs. Much more telling however is that none of the anthropomorphic spirits dressed in military uniforms interact: they take the form of a static portrait, as shown in Figure 4.11. The spirits dressed in Arab garb, including a headdress with headband, are also not waving or greeting: instead, they firmly grasp their sword with both hands. Only one of them holds his sword with one hand and presents a flower (sample coll. 715)[394]. I believe this to be very relevant to the world these spirits reflect, and will address this in the final part of this thesis.

Powerful objects are worn by the possessed and by the ritual specialist. The possessed will only wear powerful objects embodying their spirit(s), while the ritual specialist may wear multiple powerful objects. The reason for this abundance is that the ritual specialist had to appease all spirits she was working with, and would try to prevent any one of them from feeling excluded; the possessed only wore the powerful objects that embodied her personal *zār* spirits.[395] Whereas for the possessed exclusivity is key, for the ritual specialist inclusivity is of prime importance.

Figure 4.10. *Zār* pendant with a spirit raising its hand (sample coll. 982). Not to scale. Collection Qilada Foundation – Eric and Marion Crince Le Roy. Photo S. van Roode.

Visibility and invisibility

As we have seen in chapter 3, the powerful objects managed to stay largely out of sight for nearly half a century. On the other hand, we find pieces with spirit images that are impossible to keep out

---

390 Duff Gordon 1902, p. 343.
391 Duff Gordon 1902, p. 12.
392 Blackman 1929, p. 116, 242, 259-260.
393 A familiar concept already in ancient Egypt: see Frankfort 1948.
394 Private collection, no inventory number.
395 Kriss & Kriss-Heinrich 1962, p. 144.

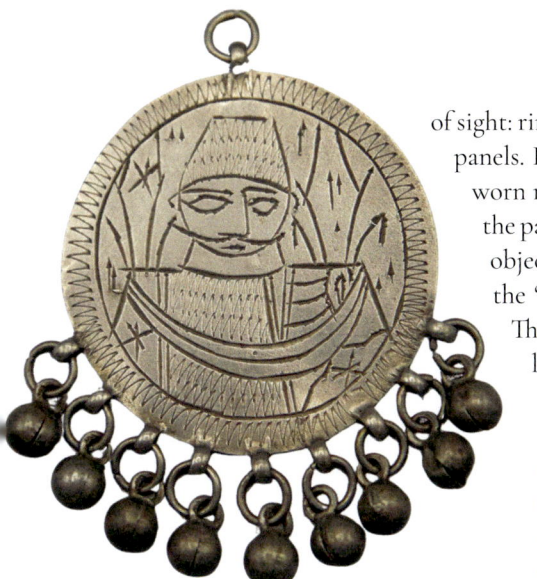

Figure 4.11. All military spirits are depicted as a bust and show no signs of interaction. Collection and photo S. van Roode.

of sight: rings with inscriptions, upper arm bracelets with large panels. How to reconcile the two? I suggest visibility when worn may be a discerning factor between objects worn by the patient, and those worn by the specialist. The powerful objects stayed out of sight because they were worn with the 'spirit-side' inward and the other side, carrying the Throne Verse, outward.[396] This is also evident from the location of the hallmark, which is usually placed on the visible side of jewellery.[397] In case the pendant is hung with southern-style bells, these also indicate the Throne Verse as the front side. When worn like this, the Throne Verse facing outward, they are indistinguishable from regular amulets. Sidqi makes mention of several silver amulets with the Throne Verse on it[398]: he may never have seen their reverse side. The upper arm bracelets and rings with spirit names engraved in them, are far too visible to be worn in everyday life as well. They serve in my opinion the ritual specialist during a *zār*.

Economics

The powerful object is purchased from a jeweller who is also, but not exclusively, specialised in *zār* items. It can be manufactured according to the instructions of the ritual specialist,[399] or alternatively, the diagnosis stage of the *zār* takes place in a jewellery store, where the possessed is drawn to a particular piece of jewellery. This in turn informs the ritual specialist about the spirit possessing her client.[400] The only author to discuss the market of buying and selling such pieces is el-Hadidi. She observes that in Middle Egypt, the craftsmen creating these pieces were part of the business network but remained outsiders to *zār* itself.[401] This illustrates the position of these items as 'terminal commodity', in the terminology of Kopytoff: a commodity that cannot be sold again, as it has turned into a singularity. El-Hadidi further describes the extent of this market, noting that during the 1960s and 1970s, approximately 60% of the production and sale of silver jewellery in the Sohag governorate consisted of *zār* jewellery.[402] I will return to this observation in the next chapter.

---

396   Bogner & Klein-Wisenberg 1979, p. 26 describe the front- and backside of the amulet correctly. Fahmy 2007 shows a necklace with the spirit side up and many newly made composite necklaces also show the spirit side. This however is not how they would have been worn.
397   See Van Roode 2017 for a short introduction on this custom.
398   Littmann 1950, p. 2, translating a manuscript by Sidqi from 1911.
399   Hadidi 2006, p. 102-103, describes how one *shaykha* was considered a business partner of the silversmiths in that respect.
400   Hadidi 2006, p. 127, describes an instance of divination in a jewellery store where 'the possessed spoke in tongues as a response to seeing the amulets that her spirit required'.
401   Hadidi 2016, p. 20-21.
402   Hadidi 2016, p. 21.

Role 2: Manifestation objects

The second role is the pieces used by the spirits to manifest themselves. These are also custom-made and *zār*-specific, but unlike powerful objects these are only active during a *zār*. These pieces, too, add to our understanding of the symbiosis between possessed, spirit and object: the beaded jewellery mirrors silver jewellery from the human world. Noteworthy in this context is that some beaded pieces visually resemble silver powerful objects (Figure 4.12). Their banded decoration evokes an abstract rendering of the lines of text visible on the powerful objects. As we have seen, these latter are worn with the spirit representation inwards and the Throne Verse outwards. When the spirit wears its beaded version, this creates a mirror image of the possessed wearing a powerful object. This reciprocity in dressing reveals the desired dynamics between human, spirit and object during the *zār*: they are indeed equals. These beaded items are not put in blood.

Colours play a crucial role in distinguishing between the various spirits manifested through these objects.[403] This is governed by particular rules: each spirit is associated with certain colours. For example, 'Abd er-Rasoul describes in 1955 how the 'Sudanese Sultan' requires a head-cover of cowrie shells and blue stones[404], much like Thompson noted the use of blue beads for a Sudanese spirit in 1913. In addition to jewellery, the visiting spirits demand to be clad in specific garments such as coloured dresses, robes and headgear. They also make use of an array of other objects such as sticks, staves, swords etc. The Schienerl collections in Dresden and Vienna also hold beaded sticks and staves as well as *zār* garments and tarbushes, all bought from a specialised *zār* dealer.[405] A few of these paraphernalia have found their way into the sample collection as well because they have been executed in silver. The silver diadem and belt (sample coll. 286 and 287)[406] and the silver wand with bells (sample coll. 1136)[407] mentioned earlier were purchased as belonging to *zār* and are most likely part of the spirit paraphernalia.[408] An ornament of three crescents (sample coll. 828)[409] may also belong in the category of manifestation objects. The manifestation set is changed when a new spirit announces itself: the possessed person in which the spirit manifests itself will change into the costume and jewellery the spirit desires. Le Brun describes this change of dress already in her 1902 account.[410]

Jewellery and dress are only 'activated' when worn by a spirit during a ceremony: before and after the ceremony they may remain in the custody of the ritual specialist,[411]

---

403   And, of course, their clothing. Many costuming elements exist that serve to identify and express the presence of a particular spirit.
404   'Abd er-Rasoul 1955, p. 6.
405   A few Egyptian *zār* garments and headdresses are also present in the Musee Quai Branly – Jacques Chirac https://www.quaibranly.fr/fr/explorer-les-collections/ , accessed on May 3rd, 2023 with search term 'zar'.
406   Private collection, no inventory numbers.
407   Indiana University Museum of Anthropology and Archaeology, inventory number DB-2149.
408   Le Brun 1902, p. 285 describes a silver-topped cane with bells being held by the possessed person.
409   Weltmuseum Vienna, inventory number 164462.
410   Le Brun 1902, p. 287.
411   Zvenkovsky 1950, p. 68 mentions that in Sudan these items are to be provided for by the client, which attributes greatly to the cost of the event. He explicitly notes that these can never be lent and that none of these items (including ornaments) can be sold or given away as long as the owner lives. Kenyon 2012, p.87 describes how most Sudanese women could not afford these items, and that they were part of the collection of the ritual specialist instead. For Egypt, Fakhouri 1972, p.94 describes how the participants arrive wearing a dress in the colour prescribed by the specialist underneath their regular black dress.

Figure 4.12. Beaded pendant with abstract rendering of lines (collection Museum für Völkerkunde, Dresden, inv. no. 86878, photo S. van Roode) and a silver pendant with lines of text (collection S. van Roode). The colours of the beaded ornament correspond to particular spirits, and the general design mirrors that of a powerful object in silver when worn. Not to scale.

but more as a collection of props than as 'loaded' objects. Simply having these objects nearby does not summon spirits. However, when spirits are invited by drumming their beat, singing their song and burning their incense they will have a need for these things to manifest themselves. The jewellery itself is, along with the clothing, obtained from a specialised dealer in *zār* necessities.[412] Like the silversmiths, this dealer is part of the business network, but remains an outsider to *zār* itself.

Role 3: Contracts

The third role of jewellery items is that of a contract. This is a role fulfilled by coins or coin jewellery. The preferred coin is the pillar dollar, of which Kriss & Kriss-Heinrich state that imitations were specifically produced for *zār*.[413] The explicit use of coins in both diagnosis and the establishing of a contract or *'aqd* between patient and spirit was described as early as 1911,[414] and remains in use until more recently.[415] To affirm the contract, the coin is put in blood.[416]

Coins are usually regarded as part of a jewellery piece, and it is this piece in its entirety that is then associated with *zār*. For example, twelve of the southern-style *kirdans* carry a coin as pendant below the crescent, resulting in the complete necklace

---

412   Kriss & Kriss-Heinrich 1962, p. 159 mention the store of one Tāhā Laqqānī as the easiest place to obtain these. In the acquisition notes of Peter Schienerl, beaded jewellery, decorated fezzes and beaded staves collected in the 1980's all came from one or more unnamed 'Zar-Händler'.
413   Kriss & Kriss-Heinrich 1962, p. 161.
414   Sidqi 1911, as published by Littman 1950.
415   Nabhan 1994, p. 177.
416   Sengers 2003, p. 100; Nabhan 1994, p. 177.

being ascribed to *zār*. However, the coin itself may have a far more important role than previously assumed. It could represent a material affirmation of a form of social contract, presenting itself in the form of jewellery.

Since coins also serve as general amulets, with this particular role of jewellery attributions begin to be more fluid: *zār* is not the only possession ritual to make use of coins, not every coin in jewellery was used in either *zār* or other ways of dealing with possession, but all coin pendants potentially may have been. As such, these items are commodities, unless they have been put in blood: they then become a singularity.

Role 4: Amulets

The fourth role that jewellery can have, is that of amulets. This role allows for bricolage, where anything with apotropaic capacities may be used in *zār*. The sample collection holds a variety of general amulets which are worn in everyday life. These include pendants with 'Allah', 'Bismillah', 'Mashallah' and 'There is no god but God': of the 297 pendants that are similar in shape to the power objects, 229 carry such texts. As we have seen in chapter 2, infertility and child mortality are the greatest concerns for women. These concerns are reflected in the large number of amulets to prevent them. The presence of women of all ages, some of which might be pregnant, some of which might be young mothers, creates an ideal hunting ground for a most notorious spirit known as the Qarina. This malevolent female spirit is intent on killing young children, causing constant worry among their mothers. As we have seen, two specific types of jewellery are as helpful against the Qarina in these circumstances: iron ankle rings[417] and an amulet called *zur'a*, mentioned by Sidqi.

Role 5: Jewellery requested by the spirit

The last category is the most fluid category. It encompasses the jewellery that the spirit requests be bought, and as such, it potentially includes any and all jewellery. For example, in 2011, the following items were presented as '*zār* amulets': bracelets, *khulkhals*[418], pendants and arm ornaments.[419] This jewellery is provided for by the patient upon the advice of the ritual specialist. Before the ceremony, the jewellery is no different from regular jewellery. Afterwards, the jewellery has become a solid part of the agreement with the possessing spirit. This position has consequences for the household economy, as I will address in the next chapter. Since these jewellery items are regular jewellery pieces, they are not present in the sample collection: they cannot be identified based on visual characteristics only and their role in *zār* has gone unrecognised. I believe this to be a feasible explanation for the jewellery mentioned by Kahle, as we have seen in above 4.1.3: jewellery of a general type, such as the Ottoman-style amulet cases that Kahle refers to (if I interpret his reference to Lane correctly), may very well have been produced at the request of a spirit, to be presented to it during the ritual. As his experience with *zār* was a staged event, the explanations provided to him may have lost significant parts of their meaning.

---

417 Kriss & Kriss-Heinrich, p. 149; see also Soliman 1970, p. 134. Iron ankle rings are present in the collection of Winifred Blackman, Pitt-Rivers Museum inv. no. 1985.54.1775 and 1985.54.1780, collected in 1929.
418 Ankle rings.
419 Ejibadze 2011, p. 140.

4.2.5 Converging worlds

The roles jewellery may have in ritual clarify how we may understand the pieces themselves. However, when we consider their roles in the wider world of spirit engagement and accept the agency of the pieces with spirit images to be that of power objects, new questions arise. These questions relate to the use of contracts, which take a material form in coins, and the position of blood-stained jewellery within the broader context of spirit engagement in Egypt. Both points in my view reflect how an African cult merged with existing Egyptian practices, and I will address both next.

The point of contracts

Why do contracts in *zār* exist? After all, the powerful object itself already cements the bond between human, spirit and object: another material form of contract is, strictly taken, not necessary, but is present nonetheless. It is worth noting that the use of contracts with a spirit also is attested for non-*zār* possession cases.[420] In chapter 2 I touched upon the *ṣulḥ*, the Arab method of settling disputes, in relation to settling disputes with jinn of one's own *qarīn*. This shows strong similarities to an element of *zār*: a dispute needs to be settled through intervention of an intermediary, and when a successful agreement has been reached a communal meal is held, involving the slaughter of animals.[421] A *ṣulḥ* is closely related to an *'aqd*: the agreement reached during a *ṣulḥ* is binding. As we have seen in chapter 2, opinions on the relationship between *zār* and *ṣulḥ* diverge. Some authors see the *ṣulḥ* as a different event altogether[422], another view is that *ṣulḥ* is the animal sacrifice in *zār* in particular[423], or consider the entire initiation into *zār* an *'aqd*.[424] In my view, the challenge of distinguishing between *zār* and *ṣulḥ* arises from their shared objective of reconciliation and their outward similarity, which extends up to the point of animal sacrifice. But in that last aspect, the two methods are different. In a *ṣulḥ*, animals are slaughtered to prepare a formal meal and honour the other party. In *zār*, the sacrifice is made to bond human, spirit and object through blood. As both methods make use of similar activities, they have become so closely interwoven that they are practically indistinguishable and have become one and the same. It is through the presence of objects related to both methods that I feel we may learn of two different systems converging.

Cultural restrictions

In chapter 2, I have argued that the presence of general amulets in *zār* indicates a twofold approach to spirits: where *zār* spirits are invited, others are actively averted. This is because of the high stakes: women can be rendered infertile or end up unmarried because of spirits. But when we consider the general tenets of spirit engagement as explored in the same chapter, we run into another challenge: the incompatibility of *zār* jewellery with cultural restrictions.

---

420   The collection of Winifred Blackman holds a piece of cotton in which several coins have been wrapped, which has been dipped in blood. It is used 'for sheikh possession' in general. Pitt-Rivers Museum inv. no. 1985.54.2877, collected in 1929
421   See Pely 2011 and Lang 2002 for a general layout of a *ṣulḥ*; Drieskens 2006b for an example from Cairo.
422   Blackman 1926, p. 198-199 and Morsy 1978, p. 601.
423   Nabhan 1994, p. 211.
424   Hadidi 2006, p. 64.

I would like to recall how a framework of strict rules was in place to protect women who are considered ritually vulnerable after a crisis-event.[425] These cultural restrictions pertain to both the possibility of inadvertently inflicting *kabsa* upon others as well as the risk of contracting *kabsa* oneself. As everything spirit related in Egypt is fluid, the 'rules' to prevent *kabsa* vary. What they do have in common is the avoidance of anything related to blood: a challenging concept, seeing how the use of blood is central to *zār*. In fact, these cultural restrictions, when combined with *zār*, potentially derail virtually every contact between women. As I mentioned in chapter 2, anything bearing a remote resemblance to blood and death is kept away from women during the period in which the risk of contracting *kabsa* is high. This includes for example actual blood (from attending a circumcision event, but also from visiting a butcher[426]), but extends as far as anything that might attract the unwanted presence of spirits, such as gold jewellery and notably that with any form of human portraits, such as coins.[427] This could potentially result in envy, which attracts spirits. Wearing jewellery with spirit images in this context is even more suspect: there is no surer way to bring a spirit to a person in danger of contracting *kabsa* than wearing one around your neck during a visit.

Theoretically, anyone who had attended a *zār* should not be visiting new mothers or brides on account of the presence of blood in which its jewellery had been placed. Given the popularity of *zār*, this would constitute an impossible restriction to maintain. Even worse, how to reconcile the possibility of the possessed and the ritually vulnerable being one and the same person...? Intriguingly, *zār* is not mentioned anywhere as polluting circumstance. How does it manage to escape these rules?

When we look at *zār* again, we see it is held precisely around crisis events: first menstruation, marriage, childbirth, and menopause.[428] Hadidi relates how a possessed woman who had had a *zār* held a second *zār*, this time to protect her unborn child.[429] Yet in 1911, Sidqi states that it is absolutely necessary for a pregnant patient to wear a *zur'a* amulet during the *zār*, or her unborn child will die. Another observation is that children, who are otherwise considered as vulnerable beings that need protecting from jinn, seem to have been present from a very young age. Franke writes that in her opinion 'it is most dangerous for children to attend the Zar exorcisms' (as they are easily impressed and will grow up believing in it), followed by a citation from Le Brun that mothers bring their children along often, and if they fall ill afterwards, they have a *zār* in their own house for the child.[430] Le Brun indeed writes that children are present, and even at such a young age they are still being breast-fed.[431] In fact, *zār* seems to have been so much a part of everyday life that already in 1913 Thompson wrote 'Indeed, in some parts of the city, the little girls have this as a performance in their play in the streets.'[432]

---

425 The importance of these restrictions is for example described in Early 1993, p. 180-181; Wickett 2010, p. 67.
426 Inhorn 1994, p. 495.
427 Inhorn 1994, p. 496.
428 Hadidi 2006, p. 113-142.
429 Hadidi 2006, p. 125.
430 Thompson & Franke 1911, p.288.
431 Le Brun 1902, p. 271.
432 Thompson & Franke 1913, p. 275.

The cultural restrictions in place around crisis-events are all aimed at ensuring a woman's fertility, successful pregnancy and healthy children. *Zār* does the same, and so I would suggest that its occurrence around crisis events may indicate its position as a counter measure against *kabsa* such as Inhorn describes, which can be both preventive or therapeutic,[433] rather than as one of the polluting occasions itself. Simultaneously, the large amount of apotropaic jewellery in *zār* does reflect uneasiness over these conflicting views. It points to the existing, and deeply felt need, to protect oneself in the usual manner against jinn and their ill intentions which may result in infertility.

4.3 *ZĀR* JEWELLERY IN EVERYDAY LIFE

4.3.1 Costs

Jewellery also played a practical role in everyday life. It constituted a financial asset and was critical to empowering women financially. However spiritually meaningful *zār* jewellery was, it still had to be purchased. And so, a major aspect of *zār* that has frequently been held against it, already from the first reports on the practice, are the costs. Zwemer, writing in 1920, calls it 'such an expensive bit of heathenism that families have been ruined through its demands'.[434] Blackman calls *zār* 'a baneful belief', providing as reason that *zār* comes with great expenses.[435]

In order to get an idea of just how expensive we should imagine a *zār* to be, I have looked into a case-study from 1913, as described in Thompson & Franke 1913 (see Appendix 1).[436] Based on this case study I have estimated the cost of a personal *zār* for a lower-class woman to amount to approximately LE 60-80, against an annual family income of LE 60. Having this ceremony would therefore constitute a very serious financial imposition. The family income offered little space for saving, which was needed for medical aid and financial setbacks.[437] The high costs of a *zār* could not be settled at once, but were often paid in instalments.[438] Given the difficulties a husband already had in providing the necessary dowry upon his wedding, and the struggle to make ends meet in general, covering another large amount of costs would be near impossible.[439] Spending an annual income or more on *zār* illustrates both the

---

433 Inhorn 1994, p. 496. If infertility is suspected to be the result of spirit possession, attending a *zār* may lift it according to Van der Most-Van Spijk 1982, p. 46-47; Haverhals-Werkman 1996, p. 16.
434 Zwemer 1920, p. 241.
435 Blackman 1927, p. 200.
436 I have chosen this case-study, even though it provides its own challenges in terms of economic value, instead of the account by Kriss & Kriss-Heinrich who list the costs of their *zār*, as, in addition to the challenges their account poses, I cannot rule out bias against foreign clients which may have resulted in higher expenses. In 2003, a *zār* might cost between 200 and 300 pounds, according to Sengers 2003, p. 100, 109.
437 See Hoodfar 1999 for a study into household economy, Kholoussy 2005 for the financial imposition a marriage constituted, Van Roode 2017, p. 73 for an introduction of the principles behind income and saving in relation to jewellery. See Yousef 2018 for a case study of poverty in 1913, focusing on a woman whose husband was no longer capable of earning an income as a shoemaker.
438 Comparable to the payment 'in degrees' for the *gallābīya* and golden earrings requested by the spirit in Blackman 1928, p. 187. Nowadays the costs can also be settled in installments, according to Granzow 2008, p. 14.
439 Although it is debatable whether the man or the woman would cover these costs, the entire family income would be stretched as a result of having a *zār*. See Hoodfar 1999, p. 162 for the general division of costs within a household.

importance of the ceremony to the patient and the realistic potential of financial ruin that critics of *zār* warned so vehemently against.

A reasonable thought might be that wealthy people could afford a *zār* more easily than less affluent women. Gordon explains that the poor had to resort to other methods of 'exorcisms', as *zār* was mainly popular by the rich because these could afford the costs.[440] 'Abd er-Rasoul notes that *zār* was mainly practised by 'uncultured rich women who do this for fun and spend a great deal of money on it'.[441] However, the cost of *zār* usually rose with the financial means of the possessed. Instead of a few birds, the sacrificial animals needed by the spirit were more expensive creatures such as cows, sheep, goat or even camels.[442] The necessities for the ritual would also be more elaborate. The jewellery would be in gold instead of silver, as we have seen in Sidqi's account from 1911. Additionally, the ceremony itself could last up to a week. In short, for every stratum in society a personal *zār* would have been an expensive affair. That these costs are indeed meant to be high, is also affirmed in 1911 when Sidqi wrote how a ritual specialist proclaimed that a cheap *zār* would not have the desired effect on the patient.[443] The weekly *zār* ceremonies involved a much smaller sum, but this still had to be provided for.[444] Critics of *zār* therefore often regard it as a shrewd way to shake hard-earned money out of superstitious people, criminally abusing their good faith and trust.[445]

The importance of jewellery in an economic sense associated with *zār* becomes apparent in a remark placed by 'Abd er-Rasoul, who notes that social customs dictated that women brought each other small presents in the form of money on the occasion of marriage, birth or *zār*-ceremonies – and that these were expected to be repaid by the recipient on the next occasion hosted by the donor.[446] This is a well-known and widely practised form of 'crowdfunding' within a community. These small presents can also take the form of jewellery, such as is often the case with weddings, and the obligation to return the gift in kind constitutes the backbone of this informal financial network. Women will contribute to the financial assets of the bride, new mother or *zār* patient, in the knowledge that they, too, will be a beneficiary in due course.

4.3.2 Marriage dynamics

The costs of a *zār* could also be employed as strategy within the marriage. Ensuring that a husband would not have the financial means to take another wife has been given as ground by women to be 'needing' several *zārs*.[447] This concurs with the general trend

---

440 Gordon 1929, p.154.
441 'Abd er-Rasoul 1955, p. 81, note 1. She reduces *zār* to a party hosted for friends with the specific outcome of receiving gifts like these.
442 Blackman 1928, p. 199, mentions a sheep. See also Kriss & Kriss-Heinrich, p. 163.
443 Littman 1950, p. 6, translating a manuscript by Mahmud Sidqi from 1911.
444 Currently several pounds and increasing; Hadidi 2016, p.44 mentions that public *zār* is costly.
445 Natvig 2014, p. 308 describes how *zār* leaders are looked upon as charlatans and frauds, in these wordings echoing the concerns regarding the expenses of a *zār*. Le Brun 1902, p. 262, notes that a *kōdiya* that connected wealthy and poor patients possessed by the same spirit, also stood to gain from this arrangement, making her skills suspect.
446 'Abd er-Rasoul 1955, p. 81 note 2.
447 Nelson 1971, p. 31; Granzow 2008, p. 14-15, note 24.

of married women preventing their husband from entering a second marriage, as this would stretch the already limited family finances even further.[448]

However, the risks of this strategy backfiring were serious. The possibility of a woman being possessed and in need of a *zār* has been claimed by critics to be leading to divorce or the breaking off of an engagement, due to the significant costs involved.[449] We need to be aware that this consequence is put forward by known critics of *zār* and might thus well be aimed at discouraging participation altogether by targeting one of the most important prospects of a woman's life: getting married. However, when divorce or the breaking off of an engagement would indeed be on the table, it would seem to me that a critical factor in using *zār* as strategy to prevent a second marriage is whether the dowry of the first wife had indeed been paid in full. If it had, divorcing would be the cheaper option on the part of the husband. This would in turn bring shame on the wife and her family, not to mention constitute a serious financial challenge. Had the dowry however not yet been paid in full, and according to Kholoussy it rarely was[450], the '*zār* strategy' had considerably more chances of success: not only his wife, but her entire family would insist he fulfil both his debt and his obligations to his wife before taking a second wife – including financing her *zār*.

The economic aspects of jewellery within the marriage also extended to *zār* jewellery in another way. The dowry jewellery a woman receives upon her wedding is theoretically hers alone.[451] It is meant as financial failsafe in case of divorce or death of the husband (hence the emphasis on the dowry actually being paid), and is not considered part of the household means.[452] However, in reality, the jewellery of the woman is used to cover large and unforeseen expenses, such as hospitalisation or major repairs – it is often the only financial reserve a family has. In this light it is of interest that *zār* jewellery apparently cannot be sold: not just the powerful objects, but also the jewellery requested by the spirit cannot be parted with. As a reason for this, property in the juridical sense is inferred by several authors,[453] but others distinguish between possession and property in their choice of words. Hadidi for example relates how a possessed woman was fine for a while, 'because the mistress (zar spirit) was wearing *my* gold bangles, *my* ankle-bracelets and *my* rings' (italics by the present author).[454]

I believe the inhibition on parting with *zār* jewellery is to be regarded in this light as well. Apart from its association with the possessing spirit, the jewellery needed in *zār* did add to the collection of jewellery, the savings' account, of the patient. *Zār* was one of the methods a woman would resort to in case of infertility. Having no children could be grounds for divorce – and with possible divorce looming on the horizon, adding to her personal assets might have been the savvy thing to do. That certainly does not replace or diminish the spiritual meaning attached to this jewellery, as that

---

448 Hoodfar 1999, p.75, describing how women feel they must manipulate their men to prevent another marriage.
449 Zwemer 1920, p. 241; Snouck Hurgronje as quoted by Thompson & Franke 1913, p. 285.
450 Kholoussy 2010, pp. 29, 69.
451 Bakker & McKeown 2021, p. 195-196.
452 See Tucker 1985, p. 45-46 for 19th century Egypt where court cases show the right of a woman to her dowry was consistently upheld.
453 Blackman 1926 p. 199 identifies the five piaster piece a present to the possessing spirit; Boddy 1989 p. 325 makes the same distinction between object possession by the host and ownership by the spirit.
454 Hadidi 2006, p. 121.

is one of its fundamental qualities, but it does provide another angle from which to understand these pieces.

4.3.3 *Zār* as integral part of life

Zār created communities. Specialists and attendees formed their own close-knit circle on a local level, and as Hadidi has extensively shown, on a larger scale anyone in the *zār* 'guild', including musicians, silversmiths and traders in all sorts of *zār* paraphernalia, contributed to the creating of the *zār* community.[455] But that community stretched well beyond the cult members itself.

Going by the indication of Hadidi, as quoted above, that roughly 60% of the production and sale of silver jewellery in Sohag governorate in the 1960s and 1970s consisted of *zār* jewellery, that not only indicates the popularity of *zār*, but it also means its material culture must have permeated everyday life. *Zār* jewellery was visible widely in silver shops: a divination of the type Hadidi describes cannot take place if the jewellery is not visible in the first place, and apparently going into trance in a store where other customers are present is accepted behaviour. The silversmiths themselves were Christians and Jews[456]: as we have seen, *zār* was practised by the three main religions, and the *zār* business extended into these worlds as well.

In addition to silver, the garments and beaded jewellery created specifically for *zār* were available for purchase as well. Where silversmiths combined their workshop with a store, the designated dealers in *zār* supplies acquired their stock from elsewhere. The making of embellished garments involved home labour by women, as Chalcraft explores: in the early 20th century, decorating textiles such as the famous silver-worked Assyut shawls, was a home-job, and one that paid very little.[457] Decorating the sequined *zār* garments and *tarbushes* or creating the many beaded pieces of jewellery is a comparable activity that would have been regarded as fitting for women, working as seamstresses.[458]

It is very well feasible that *zār*, in one way or another, was present in many homes: either because its residents practised *zār*, or because they were involved in purveying its supplies. *Zār* was integral to everyday life, not just in a spiritual sense, but also from an economic point of view. When we observe the jewellery spirit images as a historic source, they may provide us with glimpses of that everyday life, and tell us more about that wider community itself.

---

455 Hadidi 2006, passim, but notably p. 77-112.
456 Schienerl 1976, p. 129; Hadidi 2016, p. 20.
457 Chalcraft 2005, pp. 112-113.
458 Remarkably little is known about the beaded jewellery market or indeed the use of beaded jewellery in general. Fahmy 2007, p. 192 writes that stringing of beaded necklaces was done by women themselves. Weeks 1986, p. 19 already noted that 'a study of the many beads… in Egyptian women's jewelry would merit a volume of its own' and mentions how women would make intricate beaded pieces themselves (p. 22). Mehrez 2023, p. 95 mentions seamstresses as responsible for the beading of traditional dresses in some cases, and in other cases the client had to bring the beads (p. 107).

5

HISTORIC OBJECTS

5.1 MATERIALISED MEMORY

5.1.1 The performance of cultural memory

A well-known element of many African possession cults is their capacity to store and transmit collective memory.[459] That goes for *zār* as well, as has been identified in, for example, the works of Boddy[460], Kenyon[461], and Hadidi[462]. During possession episodes, historic realities relevant to a community are remembered, re-experienced and transmitted through enactment and personae. This quite literally takes the form of a performance: during a possession episode, *zār* devotees change their manner and appearance completely. They act differently from their regular behaviour, and they also look differently. Items of dress serve to embody a variety of spirits: items like *tarbushes*, sashes and a variety of garments are changed for the next spirit to manifest itself.

However, where the performance itself is only temporary, and the manner of acting may no longer be observed, the images of spirits engraved in jewellery provide a lasting view on what they were believed to look like. If performance is, as Hadidi explains for *zār* songs, aimed at preserving the identity of a community through its cultural memory,[463] could studying these images in reverse tell us more about that identity and cultural memory?

First, I would like to briefly address why my focus is on the images, and not on the texts. The texts on the *zār* power objects are renderings of the Throne Verse: incomplete, with spelling mistakes and sometimes abbreviated to a few words only. Redman has shown how the Throne Verse is misspelt on Omani pendants on a number of occasions and explains this as characteristic of illiterate wearers: the wearer knows the Throne Verse by heart, and seeing an inscription that is more an impression instead of an accurate rendering of the verse, still activates its powers through inner

---

459   See Behrend & Luig 1999, p. xviii-xx 'Spirit possession as performative ethnography and history 'from below'' for an introduction. Also Motta 2005, p. 298 for an example of an Indian spirit in Brazil, referring to a rebellion leader, and Della Subin 2021 for both *zār* and an introduction into similar phenomena worldwide.
460   Boddy 1989.
461   Kenyon 2012.
462   Hadidi 2006.
463   Hadidi 2016, p. 130-132.

Figure 5.1 Sultan al-Habashi on a pendant from 1913-1916 (left, sample coll. 071) and 1919-1920 (right, sample coll. 089). Not to scale. Both collection Landesmuseum Oldenburg, photo S. van Roode.

reciting.[464] Assuming the same holds true for *zār* power objects as well, that makes the side with text to more of an 'image' of the intended text, while the actual narrative is in the image on the other side.[465]

That this visual narrative indeed does contain a form of collective memory becomes apparent from at least one spirit depicted on *zār* jewellery, which is directly linked to historic events: Khedive Abbas Hilmi II. This spirit appears in jewellery dated from 1913-1916: the Khedive was deposed and banished in 1914. Understanding these images as historic source, however, is not as straightforward as simply matching an image to a spirit and from there to a historic event: only the appearance of Khedive Abbas Hilmi II is that specific because he has his name and title written next to him. This is rare: as individual spirits are rarely depicted most images go without text. Two other rare instances where a spirit is labelled are shown in Figure 5.1.[466]

The two images both depict Sultan al-Habashi, the Ethiopian Sultan. But they do so very differently: the only thing they seem to agree on is that the sultan sports a moustache. Does that mean all male spirits with a moustache are Sultan al-Habashi? That is unlikely. So, how do we recognise and 'read' historical information present in *zār* images, if a single spirit can take two totally different forms, and the majority of spirits are not as helpfully labelled? Observing the spirit images as expression of <u>collective</u> memory and identity, in my view, requires a different approach than looking for <u>individual</u> identities of spirits – these are rarely presented as such. However, this is the path that has thus far been chosen by researchers, and so I will discuss this first.

---

464 Redman 2020.
465 They are both *grammae* in the sense put forward by Elkins 1999, p. 83-91. See also Garcia Probert 2022, p. 255 for a discussion on approaches to the study of collected amulets beyond their texts.
466 Translation by Yasmine el-Dorghamy.

5.1.2 Challenges in identifying individual spirits

From the moment jewellery with spirit images started to be sold and subsequently collected by cultural outsiders, attempts have been made to identify these depictions as this or that spirit based on their appearance and attributes. Schienerl formulates this active pursuit of identifications as follows: 'The naming of *zār* spirits based on their attributes has not yet been scientifically established. Kriss introduces in his book V.B.I.II[467] over 200 names, among which Adam, Eve, Gibrail (Gabriel), etc. The identifications we chose all follow this book. Even so, an attribution of Sitt and Sid with Adam and Eve etc would also be possible'.[468]

The need for identification is still strongly felt in the world of collectors: descriptions of *zār* images often provide a name for the spirit depicted. That name is, in most cases, Yawri Bey, the officer, or Sitt Safīna, the mermaid. Schienerl shows a selection of male spirits wearing different uniforms and a male spirit in *gallābīya*: the caption says these all represent Yawri Bey.[469] Following the popularity of his publication and due to the repetition of bits and pieces of information, notably online, the name Yawri Bey is now often applied to any and all male spirits, not necessarily officers.[470]

Spirit pairs are often labelled as 'Sitt and Sidi'. Many forms of classifications have emerged over the decades; in every account, the number, names, and group associations of the *zār* spirits vary. Family relations between spirits change, too. The officer Yawri Bey is nowadays accompanied by the girlish Rakkusha, who is claimed to be his daughter or sister.[471] In older songs, any relation between the two is not apparent, and when looking at the spirit images on jewellery none of the officers is accompanied by a female spirit.

This organising of spirits into groups, families, and hierarchies is already mentioned in older accounts but seems to be taking flight from the 1960s onwards, so from the moment *zār* jewellery started to be sold. And finally, attempts at identifying or classifying spirits depicted on jewellery reach dead ends because the spirits they vary not only over time but also geographically.[472]

Apart from the need to identify and classify, the interpretation of these images has also been influenced by a desire to see ancient Egypt lingering in today's popular religion. Two examples are the 'sphinx' and the 'obelisk' (Figure 5.2).

---

467   This is Kriss & Kriss-Heinrich 1962.
468   Bachinger & Schienerl 1984, p. 82: 'Die Benennung der Zargeistern aufgrund ihrer Attribute ist bis heute nicht wissenschaftlich festgelegt. Kriss führt in seinem Buch V.B.I.II über 200 Namen an, darunter Adam, Eva, Gibrail (Gabriel) usw. Die von uns gewählten Bezeichnungen folgen alle diesem Buch. Allerdings wäre auch denkbar eine Zuschreibung der >Sitt< und des >Sid< mit Adam und Eva etc.'
469   Bachinger & Schienerl 1984, p. 74.
470   https://ethnicsilverjewels.wordpress.com/2018/05/22/egypt-zar/ showed a *zār* pendant featuring a man in *gallābīya*, named as Yawri Bey, as well as a coin of King Farouk mentioned as symbolizing Yawri Bey. Website consulted on January 25, 2023. Mörike 2021, Tafel VII, abb. 9 presents a *zār* pendant featuring a man in Arab dress as Yawri Bey. Weeks 1984 however also mentioned '*Askari*', meaning 'soldier' as name for military spirits, and there are more – Yawri Bey is not the only military spirit.
471   Darmody 2001, p. 71 lists Rakkusha as daughter; Granzow 2008 p. 41 as 'daughter or sister'. Granzow also mentions Yawri Bey and Rakkusha to be the most popular spirits at the time of her research.
472   Hermann 1969, p.33 for example states succinctly that the world of demons varies substantially from a geographical point of view. See also Drieskens 2008. Hadidi 2016, p. 22 relates how ritual specialists in Cairo did not know much about the *zār* jewellery she had collected in Upper Egypt.

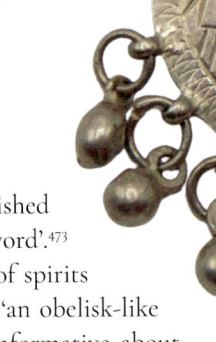

Figure 5.2. Zār pendants showing imaged identified as 'sphinx' (left, sample coll. 344) and 'obelisk' (right, sample coll. 329). Not to scale. Collection and photo S. van Roode.

The image on the left has been published by Schienerl as 'Sphinx-demon with sword'.[473] The image on the right shows a pair of spirits flanking what Schienerl described as 'an obelisk-like pillar'.[474] Both descriptions are very informative about how Europeans viewed Egypt. By the time these images were created, obelisks were a more familiar sight in Europe than in Egypt itself. The stone needles have been dragged off to Europe since the Roman period, and in the early 20th century, only a few were left standing in Egypt.[475] But the attractive notion of a surviving connection from ancient Egypt held sway over Egyptian scholars as well. El-Adly described a stylised version of the 'sphinx'-image as 'The head-dress is similar to that of a mummy'[476] and Nabhan pondered whether the 'obelisk' could not rather be a *djed*-pillar[477].

While it is certainly possible that ancient monuments feature in popular belief, I feel that the identification of these images with ancient Egyptian monuments is unsubstantiated. The 'sphinx' is actually a male spirit in Arab Bedouin attire, and the explanation for the 'obelisk' might be found much closer to home – as I will argue below in 5.2.

---

473 Bachinger & Schienerl 1984, p. 83. Cited by later authors, including myself, and for example Mayer 2021, p. 84.
474 Bachinger & Schienerl 1984, p. 82: Zwischen >sid< und >sitt< befindet sich eine obeliskenartige Säule.
475 The obelisks of Heliopolis, Luxor and Karnak are the only ones standing at their original location.
476 Adly 1984, p. 664. He also interprets the spirit as a female jinn.
477 Nabhan 1994, p. 66 note 319. A *djed*-pillar is an ancient Egyptian amulet, which does not look like an obelisk or the object shown on the *zār* power objects.

5.1.3 The pivotal role of the ritual specialist

The approach as worded by Schienerl expresses a thoroughly Western view: scientific, measurable, and orderly. One should be able to recognise spirits by their attributes as if they were Catholic saints. However, as we have seen, the majority of images do not represent a particular spirit. They are rather 'stock images', to be interpreted by the ritual specialist. They become embodied spirits during a *zār*, and only then their identity becomes known. All we are left with today is the material culture of this event, and without the original interpretation of the ritual specialist we cannot determine by visual characteristics alone which spirit is meant to be represented. An example is again shown in Figure 5.1, the power object with the name of the spirit engraved above his shoulders: Sultan al-Habashi.[478] But across his chest another name has been added, in a different hand: Shaykh al-Meccawi al-Malt(?).[479] This pendant has been reinscribed for another spirit, or perhaps the single image sufficed for two different spirits. The ritual specialist and her client would have known, and apparently its visual appearance was not the decisive factor.

So, could we ask a ritual specialist to identify the spirits on the power objects? This reverse approach has been chosen by Darmody. In her study, the first that places the collected jewellery items with spirit images in the context of *zār*, she has combined her own experiences with *zār* with the knowledge of its ritual specialist.[480] She is the first to put together 'spirit charts', tracing the occurrence of spirits through time based on the identifications presented to her.[481] This tracing of spirits over time is an essential insight. A complication with Darmody's excellent approach, however, is, in my view, that identifying the images on jewellery of a century old using knowledge about spirits manifesting today is problematic when the purpose of that identification is to get a clearer view on the spirits of the past. It presupposes a static and universal spirit 'pantheon', still based on visible characteristics, much like Schienerl assumed.

Sidqi, writing in 1930, shares an incredibly relevant observation about the hierarchy in spirits he describes: this was the hierarchy used by the specific ritual specialist interviewed.[482] This ritual specialist, in turn, commented on his endeavour that writing a book about *zār* was completely impossible, and that she did not even want to hear how other specialists approached *zār*.[483] Her comment emphasises how a firmly established number, order, and visual appearance of spirits is not in keeping with the adaptive capabilities or the fluid nature of the *zār*, or indeed with the spirit world itself.

The person tying it all together is the ritual specialist: each village, town, or region has its own tradition, and within these communities every ritual specialist follows her own instincts and training to determine which *zār* spirit is possessing her client.[484]

---

478   Translation by Yasmine el-Dorghamy.
479   Translation by Yasmine el-Dorghamy. Al-Meccawi is certain, al-Malt is not.
480   Darmody 2001.
481   Darmody 2001, p. 40 ff.
482   Littmann 1950, p. 35-36.
483   Littmann 1950, p. 35-36.
484   Hadidi 2016, p. 41 mentions 66 spirits and their organisation in extended families, and she also notes that there are discrepancies between cults. Sengers 2003 p. 104, citing Kriss & Kriss-Heinrich and Littmann, notes the classification by the authors mentioned and the spirits familiar to the respondents in her research differ.

Backtracking old spirits and their historic meaning based on knowledge of today's spirit world, which by its very nature differs from that of, say, the 1920s, therefore in my view is not feasible.

That is not to say that old power objects cannot be reinterpreted by today's ritual specialists: after all, the interpretation of the ritual specialist is and remains key. Whichever spirit her training and abilities allow her to recognise today on an old object, her interpretation is completely valid in the context of *zār* as it is currently practised. In fact, that old objects continue to have agency in my view is perfectly illustrated by the pieces that Carl Axel Silow acquired when he purchased the complete contents of an herbalist's shop in 1978 (see chapter 3), or the reinterpretation of sample coll. 0071 from an Ethiopian to a Meccan spirit.[485]

5.1.4 Time is of the essence: changing narratives

If we want to catch a glimpse of the historical realities *zār* jewellery reflects, their place in time is very relevant. Because the collective memory stored in *zār* is not equal to a series of facts in chronological order: histories are kept alive in the tradition of the *zār*, up until a point where they are replaced with other stories. This is linked to the perception of history in African knowledge traditions. To better understand this aspect of *zār*, I have used the study on knowledge traditions of the Oromo by Megerssa & Kassam;[486] as we have seen, one of the components that constitute Egyptian *zār* may well find its origins with the Oromo.[487]

The study by Megerssa & Kassam provides a framework for understanding other methods of historical narration than factual chronicling. Possession is one of those methods. Both the definition of history in Oromo culture and the way it is communicated present a different form of historic awareness: history is something that has been experienced and is considered to be a message from the ancestors that carries relevance and meaning for the community.[488]

Megerssa & Kassam point out how Oromo history is to be regarded as living history, as it is orally reproduced and transferred. Writing down history, they argue, is 'a closed history, a history of the past, whilst the Oromo narrative is a religiously inclined, unfolding history that seeks to understand how the past lives on into the present and can serve as a meaningful guide for the future'.[489]

That ever-unfolding history is clearly visible in the temporal nature of *zār* narratives. From *zār* songs and spirit personae, it becomes apparent that the oldest spirits reflect the state of affairs around the end of the 19th century and the beginning of the 20th century.[490] Most countries where *zār* was practised were part of the Ottoman Empire at that time, followed by British rule. In Sudan for example Lord Cromer, Gordon and Kitchener are included in the *zār* pantheon.[491] In Egypt, the banishing of

---

485   Schienerl 1984, p. 10, also notices old *zār* jewellery being resold.
486   Megerssa & Kassam 2021.
487   *Zār* as known in Egypt is an amalgam, and one of the components of the Egyptian *zār* comes from Ethiopia: as Natvig 1987, p. 685-686 proposes, notably from the Oromo.
488   Megerssa & Kassam 2021, p. 150.
489   Megerssa & Kassam 2021, p. 159.
490   See for example Kramer 1987.
491   See Boddy 1989, Granzow 2008 for the *zār*.

Khedive Abbas Hilmi II was memorialised in *zār* as we have seen above – but only very briefly. There are no power objects with his image hallmarked after 1916. After British rule had ended, *zār* in Hofriyat (Sudan) reflected the growing importance of Saudi Arabia in Sudan through the increased activities of a *zār* spirit called al-Qurayshi between 1977 and 1983.[492] Another telling example about the limited longevity of the collective memory is the appearance of a foreign, Canadian *zār* spirit, called Sitt an-Nisa, in the same Sudani village. This spirit announced itself by the clanking of metal and turned out to be the spirit representation of the researcher herself, down to her recording gear and cameras.[493] She only appeared for a few years – after a while, the collective memory of the researcher's activities apparently lost immediate importance, and faded.

This, in turn, has consequences for the way we may approach the historic aspect of the images on Egyptian *zār* jewellery: what we are looking for is not a series of facts, but a rather a rendering of those aspects of their world that the *zār* community felt to be of direct impact on their collective identity. I will now first propose how we may understand the images as expressions of a collective memory, followed by three case studies in 5.2. I will then add the temporal factor in section 5.3.

5.1.5 A collective representation: the personal front

As I have said at the start of the section above, *zār* literally takes the form of a performance. Through items of dress and accessories, devotees express the identity of the spirit that possesses them and enable it to manifest itself. This particular dressing does not only involve the possessed and the spirit. As in any performance, it also serves to convey a message to the onlookers. The choice of items therefore needs to make sense to the onlookers as well: they need to recognise this way of dressing and what it stands for. In other words, the costumes and accessories chosen in *zār* constitute a 'personal front', as coined by Goffman.[494]

Goffman discerns three elements for a performance: the setting in which the performance takes place, and for the performers themselves their manner or behaviour, and their appearance.[495] These last two form the personal front – the way a person presents themselves. The three elements interact: the people that have a role in the public defence of this thesis will both dress and act differently during the defence itself and at the hopefully celebratory dinner afterwards. All participants will adhere to a broader bandwidth of acceptable appearance on both occasions: no one is likely to don a space suit during either event. That broader bandwidth presents the range in which a given appearance still makes sense to the onlookers, because it fits in how they experience their world: the collective representation.[496]

Spirits may appear in a variety of costumes, but all of these have to make sense to the community that needs to recognise itself and its values in these forms. In *zār*, the

---

492 Boddy 1989, pp 302-303. Al-Qurayshi means 'he of the Quraysh', the tribe of the Prophet. This spirit was said to came from Mecca.
493 Boddy 1989, p. 359. *Sitt an-Nisa* means Lady of Women, a clear reflection of her interactions with female population of Hofriyat.
494 Goffman 1959.
495 Goffman 1959, p. 23-24.
496 Goffman 1959, p. 27.

separation between possessed and 'audience' is not that strict: anyone in the room may at some point feel compelled to enter the trance stage, in particular at the weekly *zār*. Dress is, together with music, songs, dance, and incense, a fundamental part of *zār*: the colours used, the moving of textiles, the jingling of silver, and the rattling of cowrie shells all add to the sensory experience of the participants.[497]

The *zār* images do not capture all of this: they reflect only part of the personal front and do not register the changes in behaviour during a possession episode. These have been addressed elsewhere.[498] What the images do reflect, however, is the appearance and the setting of that collective identity: the spirit images show them dressed in a variety of costumes, holding objects and placed in landscapes. I suggest observing these may shed light on that collective identity as it was experienced throughout the timeframe these objects with spirit images were in use. In the next sections, I present an overview of that personal front.

Female dress and adornment

A first observation that stands out for the hand-engraved pieces is that female human-shaped spirits wear traditional dress. The majority wear a v-necked *gallābīya*, sometimes detailed with an inset of sorts. Elaborate necklines occur in a few cases. The dresses are shown either as falling straight to the ground or with a widening lower part. A different form of dress, worn by only five female spirits, is what looks like a short tunic over a pair of trousers. This outfit is identical to that of their male counterparts depicted on the same object.

Female mermaids also wear clothing on their human upper body, and based on its similar neckline as fully human spirits wear, I interpret these to be representations of traditional dress as well. A noteworthy detail is that a small number of mermaids are depicted nude, sometimes with visible breasts. An interesting depiction is that on sample coll. 0978[499] (see cat. no. 009 in the catalogue): here, a pair of mermaids is clearly wearing v-necked garments, but their breasts are also indicated.

Another observation for the hand-engraved pieces is that the vast majority of the female *zār* spirits do not wear a face veil or hair covering. A few spirits are shown wearing a long head-veil falling down their back, and every spirit wearing such a head-veil carries a jug or basket on her head (see figure 3.8 for an example). Only one spirit might be wearing a face-veil.[500] It is, however, impossible to be sure, as the execution of the piece is quite sketchy, and it has no parallels. In this absence of veils and hair coverings, female spirits are often depicted with a visible, neat partition of the hair. Nothing else of their hairstyle is visible. The exception are eleven bald spirits, of which seven are water spirits.

Finally, most female *zār* spirits are depicted wearing earrings. These are similar in shape throughout time, and therefore probably serve as a general indicator of the presence of earrings rather than representing actual existing types of earrings. The earrings are the only jewellery pieces to be identified with certainty: other elements

---

497 See Gouy 2023, p. x for a brief description of the connection between dress, dance, ritual and community.
498 The psychological aspects of this behavioural change in *zār* have been addressed by scholars such as Okasha 1966 for the UAE; Fakhouri 1968 and 1972 for Egypt; Lewis 1991 for *zār* in general.
499 Collection Qilada Foundation – Eric and Marion Crince Le Roy, inventory number 63n.
500 Sample coll. 277, dating from 1978-1979. Private collection, no inventory number.

such as necklaces and bracelets (see cat. nos. 006 and 022 in the catalogue for an example) might also be renderings of an embellished neckline or ends of sleeves.

The predilection for traditional dress changes on machine-tooled, stamped pieces: here, the majority of female spirits are seen wearing a blouse. As they are depicted from the hip upwards, it is impossible to tell whether they pair this with trousers or a skirt, but the difference with traditional dress is obvious. The female spirits on the stamped pieces, both human and water spirits, wear their hair loosely hanging down, as opposed to the spirits on the engraved pieces.

Male dress and adornment

On the hand-engraved pieces, male human-shaped spirits also appear for the majority in *gallābīya*. Here as well, a variety in *gallābīya* is present: most wear a v-necked *gallābīya*, but more ornate necklines exist as well. On their heads, they generally wear a *tarbush* or what looks to be a tight-fitting skullcap: it is not always possible to see the difference. The second largest group of human-shaped male spirits wears a military uniform, paired with a *tarbush* or in some cases a helmet with plumes.

Other male spirits appear in attire from the Arab Peninsula, wearing a headdress with band and holding a sword, and a few are shown in long robes with a turban. Many spirits sport a moustache, while just one spirit, dressed in long robe with turban, has a full beard.

This preference for traditional dress or military uniform changes, too, on the machine-tooled pieces: here, the majority of the male spirits are shown in a shirt with pockets and sometimes a visible collar. They are clean-shaven and wear a *tarbush* on their heads.

Setting and accessories

It is not just the images of the spirits alone that constitute a visual reflection of collective identity, but their setting is relevant to that identity too. Male and female spirits, in pairs or on their own, are placed amidst undulating hills or, in the case of mermaids, in bodies of water. Where such a setting is depicted, it consistently is a rural, outdoor setting, with only one piece showing a decidedly urban context (see 5.2). Stars twinkle over their heads, and in their hands, they hold plants or objects that apparently carry meaning. That meaning is not always straightforward, and some objects cannot be identified at all. For example, a few spirits are shown wearing wide skirts, their arms outstretched, holding sticks or curved objects that might be scrolls, pieces of textiles, or something else entirely (see cat.no. 044 in the catalogue for an example).[501] Where spirits appear as pair, they are seen flanking a plant (75), a fish (10), or a pillar (13). A remarkable image is that of a female spirit holding a miniature spirit.[502] The structure of this composition is also found in Coptic visualisations of the Virgin Mary with her child. Christian saints and even Christ himself are known to feature as *zār*-spirit, too, but whether that is the case here is impossible to say. On the machine-tooled pieces, the setting is either absent or limited to plants or an incense brazier.

---

501   Sample coll. 397, 1026 and 1068.
502   Sample coll. 703, private collection, no inventory number.

So, what world do these details represent? The following three case studies will explore that question – and where we meet the limits of these images in answering it.

5.2 THREE CASE STUDIES

The images reflect a form of self-presentation, and harbour direct and indirect references to historic realities as experienced by the women of *zār*. In this section, I present three case-studies that illustrate how we may understand these realities in *zār* jewellery: a case study with a clear direct reference, a case study with an indirect reference to historic events that may be placed in a particular timeframe, and finally an indirect reference to the world of women in general.

5.2.1 Direct reference: khedive Abbas Hilmi II

Thirteen pendants show the bust of a man in military uniform, with 'Abbas Hilmi' written above his shoulders. They all date from 1913-1916, and reflect a single historic event: the deposition of khedive Abbas Hilmi II. Abbas Hilmi ascended the throne of Egypt in 1892. Formally, he was viceroy (khedive) of Egypt, serving the Ottoman sultan, but in reality, Egypt had been firmly under British control for ten years.[503] Abbas' relation with the British was complicated: on the one hand, he harboured nationalist aspirations[504], while on the other he backed the extension of the British hold on the Suez Canal in 1910[505]. It was not just his relation with the British that was complicated: when visiting Constantinopel in 1914, he was shot by a pro-Ottoman Egyptian student. The wound took months to heal, and as a result, Abbas Hilmi was in Constantinopel when the First World War broke out.[506] Seizing the opportunity, British consul-general Lord Kitchener refused Abbas' return to Egypt on the grounds that his prolonged stay in Turkey made him suspect as pro-Ottoman. Egypt was declared an official protectorate on December 18, and the next day Abbas Hilmi was deposed. His uncle, Hussein Kamal, generally perceived as more malleable, was installed as Sultan of Egypt.[507]

The thirteen pieces displaying the figure of the khedive reflect these events. But only two images show the name of the khedive only: the others also contain several other features that I feel are important, but that I have so far not been able to find an explanation for (see Figure 5.3). On the right side, three images show Arabic numerals:

Figure 5.3. *Zār* pendant showing Khedive Abbas Hilmi II (sample coll. 348). On the right side an additional 7 and 5 may be seen, on the left side a twisted and an undulating line. Not to scale. Collection and photo S. van Roode.

---

503 Thornhill 2004.
504 Ellis 2018 offers insight in how the khedive attempted to establish independent political power in the Western Desert through his khedivial landholdings and the development of a railway.
505 Thornhill 2004.
506 McKale 1997, p. 21.
507 McKale 1997, p. 24.

a 7 and a 5 written above the name. Three other images show only the 5. On the left side, five images carry an engraving in the form of a twisted and an undulating line.

After 1916, there are no other pieces showing Abbas Hilmi in the sample collection: this reality seems to have disappeared from the collective memory rather fast. Or does it...? Apart from the pieces where the name of the khedive is written next to his image, Abbas Hilmi may be hiding in other images, too. A type of bracelet worn in the Western oases shows the image of an officer, with two flags crossed behind him. This image is also present in the *zār* power objects. The bracelet is called an 'Abbas bracelet' – could the officer with flags be another personification of the khedive?[508] In that case, the khedive dwelt longer in the collective memory: of the three dated images of an officer with flags, one is from 1913-1916, one is from 1923-1924 (shown in the catalogue, cat. no. 036), and one is as late as 1925-1926. The direct reference to Abbas Hilmi is also the only direct reference to historic realities in *zār* in the sample collection, an observation I will go into in chapter 6.

5.2.2 Indirect reference: the *maḥmal* festivities in Cairo

An indirect reference to historic events that affected the community is in two representations which may be considered together: that of the spirit dressed in Arab costume, and the camel with a canopy on its back. Both are connected to the *hajj*, the pilgrimage to Mecca. Le Brun already mentions *hajj*-spirits in 1902[509], and Arab costume in connection with the pilgrimage is attested in *zār* songs: the song for an Arab spirit mentions the placing of the headband, the girding of a sword and the pilgrimage.[510] Spirits dressed in Arab costume are seen consistently throughout time until the 1950s: see for example cat. nos. 040, 047 and 081 in the catalogue. With the *hajj* being an annual event, this is to be expected. For the camel with a canopy on its back, the spread is not that consistent: what does this image represent?

The camel occurs 30 times in the sample collection, of which 28 show it with a canopy on its back, as depicted in Figure 5.4. Other examples are cat. nos. 074 and 075 in the catalogue. El-Adly explains a *zār* pendant featuring a camel with canopy as powerful spirit in its own right: he argues the camel is known as a king of the jinn, and it is the camel that knows the secret name of God.[511] More likely, the camel in combination with the litter on its back is related to the *maḥmal* or festive canopy that travelled at the head of the pilgrim caravan to

Figure 5.4. *Zār* pendant showing a camel with a canopy on its back. Not to scale. Collection and photo S. van Roode.

---

508 Fahmy 2007, p. 46.
509 Le Brun 1902, p. 290.
510 Littman 1950, p. 29; also Schienerl 1984, p. 18 for the clothing to be worn by a patient possessed by Sultan al Arabi.
511 El-Adly 1984, p. 665, presents this as an explanation for a *zār* pendant featuring a camel with canopy.

Figure 5.5. *Maḥmal* arriving in Cairo in 1899. Photo: Library of Congress LC-DIG-stereo-1s21027.

Mecca, a tradition that dated back to the reign of the 13th century Mamluk sultan Baybars.[512] This canopy on a camel featured on three separate occasions. First, during the tenth month of the Islamic year, the *maḥmal* headed the procession through Cairo in which the coverings for the Kaaba were carried around on public display. These coverings were traditionally produced in Cairo and shown to the public in a festive procession before being transported to Mecca. The second and third occasions were the departure procession and the returning procession marking the start and the end of the pilgrimage to Mecca, in the twelfth month of the year. Relevant to our story is that each of these processions was accompanied by large festivities in the city.[513] For many inhabitants, the *maḥmal* was the closest they could get to Mecca, and both camel and canopy served almost as a contact relic.[514]

These public festivities were cancelled in 1927 as a result of a political incident with Saudi-Arabia the year before.[515] It would take ten years for the streets of Cairo to be filled with bustling festivities around the *maḥmal* procession once again: the new king, Farouk, signed a treaty with Saudi-Arabia and in 1937, the coverings for the Kaaba were on their way again. But although the *hajj* caravan might be headed once again by the *maḥmal*, the camel with litter itself proceeded no further than Jeddah and was not allowed to enter the holy places. From 1938 onwards, the *maḥmal* was still heading the processions through the streets of Cairo during the display of the coverings and the beginning and end of the pilgrimage, but it never again actually left Cairo for

---

512 The first description of the *maḥmal* dates from 1266. Jomiers 1953, p. 10.
513 The festive nature of these events is best worded by Mayeur-Jaouen 2005, who calls them 'carnavalesque'.
514 Schienerl 1984, p. 16; Mols 2013, p. 160.
515 The incident and its consequences are presented in detail in Jomier 1953, p. 67 ff.

Saudi-Arabia. While *maḥmal* festivities were still celebrated in Cairo itself [516], their relevance gradually dwindled: the procession was shortened, and the procession route was altered because the overhead lines of the newly introduced electric trams were too low for the *maḥmal* to pass. In 1952, it was paraded around on only 25 meters, and that was the last time: following an official fatwa, in 1953 the ministry of Interior Affairs decided to remove the *maḥmal* from the pilgrimage altogether.

I believe that what these *zār* images show us is not so much the importance of the *hajj* itself, but of the public festivities surrounding the *maḥmal*. The first hallmarked image dates to 1922-1923. One is from 1924-1925, and one from 1925-1926. Their number increases around 1927, when four pieces were hallmarked: the first year there were no public festivities surrounding the procession.[517] From both 1929-1930 and 1931-1932 one image has survived, and after that the *maḥmal* is not featured among the *zār* spirits. Then, in 1938, this image shows up again three times, right when the festivities resumed. It continues to appear off and on during the 1940s, but after 1950, the camel with *maḥmal* is not seen again.[518]

The most compelling of these images is sample coll. 0180[519] shown in Figure 5.6. It shows a camel with *maḥmal* in great detail, flanked by two mosques. Rather than interpreting these mosques as an added visual reference to the religious context of the

Figure 5.6. *Zār* pendant showing the camel with canopy and two buildings (sample coll. 180, collection Landesmuseum Oldenburg, inv. no. Sch 1099), against a modern photo of the mosques of Sultan Hasan and al-Rifa'i, seen from the Citadel. Background photo licensed via Canva, photo pendant and collage by S. van Roode.

---

516 Except in 1947 due to an outbreak of cholera. Jomier 1953, p. 69.
517 The undated pieces add another five to the decade 1920-1930 based on their iconographical details and execution.
518 Two pendants (cat. no's 1019 and 1088) with a camel and *maḥmal* are hallmarked in 1979-1980, but their style and pose are identical to pendants from the 1940's. Cat. no 1017, hallmarked during the 1940s, is identical. I suspect these to have been hallmarked upon their sale after a lifetime of use, rather than their initial purchase.
519 Collection Landesmuseum Oldenburg, inventory number Sch 1099.

maḥmal, as Schienerl suggested[520], I propose the image shows an actual world, closer to home: Salah ed-Din square[521] in Cairo, historically the departure and return point of the *maḥmal*. I suggest the mosques depicted may be those of Sultan Hasan and al-Rifa'i, placing the pendant after 1912, when the latter was finished.

5.2.3 Indirect reference: women and their world

The images on *zār* jewellery also offer potential for further research into their value as a historic source in references that are not immediately pinpointed in time. An example of such a reference are the pillars, jugs and fish that occur on the images. For these, I suggest they may be placed in the context of fertility issues, as described in chapter 2: I would like to recall how fertility problems are often ascribed to possession, and how attending a *zār* may lift these.

The pillars, interpreted as 'obelisks', I already mentioned in chapter 5.1. If these are not obelisks, then what are they? Of course, a first association would be with faith: it might be a rendering of a minaret. But looking at the general setting of the *zār* images with their outdoor, rural context, they might also represent another feature that can be found in abundance in such context: a pigeon tower. Notably in Upper Egypt, pigeon towers feature as a metaphor for fertility.[522] The design of these mudbrick dovecotes presents a visual similarity to the zigzag lines and horizontal lines shown on the *zār* pillars. As *zār* is often practised in the context of fertility, an explanation of the pillar in this context would make sense.

That goes for the jug that eleven female spirits carry on their heads, too: jugs have a strong connotation of fertility as well and are used in informal ritual practices to combat infertility.[523] That fertility may also be hinted at in the images of spirit pairs flanking a fish. Of course, this may be a visual indicator of their identity as water spirits. However, fish also represent fertility due to their many eggs and feature in informal rituals aimed at battling male impotency.[524]

I do not propose the imageries of the pillar, the jug and the fish are to be interpreted this way exclusively, but I do suggest they would have been recognised in the context of fertility by the participants: a theme that deeply permeates everyday life. Their presence in the *zār* images reflects this importance.

A second example is the presence of military spirits. These are the first spirits to appear on *zār* jewellery besides water spirits, and given the omnipresence of the military in everyday life, its presence in *zār* is hardly surprising. But which military presence is it that we see?

The *zār* spirits are not simply lower-ranking soldiers or conscripts, of which there must have been many, too, but higher officers: they appear in dress uniform with

---

520 Schienerl 1983, p. 17.
521 Also known as Rumailah square, Citadel square or Muhammad Ali-square.
522 Wickett 2010, p. 82.
523 El-Aswad 2002, p. 111 mentions a *qullah* or jug as symbolizing femaleness because of its wide opening and absence of a spout in the context of the seventh day celebration after a birth; Haverhals-Werkman 1996 describes the use of jugs in informal fertility rituals.
524 Hansen 2006, p. 154, presents several examples of informal ritual involving fish to cure male impotency. Adly 1984, p. 664, also draws attention to the fact that while fish may be 'symbols of sea-demons, but it must not be forgotten that the fish is also the symbol of the phallus and of fertility'.

epaulettes, lanyards, and insignia. This distinction is relevant because, unlike regular soldiers, officers spoke Turkish: they are Ottoman.[525] That identity is still present in one of the most popular spirits, Yawri Bey, who, judging by his name, is unmistakably an Ottoman officer.[526] The explanation most offered for his name is that Yawri is a rendering of the Ottoman rank *yaver*, equivalent to *aide-de-camp*.[527] By proxy, every military spirit on *zār* jewellery is in general thought of as an Ottoman officer. But are all of them Ottoman?

After all, most of these images were created after 1914, when army and police became British-run instead of Ottoman, and British armed forces would remain in Egypt until the 1952 Revolution. I have looked at the uniforms depicted to see if there were any relevant differences. The majority wear a *tarbush*, which was widely worn by both Ottoman and British armed forces in Egypt. Their epaulettes are mainly braided, and in a few cases, epaulettes with tassels hanging from the shoulder[528] are depicted. These, too, were worn by both armies. A difference between the two appears in the plumes that some of the spirits wear on their headdress (see cat. nos. 049 and 050 in the catalogue): a headdress with the plume on top of the head was not worn in the Ottoman army, but it was in the British.[529]

Except for this difference, we cannot definitively discern between British and Ottoman uniform in the images, and the main military spirit to possess women until today continues to be Ottoman Yawri Bey. Here again, looking for exact realities and categories is not feasible: the *zār* objects present 'stock images' of a military presence. Rather, their presence in *zār* may have started out as a collective memory of what the military, regardless of their affiliation, *did* that directly affected the lives of the community: take their husbands and sons, and control their everyday life.

From the moment Muhammad Ali began his military reforms, he met with resistance among the Egyptian population.[530] To counter this, the state began to exercise much greater control over everyday life.[531] Forced conscription continued when Egypt was declared a British protectorate, even though it took a slightly different form. Egyptian peasants were offered a way out of mandatory military service in the British Army in 1917, by joining the Egyptian Labour Corps or other auxiliary services.[532] Between March 1917 and June 1918, over 300,000 men joined and were deployed to Palestine,

---

525 Fahmy 2003, p. 245 notes that in the time of Muhammad Ali regular soldiers, conscripted from the Egyptian population, spoke Arabic, while officers spoke Turkish.
526 Yawri Bey has even found its way 'back' into the heart of the Ottoman world via the slave trade through Egypt: he appears as zar-spirit in Istanbul and Izmir under the name Yavroube. Toledano 2007, p. 224-225.
527 Already suggested by Kahle 1912, p. 26.
528 An example of Turkish epaulettes worn in 1917 in the Imperial War Museum is IWM sample coll. INS 7445.
529 Flaherty 2012 does not show a feathered headdress for the Ottoman military in Egypt, nor does his website www.ottoman-uniforms.com, accessed on August 24, 2020. Feathered Ottoman headgear does exist, but the feather is placed on the forehead instead of on top of the headdress. The British Household Cavalry wears a helmet with a plume on top.
530 Fahmy 2003, p. 78.
531 Idem.
532 https://khaledfahmy.org/en/2019/11/11/the-great-theft-of-history-the-egyptian-army-in-the-first-world-war/ accessed on January 21, 2023.

current-day Iraq, Greece and France.[533] Many did not return. Those that did found that in their absence their land had been taken and the circumstances of their families had deteriorated. The last months of 1918 saw increasing unrest and sabotage across the country, and when in March 1919 the very popular Wafd-leader Saad Zaghlul was arrested and exiled by the British, the country erupted in what would become known as the 1919 Revolution.

5.2.4 The limits of *zār* images

But why do we not see anything of Saad Zaghlul's arrest in *zār*, where the exile of khedive Abbas Hilmi II only five years prior is well attested? Or, later, anything pointing to the 1952 revolution? In fact, only two pieces *may* present a reference to the 1919 revolution.

Sample coll. 125[534] might be refashioned in the context of the 1919 revolution. The pendant bears a hallmark placing it in 1913-1916, and the underlying decoration on pendant shows a male figure wearing a fez. Over this a crescent and star have been incised, the deep contours of which have been filled in with zigzag lines, obscuring the earlier decoration. The star and crescent served as a nationalist symbol in this timeframe and their presence here may be seen in this context, although it is not clear whether this pendant has not rather been worn outside a *zār* context. Sample coll. 847[535] has been recut into a rough crescent and star-shaped pendant. These two altered pendants are the only possible references to the 1919 revolution.

Here, we reach the limits of these images as historic source. Before going into the reasons behind this limitation, there is one other avenue left to explore: observing the collection as a whole in its temporal context.

5.3 THE SAMPLE COLLECTION AS HISTORIC SOURCE

What does the sample collection reveal about *zār* jewellery? Studying collected jewellery items in large numbers allows us to approach the role the power objects played in the Egyptian *zār* over time. I focus on the power objects in this section, as these are the only objects that can both with certainty be ascribed to *zār* as well as reasonably dated based on their hallmarks.

I will approach the sample collection statistically by looking at its general distribution over time, and observing variations of techniques and iconography. In order to keep the overview as clear as possible, I have aggregated the dates of the pieces, based on their hallmarks, into decades. I will present the observations first, and will draw conclusions from these in the following chapter of this thesis.

5.3.1 Distribution over time

First, I have analysed the total number of dated pieces with spirit images in the sample collection and their occurrence over time. Their temporal distribution is shown in Figure 5.7.

---

533   Idem. A film of 15 minutes, now in the Imperial War Museum, shows the arrival of Egyptian men from the provinces, their outfitting and finally their arrival and work in France: https://www.iwm.org.uk/collections/item/object/1060022562, accessed on January 21, 2023.
534   Collection Landesmuseum Oldenburg, no inventory number.
535   Collection Welt Museum Vienna, inventory no. 153-893.

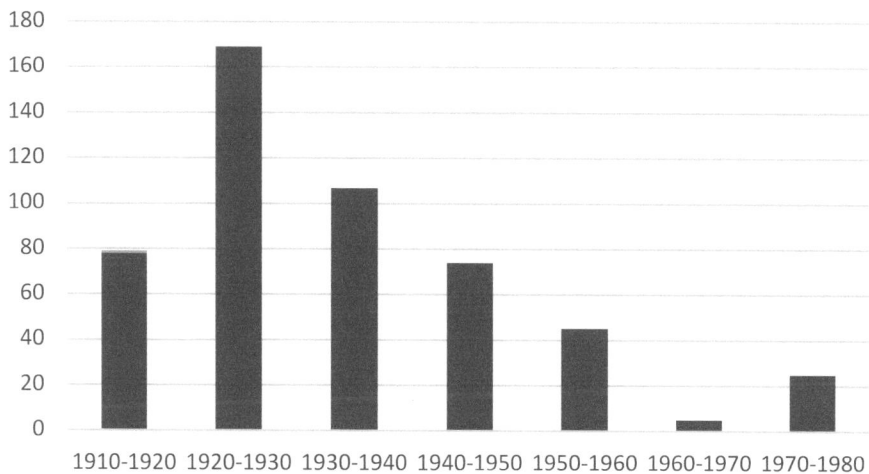

Figure 5.7. Amount of pieces with spirit images per decade.

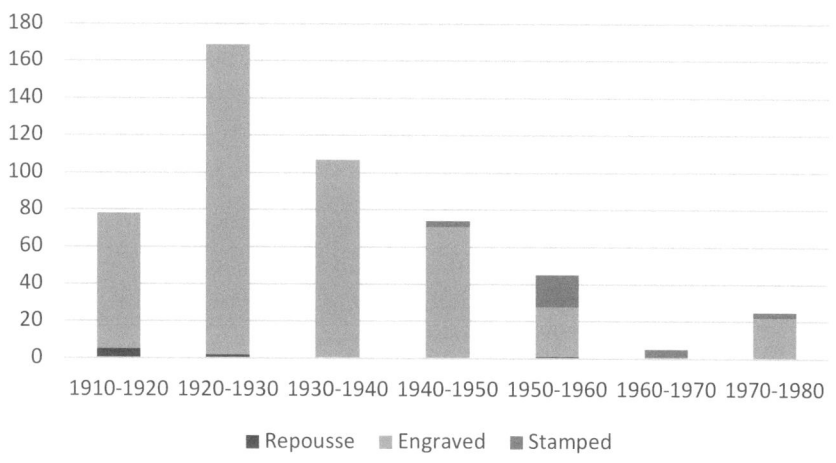

Figure 5.8. Techniques used in pieces with spirit images per decade.

The dated pieces show a clear peak in the 1920s. Within that decade, 74 are from the first half, and 95 in the second half. From the 1930s onwards, their number decreases steadily until they are almost gone in the 1960s, to reappear in the 1970s. Of the pieces that can only be ascribed to before or after 1946, based on the presence of either a cat or a lotus in the hallmark, 26 date from before 1946 and thirteen from after 1946. Another 120 pieces do not bear a hallmark: I return to these at the end of this chapter. This shows the use of powerful objects was at its highest in the 1920s, and steadily declined from there.

5.3.2 Techniques

The pieces with spirit images have been created in various techniques: they have been engraved, stamped and executed in repoussé. The engraved pieces are creations of individual craftsmen, while the stamped and repoussé pieces have been created using a mould.

The engraved pieces form the majority in absolute numbers. This may be the effect of collecting: for collectors, the engraved pieces are more attractive. They are larger, heavier, and more varied in their imagery, and so in this respect our view may be coloured.

Stamped pieces make their appearance in the 1940s, and this technique gains ground in the 1950s. One would expect to see the number of stamped pieces increase as the engraved pendants diminish, but that does not seem to be the case: engraved pendants continue to be made during the 1970s and form the majority of that decade in the sample collection. I attribute that discrepancy to two factors: a lack of securely datable pieces, and the collecting preferences mentioned above. Of the 56 stamped pieces, ten are only datable to the period after 1946 in general and 22 bear no hallmark at all. That means that the majority (32 pieces) is of an uncertain date. For the presence of the engraved pieces, another explanation may be possible, and I will go into that in chapter 6.

The repoussé pendants are all mermaid pendants (n = 10), and seem to have been made in the early 20th century only. One has been hallmarked between 1959 – 1962.[536] Given that this pendant is stylistically and technically identical to the earlier pendants, the hallmark may also have been added when the pendant was eventually sold, or alternatively, an old mould may have been used to create a new pendant. This analysis shows a change of technique from hand-engraved to machine-tooled taking place in the 1950s.

5.3.3 Execution

The pieces with spirit images show differences in detailing and execution. I have set up 5 main categories, as listed in Table 5.1. Although these are arbitrary, I have attempted to establish visible parameters.

Category	Spirits	Setting	Execution
Fine	Elaborate detail on hair, dress, hands, attributes. Gender clearly visible.	Elaborate detail on setting such as hills, water, plants in engraved pendants; considerably less on stamped.	Flowing, careful lines. Large pendants when engraved; small when stamped.
Regular	Clear detail on hair, dress, hands, attributes. Gender clearly visible.	Clear detail on setting such as hills, water, plants.	Angular lines. Medium-sized pendants.
Regular, no setting	Less detail on hair, dress, hands, attributes. Gender clearly visible.	No setting.	Angular lines. Medium to smaller-sized pendants.
Mediocre	Little detail on hair, dress, hands, attributes. Gender not always visible.	No setting.	Angular lines, crudely engraved. Small pendants.
Crude	No detail: hair indistinguishable from headdress, hands and eyes, not separately visible, no/unclear attributes. Gender mostly indistinguishable.	No setting.	Sketchy and crudely engraved lines. Small pendants.

Table 5.1. Categories of execution in the objects with spirit images.

---

536 Sample coll. 356, collection of the author, no inventory number. See cat. no. 002 in the catalogue in this book.

Figure 5.9. Level of execution over time.

I have first looked at the spirits themselves: the level of detailing in their dress and adornment, and the gender depicted. Next, I have observed their setting: the visibility and recognisability of hills, water bodies, stars etc. Finally, I have noted their technical execution. These categories plotted over time present a development in the engraved pendants from careful execution to sketchy outlines as time progresses, as Figure 5.9 shows.

From the 1940s onwards, we see an increasing number of images in which the setting is no longer included, and only the spirits themselves are shown. These pieces are also smaller than the pendants with a regular execution. Notably for images made during the 1960s-1980s, it can be difficult to distinguish what an image is supposed to represent if one is unaware of the stylistic evolution that preceded it.[537] During the 1950s, the stamped pieces show a great level of detail, while small engraved pendants appear with an increasingly crude execution. This development coincides with the change in technique as presented in the previous section.

5.3.4 Variety in images

Spirits can appear as hybrid water spirits, as humanoid spirits both in pairs and single, and finally as camels. Their distribution over time and the variety within these categories, as shown in Figure 5.10, is also revealing.

Individual female spirits are depicted the least: male spirits depicted individually occur the most, followed by humans in pairs. In the first decades of the 20th century, male individual spirits and water spirits are shown most often. Within these categories, variety decreases over time. The variety in water spirits, shown in Figure 5.11, illustrates this point further.

---

[537] These difficulties in interpretation are for example visible in Mayer 2021, but also in descriptions by vendors.

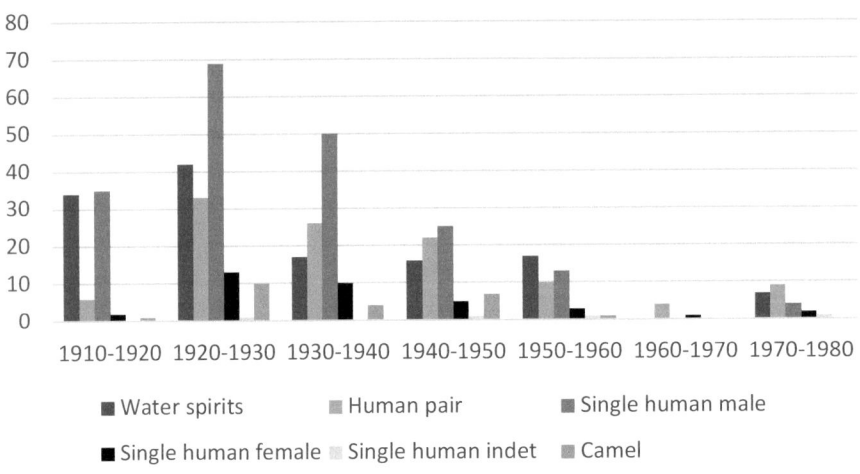

Figure 5.10. Variety in spirits over time.

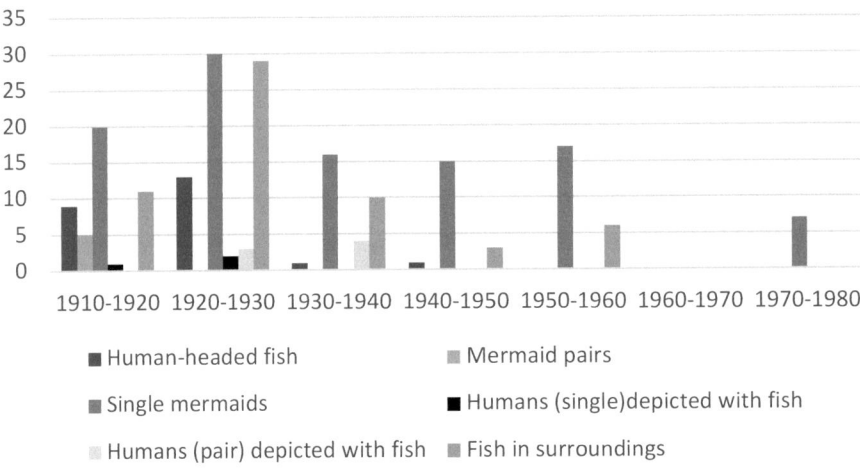

Figure 5.11. Variety in water spirits over time.

In the early 20th century, human-headed fish seem to be most popular. They appear in pairs, except for two pieces showing a human paired with a human-headed fish.[538] The single piece from the 1940s in figure 5.10 may have been hallmarked later: stylistically, it is closer to the first two decades of the 20th century. Apart from human-headed fish, mermaids with the upper body of a human and the tail of a fish also occur in pairs, but only in the first decades of the 20th century. After that, only single mermaids continue to feature until the 1980s. Actual fish are also present in the images: pairs of humans may flank a fish, and single humans stand next to it. A final category is smaller fish depicted around the spirits, much like the other elements of their setting. As we have

---

[538] Sample coll. 0039 (1923-1924, collection Landesmuseum Oldenburg, no inventory number) and 0266 (1928-1929, private collection, no inventory number).

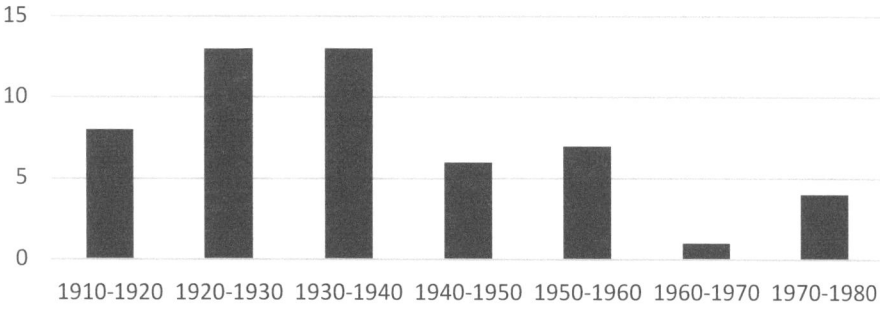

Figure 5.12. Distribution of wear traces over time.

seen in the previous section, their significance may be dual and allude to fertility issues as well. After the 1940s, only single mermaids and small fish remain; the variety in water spirits has diminished from six different ways of depicting them, to two.

5.3.5 Wear pattern

70 pieces with spirit images show visible traces of wear (see Figure 5.12). Due to consistent contact with clothes or the body, the engraved lines have softened. This is visible in only a little over 10% of the pieces with spirit images in the sample collection: 90% of those shows no signs of wear. This sheds light on the intensity with which these pieces were worn. Written accounts on *zār* propound that jewellery should be worn every day.[539] Their lack of wear, however, is inconsistent with a daily presence. The pieces that do show signs of wear are spread evenly over time, reflecting the general spread over time of jewellery with spirit images, and do not seem to indicate a change in wear preferences in a given timeframe. A possible explanation for this lack of wear could be that the majority of the pieces with spirit images may have been actually worn only on the occasion of a *zār* (including the weekly *zār* that many devotees attended).

5.3.6 Undated pieces

The sample collection of power objects also holds 120 pieces that bear no hallmark. Based on the elements presented above, notably the level of execution and the iconography, I have assigned 92 pieces to a decade. This results in the spread of total pieces over time as shown in Figure 5.13.

The distribution over time is more or less the same, except for the 1950s. The pendants I placed in this decade are stamped: many of these are undated in general and as their method of production creates identical pieces, they could easily also be from the 1960s or 1970s.

The remaining 28 pieces that I could not date all show an iconography very different from the majority of the pieces with spirit images. Five of these share a similar style, with their imagery schematic and executed in wavy lines. There is no zigzag border around the image, and only three of them carry text on their reverse side. In their iconography, they share similarities with the spirits in military uniform:

---

[539] See chapter 3; Bachinger & Schienerl 1984, p. 11.

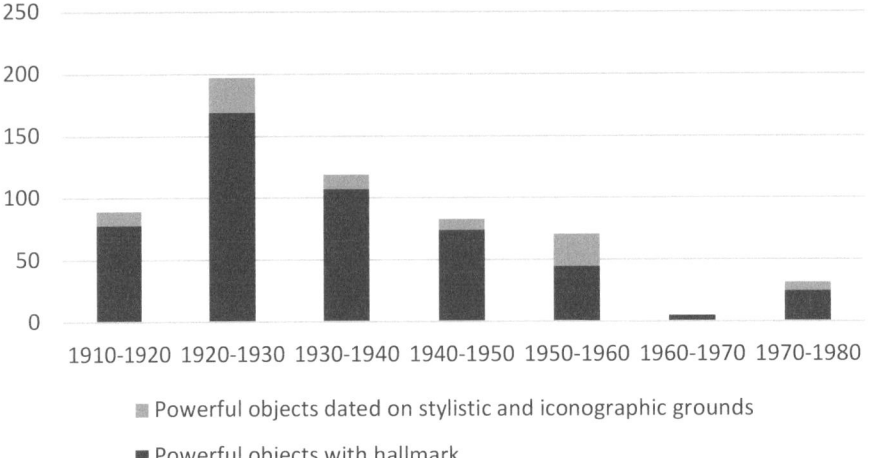

Figure 5.13. Undated pieces, ascribed to a decade.

they are depicted as a bust, with plants and/or birds above their shoulders. Based on these similarities, I believe these do belong to *zār*, but may have been locally made. Other pendants are not as similar[540], and I have not been able to establish whether they are *zār* pendants or other forms of amulets that found their way into the sample collection. A few examples are shown in cat nos. 090-094 in the catalogue.

In this chapter, I have attempted to illustrate how the images on *zār* jewellery and the way this jewellery developed over time may function as a historic source. What can this source tell us about its people?

---

540   An example is shown in Mörike 2021, Tafel VII, abb. 10.

6

THE WORLD OF *ZĀR* JEWELLERY

6.1 THE PEOPLE OF *ZĀR*

6.1.1 The lower classes

Whose world is reflected in the spirit images? In the beginning of the 20th century, Paul Kahle felt the need to state clearly that *zār* was not just the prerogative of women in the elite, but that it was <u>also</u> widespread among the middle and notably the lower classes.[541] Half a century later, Kriss and Kriss-Heinrich explicitly noted that the belief in the healing properties of the *zār* was in no way limited to the simple folk people, but that members of the upper strata of society were equally convinced of the benefits of the *zār*, especially in Cairo.[542] The matter of who practised *zār* has been addressed by many scholars: it is my understanding that *zār* was practised widely, and in different social strata, but I suggest the jewellery with spirit images initially reflects the world of the illiterate lower class. With the lower class estimated to be 80% of the population until 1952[543], this would make *zār* jewellery an emic historic source for an underrepresented part of the Egyptian population.

I base that idea on the collective representation, the bandwidth in which a personal front makes sense to the people who are looking at it. The outlines of a collective identity as they emerge are that of a community with a penchant for the traditional and with strong ties to the rural environment of Egypt. The invariably outdoor setting of hills, plants, water and the occasional pigeon tower suggests the community that used this jewellery with spirit images in *zār* was at home in a rural environment, rather than in the predominantly urban context in which we encounter *zār* today. This suggestion is not that far-fetched when we take into account how around the middle of the 20th century, about 70% of the people lived off agriculture.[544] The choice of material, silver, fits in that community, too: as we have seen in the description of Sidqi from 1911, affluent people would use gold jewellery.[545]

Another element that points to a lower-class community is the consistent absence of veiling among *zār* spirits. During the first decades of the 20th century, the gradual

---

541 Kahle 1912, p. 3.
542 Kriss & Kriss-Heinrich 1962, p. 142.
543 Mellor 2015, p. 63.
544 Gordon 2010, p. 379.
545 Littmann 1950, p. 5.

unveiling of women formed part of an emancipation process that had social, political, and religious aspects.[546] However, this debate was conducted mainly among middle- and upper-class women: lower-class women already went unveiled.[547]

The collective representation further indicates its people enjoyed public religious festivities, as is visible in their concern for the *maḥmal*-festivities. Processions such as these, either in local festivals or the *maḥmal*-procession as national symbol of the *hajj*, served as affirmation of collective values and instilled pride in the community.[548] But they also served another purpose, as De Jong brings up: festivities such as these, including the weekly visiting days for local saints, catered to the need of the lower classes through the presence of peddlers of a variety of wares as well as, depending on the occasion, free food.[549] This close relation between the *hajj*-festivities and local saints' days is also apparent in a *zār* song noted by Nabhan, where the lines on pilgrimage are interspersed with references to popular Cairene saint Fatima an-Nabawiyya, who is venerated in at least five different shrines.[550]

The people to whom this collective representation made sense, were also concerned for their capacity to start a family. This is not only apparent from the popularity of *zār* itself, but also reflected in references to fertility such as the fish, jugs and pigeon towers. The lack of traces consistent with daily wear observed in the power objects fits in with that concern: as we have seen, bringing images of spirits along might inflict *kabsa* and thus prevent a woman from getting pregnant. But having children is not a concern of the lower classes only: De Jong mentions how the shrine of Abu Su'ud, who is considered a powerful saint to consult when a pregnancy is desired,[551] is visited by women of all classes[552] – and it is here that many *zārs* are held.[553] What about those other classes practicing *zār*?

6.1.2 The 'others'
With *zār* practised across social strata in Egypt, and the spirit images reflecting the world of the lower classes, how would these be received by the middle and upper classes? A quick look at the middle and upper classes shows a different personal front being put forward than what we encounter on the jewellery with engraved images.

Magazines and newspaper advertisements actively targeted upper- and middle class-women through advertising, creating an image of a fashion-forward, modern Egyptian woman that embraced her national values, all in a bid to secure her clientele at one of the modern department stores – a relatively new development in Egypt in the early 20th century.[554] Personal photos of women also show a preference for European dress. In the 1920s, women had themselves photographed in studios, wearing the latest fashion such as flapper dresses, but evidence suggests more than once they

---

546 See for example Baron 1989.
547 Baron 1989, p. 372; Zuhur 1992, p. 40-42.
548 Mayeur-Jaouen 2005, p. 224-228.
549 De Jong 1976, p. 37.
550 Nabhan 1994, p. 203-287 and 273.
551 De Jong 1976, p. 32.
552 De Jong 1976, p. 42.
553 As mentioned by Kahle 1912, De Jong 1976, and Drieskens 2008.
554 Russell 2001.

brought this outfit along for the purpose of the photo, and possibly even shared a single outfit among a group of friends and relatives: in everyday life, they would be wearing traditional dress.[555] Possibly, at least the lower middle class would still recognise themselves in the collective representation. For the upper middle class and upper classes, the collective representation would not be something they recognise themselves in. However, that might exactly be the point.

Zār deals with 'otherness': not just in the state of being possessed by another entity, but also in the form that entity takes. As Kramer put it, that form, 'whether bygone or distant, is absent and inaccessible.'[556] For both the lower and middle classes, that 'otherness' manifests in the social position of the spirits: they are doctors, pashas, judges, officers or foreigners, but never simply manifestations from their own world, such as farmers. Could 'otherness' come in a different form altogether for the upper classes: spirits that look like they come from the distant and inaccessible world of the lower classes?

On the machine-tooled pieces that appear from the 1950s onwards, the collective representation changes. Here, the emphasis does seem to be on the middle class: the spirits wear mostly Western dress. This was the up-and-coming stratum of society after the coup by the Free Officers[557] – but simultaneously, the collective representation shows male spirits wearing a *tarbush*, where in reality this custom was abolished. While the human world underwent significant changes throughout the 20th century, the spirit images do not follow suit: I will explore their development in the next section.

6.1.3 Changes in the visualisation of the people of *zār*

Over the course of 80 years, four main developments are visible in the jewellery with spirit images: the variety in the personal front decreases over time, the personal front ceases to conform to everyday reality, and the jewellery itself becomes much smaller and lighter before disappearing altogether. What is more, it ends up for sale, as raw material for silversmiths and as curiosity for cultural outsiders.

The changes with regard to the personal front are very visible in the spirits in military uniform. Although a 'standard' uniform forms the majority throughout time, up until the 1940s, two other varieties of uniform are present, paired with five different forms of headdress. From the 1950s onwards, however, a single form of officer is represented, wearing only a *tarbush*. And that presence of the *tarbush* forms a case in point.

In the early 20th century, wearing the *tarbush* by military spirits makes perfect sense, given their social position and the actual wearing of a *tarbush* by higher ranks in both the military and police in reality. The *tarbush* was worn by male persons of social standing: the elite and educated men, mostly from the urban middle class. However, in the images, male spirits dressed in *gallābīya* also wear a *tarbush*. In the human world, the lower class would not be wearing a *tarbush* with a *gallābīya*, but a lower woollen or felt cap around which a shawl was wound.[558] In some cases, the details of the image

---

555 Ryzova 2021.
556 Kramer 1987, p. 69.
557 Granzow 2008, p. 46.
558 Rugh 1986, p. 15.

are not sufficient to determine what headdress the spirit is wearing, but there are a number of male spirits pairing a *tarbush* with a *gallābīya*. That could of course be a sign of respect for the spirit itself, by depicting it as a person of standing.

A second possibility is the role of the *tarbush* as an expression of nationalism. Here, the personal front serves as communicator of sentiment. Wearing a *tarbush* was a sign of being Egyptian, as opposed to identifying with Western dignitaries: although Egypt had become nominally independent in 1922, British influence and power continued to permeate every level of government and industry.[559]

The role of the *tarbush* changed again after 1952. It became a reminder of the previous colonial era and the Egyptian royal family that was associated with it, and as a result, was banned from all layers of government.[560] But while wearing a *tarbush* was by this time well and truly a fixture of the past, the *zār* spirits continue to appear wearing one. The personal front of the spirits at this point no longer conforms to reality: it has become a fixed image.

That fixation turned even more literal when the production of these items changed from hand-engraved to machine-tooled, after a gradually diminishing variety in the personal front since the 1920s. The variety of spirits on prefabricated, much lighter pendants from the 1950s onwards is limited to a male/female pair of spirits, a mermaid, and a woman sitting in front of a brazier with incense.

The very process of machinal prefabrication is at odds with *zār*'s capacity to digest changing political and social circumstances. That development towards a 'fixed' set of spirits is not just present in jewellery, but also visible in *zār* in general.[561] Eyewitness accounts of recent years attest the presence of *zār* spirits such as Yawri Bey and Sitt Safina, although the Ottoman army is long gone from Egypt and the Nile has become more reliable since the construction of the Aswan High Dam. And where the exile of Abbas Hilmi II resulted in his *zār* presence, the murder of president Sadat in 1981, for example, does not appear to have caused significant traces in the material culture of the spirit world.

The shift in the images from reflecting the world of their wearers to becoming prefabricated and limited suggests a change in their context. Additionally, the availability of these items for reuse or sale to cultural outsiders indicates a shift that allowed these objects to once again become a commodity, and to move to a next stage in their social life, ultimately becoming the collected objects they are today. What drove this change?

6.2 LONG-TERM CHANGES IN *ZĀR*

The obvious suggestion would be that *zār* became less popular. This decline in popularity, however, despite claims to the contrary, is not supported by the many recent studies into *zār*. *Zār* continues to be practised today, and is still a much-needed safe space for women.[562] But the changes both in jewellery itself, as well as in the

---

559 Dunn 2011, p. 106.
560 Dunn 2011, p. 86, 91 and 106.
561 Also noted by Granzow 2008, p. 50, who writes the *zār* pantheon has not expanded since the 1950s: I would argue it even diminished.
562 Granzow 2008, p. 52 states that it is still practised, although its number of members dwindles. Hadidi 2016 describes a flourishing *zār* community.

context that accommodated their transition from a singularity into a commodity again, do suggest that *zār* as it is practised today is different from that of a century ago. Various factors combined may have contributed to these changes: political and economic developments, the increase of religious peer pressure, and particularly, in my opinion, the passing on of the craft and knowledge through generations of ritual specialists.

6.2.1 Political and economic changes

As mentioned earlier, *zār* deals with 'otherness'. *Zār* flourished in Egypt during the same timeframe as 'otherness' increased on a national level due to British colonial involvement. Such incongruity, occurring in contact zones with strongly asymmetrical power relations, is often processed through ritual expressions.[563]

As Egypt transitioned from a nation under foreign rule to an independent republic in the 1950s, a new search for 'own' values distinct from those of 'others' ensued. This period also marks the disappearance of spirit images associated with actual events, alongside changes in the production of *zār* jewellery items, before they stop being produced altogether. The end of colonial incongruity undoubtedly played a significant part in the changes in *zār* and its jewellery.

However, the sample collection shows a clear change preceding the 1950s: from the 1940s onwards, the objects with spirit images start to be significantly smaller. This, I suspect, is the consequence of economic developments.

An economic study by Yousef shows a sharp decrease in agricultural productivity and abruptly rising prices in the 1940s.[564] At the end of the 1940s, Egypt severed ties with the U.K. by leaving the Sterling Area[565], after the Egyptian pound had been pegged to the British pound since 1914. Additionally, from the 1950s onwards, the power objects become even smaller with the introduction of the machine-tooled pieces with spirit images, which were much lighter and thinner than the hand engraved pieces. This decade saw the large-scale nationalizing of foreign businesses, houses and land, which led to gradual economic decline.[566]

The question that arises is whether the regular-sized pieces of jewellery were simply becoming too expensive for the community, that could no longer afford larger, hand engraved pieces, prompting a shift towards smaller, more affordable options.

Viewed from this perspective, the emergence of older, hand-engraved *zār* jewellery in the market from the 1960s onwards makes perfect sense. After all, jewellery was a commodity, to be sold when needed. The economic decline reached a new low in the 1970s, prompting many Egyptian men to seek employment in the burgeoning Gulf states to support themselves and their families.[567] In 1977, the Egyptian government cut subsidies on essential items like bread and other basic foodstuffs as a condition for securing a much-needed loan from the IMF. This sparked large-scale rioting in the cities, compelling the IMF to extend the loan without this condition. It is during the

---

563   Chidester 2018, p. 122.
564   Yousef 2002, p. 564 and 568.
565   Yousef 2002, p. 576.
566   Mellor 2015, p. 65-67.
567   Granzow 2008, p. 47.

spiralling economy at the end of the 1970s, that the last hallmarks on jewellery with spirit images appear: apparently, they ceased to be made after this.

From an economical point of view selling jewellery is a rational decision for families facing economic hardships, but how did women come to feel comfortable to part with this jewellery in particular?

6.2.2 Religious peer pressure

The perceived decline in the popularity of *zār* is often attributed to religious factors, notably since the 1950s. But when we look at it, *zār* has <u>never</u> been well received by formal religious institutions, and as such has been under pressure from the moment it arrived in Egypt. The core of the objections is that *zār* is un-Islamic, whereas *zār* specialists and attendees argue that everything falls under the authority of God, and therefore *zār* in their point of view is regarded to be compliant with Islam.[568] The practice involves direct contact with jinn, instead of turning to God for help. From that point of view, *zār* belongs in the realm of magic, which is forbidden. Additionally, negotiating with spirits implies attributing power to them. This contradicts traditional orthodox Islam belief that attributes all power to God alone.[569] Although these objections are not particular to *zār*, seeing as how other folk beliefs involve jinn as well, the popularity of *zār* in combination with the high costs has caused it to attract more than general attention.

While *zār* has always been at odds with formal religion, this increased in the 1950s, when it was forbidden officially.[570] But it is only during the 1970s that we see the last of the items with spirit images being made. Apparently, not even an official ban could stop *zār* jewellery with spirit images from being produced, even though they became increasingly smaller. Why did they eventually disappear at the end of the 1970s?

I believe that not so much to be the result of changed official religious stances, because those have remained largely unchanged since *zār* first arrived in Egypt, but rather the outcome of a process much closer to home. For from the 1970s onwards, Islamic revival gained widespread ground. That was not just among men, who found employment in the Gulf states, but also among women.[571] Mahmood suggests that this form of piety is the result of the greater mobility women acquired after the colonial period: having access to education, they started out to teach each other religious lessons in an informal framework spread around the many mosques, notably in Cairo.[572] This is the first time, Mahmood writes, that 'such a large number of women mobilised to hold lessons in Islamic doctrine in mosques'.[573] One could say these religious informal networks replaced the previously existing networks of *zār* to a certain extent. Therefore, I suggest that in addition to the economic reasons given above, the changing attitudes

---

568 Hadidi 2016, p. 41 suggests that the objections may also be related to the fact that the *zār* is a woman-centered practice.
569 Sengers 2003, pp. 31-32; Rashed 2015, p. 20.
570 Pielow 1997, p. 369; Mörike 2021, p. 36. According to Okasha 1966, p. 1217 '*zār* is contradictory to religion and it is government policy to try to suppress its very occurrence'. The point of unislamic practices is reiterated by many authors, such as Drieskens 2006, p. 64, Natvig 2014, p. 308.
571 Mahmood 2006, p. 32.
572 Mahmood 2006, p. 34-35.
573 Mahmood 2006, p. 34.

among women themselves contributed to the decline of jewellery with spirit images: change on a grassroots level.

In particular, in my view these changing attitudes and increased religious activities would present a direct challenge on the level of peers when it comes to *zār*. As Drieskens emphasises, keeping up appearances in line with what is considered proper behaviour is imperative.[574] This means a form of plausible deniability must be present: if there is no way of formally knowing someone is deviating from proper behaviour, the deviation itself does not have to be addressed.[575] An example is the case of a woman who regularly partook in a *zār* but objected to the presence of an outside researcher, for fear she might become known as a *zār* devotee.[576] As her immediate family would have known she attended *zārs*, the objection was not so much with her own inner circle in mind, but her fears concerned her image with a larger audience.

I believe it is precisely this social peer pressure of a growing number of religiously involved women in the immediate social circles of any woman, that would affect the use of jewellery with spirit images: it was publicly being seen with *zār* jewellery, buying and owning it that, in my view, became increasingly problematic from a religious point of view – and that is even without the matter of affording such jewellery. Mörike suggests that this religious peer pressure is why ritual specialists nowadays are less keen on continuing the craft.[577] But while that certainly may be one reason, in my opinion, the jewellery offers a more complex picture here, too.

6.2.3 Syncretizing worlds: the pivotal role of the ritual specialist over time

The previous two factors, political and economic changes as well as religious peer pressure, can be correlated with changes in the jewellery in both the 1950s and the 1970s. The power objects become smaller in the 1940s and significantly change shape in the 1950s, as they become lighter and machine-tooled, and they cease to be made at the end of the 1970s.

But before that, their number had already been decreasing steadily since the 1920s. This points not so much to an abrupt change, but to a slow and gradual process: the dialectic processes that Hansen introduced for magical practices being passed down generations.[578] I believe the generational succession of ritual specialists in a changing context to be of importance as well.

During the first decades of *zār* in Egypt, so from the 1860s onwards, the ritual specialists were enslaved women that were brought in from Ethiopia via Sudan. They would have understood the world along the lines of their own knowledge structures, as Megerssa & Kassam provide insight in, before they were forcibly abducted from

---

574 Drieskens 2008.
575 Drieskens 2008 provides examples of how this keeping up appearances is achieved. My own experience with this in the 90s is that one could easily purchase alcoholic beverages with soft-drink sellers: these would be hidden from view under stacks of Coke-bottles. As they were not directly visible, there was nothing untoward to be observed.
576 Natvig 2014, p. 308. See Drieskens 2006, p. 66 and further 2008 for an illuminating introduction on the various levels of perception of the self and the family by a range of 'others'.
577 Mörike 2021, p. 36.
578 Hansen 2006, p. 112-113.

that world.⁵⁷⁹ Assuming that these were (young) adult women in the second half of the 19th century, the generation of ritual specialists active in the 1920s is likely to have been the second or third generation: a generation already born in Egypt. According to early accounts, the role of the specialist is hereditary, but in more recent publications one can also become a specialist by training.⁵⁸⁰ The generation of ritual specialists practicing *zār* today is the third or even fourth generation, who may pass on their knowledge vertically to their offspring, but also horizontally, to new specialists.

This means that the world view of the first generation of ritual specialists is no longer familiar to the generation of ritual specialists currently active: they have been raised in a different world. Three to four generations later, the knowledge inherited from their ancestors has syncretized with Islamic thought, much as candomblé has merged with Catholicism. The association of *zār* with women of colour from the south however may echo in the lingering predilection for southern-style jewellery. *Zār* leaders of colour were often of southern descent, and so it seems likely that jewellery worn by southern women became faster and more firmly associated with *zār* than other regional styles.

I believe this combination of factors, visible in the changing commodity situations of the jewellery, illustrates the gradual absorption of an African cult into a monotheistic framework under the influences of political, economic, and religious developments. *Zār* continues to function as an outlet on a personal level, a form of coping mechanism, but it finds itself more and more transformed into a tradition itself, subject to set rules and strict formulae. Its capacity as adaptive mnemonic device, reliving and passing on actual events, is disappearing.⁵⁸¹

6.3 THE ORIGIN OF THE EGYPTIAN POWER OBJECTS

And at the very end of this study into *zār* jewellery, I address the origin of the jewellery. Because one last remaining question is what prompted the form of these silver items with spirit images in the Egyptian *zār*: where do they come from?

The earliest objects with spirit images bear hallmarks of the period 1913-1916: as this was the start of official hallmarking in Egypt, still under the Ottoman system, some of these may actually be older. What this hallmarking does tell us is that by 1913, the use of silver objects with spirit images was already an established practice. Looking at these earliest power objects (n = 60 out of 681), half of these show mermaids⁵⁸² (n = 29). Apparently, in the early days of *zār* jewellery, water spirits were popular. But are these actual *zār* pieces? There are two observations that stand out.

First, their popularity is at odds with the limited references to water spirits in possession cases. *Zār* songs frequently mention Sitt Safīna as a female mermaid and Sultan al Bahr as a male water spirit, but actual possession is not mentioned as

---

579 Megerssa & Kassam 2019.
580 Nabhan 1994, p. 69-71 explains how ritual specialists that did not inherit the craft but were accepted through training do not hold the same esteem that hereditary specialists do; Hadidi 2016 shares how she was accepted into a *zār* community and from there became a specialist herself.
581 Sengers 2003, p. 106 notes that is no longer known today which situations the Egyptian *zār* spirits were associated with.
582 Mermaids: hybrid creature with the tail of a fish. I have included all hybrids in this count: both beings with the tail of a fish and a human upper body, and beings with only a human head on a fish body.

clearly.[583] In comparison, possession by an officer, the second largest group of spirits, is described far and wide.

Second, *zār* spirits are never encountered outside of *zār* – but water spirits do exist outside of *zār*. These two observations lead me to believe that perhaps their presence in *zār* is comparable to that of the *madīh* songs as I have introduced in chapter 2: they may not be among the possessing spirits, but they are included. Why could that be?

As early as 1916, Meyerhof brings up that water spirits are much feared as a source of disease.[584] He lists the mermaid Safīna along with the Qarina in the category of female 'demons', and notes that she is, much like the Qarina, responsible for harm brought upon children, especially in Cairo. Meyerhof adds that she occurs frequently on amulets. These, often made in silver, were readily available and were meant as an amulet to protect the wearer from Safīna.[585]

In his enumeration of jewellery of the *zār* leader from 1911, Sidqi mentions an amulet showing Sitt Safīna as a separate item, apart from the other jewellery items.[586] As we have seen in chapter 12, this must have been an amulet that differed in appearance from the 'regular' *zār* pendants because the depiction apparently was visible. What Sidqi, in my view, describes is a Safīna amulet as mentioned by Meyerhof, being worn during a *zār*. A pendant in the sample collection, hallmarked in 1933-1934, shows a mermaid with the text 'Oh God, protect the newborn' – apparently, amulets to protect children from river spirits continued to exist.[587] An even older amulet with water spirits is the piece collected in 1889 in Cairo, currently in Basel and introduced in chapter 3. It shows two water spirits with the body of a fish and the head of a human (Figure 6.1, right) This amulet was collected as head ornament. Whether it is, in fact, a head ornament is debatable: the image in Lane referred to in the museum registration shows indeed head ornaments, but none of the depicted items look like the Basel piece. I personally believe this to be a mix-up in the records and the object to be a regular amulet.[588] This amulet in Basel is similar in design, and identical in its depiction of two water spirits, to a piece in the sample collection (Figure 6.1, left). The text on that amulet is a garbled version of the Throne Verse.[589]

I propose that the form of *zār* power objects evolved from regular amulets to protect from river spirits. These formed a perfect carrier to adapt to feature other spirits. Using spirit imagery in amulets worn on the body may have come from Ethiopia as

---

583 Littmann 1950, p 66, relates how his spokesperson explained to him that a woman possessed by a *zār* would play with living fish in a bowl of water and dunk her head in the water when the song for Safīna is sung. Whether the person is possessed by Safīna however is not clear. Winkler 1936, p. 34 mentions Safīna among other *zār* spirits in a general description of *zār* songs. Al-Guindi 1978 mentions possession by the angels of the river. Water spirits do possess humans in other cultures, such as for example Mami Wata in Nigeria, but for Egypt this is not as clearly attested.
584 Meyerhof 1916, p. 317-18, see also p. 314.
585 Meyerhof 1916, p. 319.
586 Littmann 1950, p. 2.
587 Sample coll. 0161, translation by Yasmine el-Dorghamy.
588 The sample collection does contain a head ornament of a type already depicted in Lane in the reference for the Basel piece: a silver pendant in the shape of comb (*misht*). This piece carries an engraved fish on one side and a text on the other. This pendant is undated, and collected by Schienerl.
589 Sample coll. 1010. Translation by Yasmine el-Dorghamy, who informed me: 'This is very poorly etched and full of spelling mistakes, but it is meant to be the Verse of the Throne, chopped up and distributed all over the amulet in no particular logical sequence'.

Figure 6.1. Amulets to protect from water spirits: *zār* pendant in the sample collection (left, sample coll. 1010, photo S. van Roode) and the piece collected in 1889, currently in the Museum der Kulturen, Basel (photo Museum der Kulturen, Basel). Not to scale.

well. Like in Egypt, *zār* is not the only form of spirit possession in Ethiopia. Many forms of spirits exist, and in exorcising these, the ritual specialist will create a magic scroll. Lombard discusses these in detail.[590] For the construction of such a scroll the ritual specialist, usually a man, consults books as well as his personal knowledge of possessing spirits.[591] The scroll he prepares will have both powerful texts on them as well as images.[592] According to Natvig, twelve out of 29 scrolls acquired by Littmann in 1906 contained the word *zār* for a spirit or group of spirits and the illness they cause.[593] Magic scrolls can be used as preventive amulet, but when used to exorcise a spirit, the images on the scroll are aimed at terrifying the spirit with the realisation that it is being seen: the images present a mirror image of the spirit believed to be possessing the patient.[594]

The Ethiopian women who brought *zār* along with them to Egypt via the slave trade, came from a world where images of possessing spirits were part of rituals to deal with spirit possession. That world may well have translated into silver jewellery, starting with amulets with images that were used far and wide when *zār* found its way to Egypt: amulets against water spirits.

---

590 Lombard 2003.
591 Lombard 2003, p. 96-109 for the process of scroll-preparing.
592 Lombard 2003, p. 101.
593 Natvig 1987, p. 676-677, and Worrell 1915, pp. 85-127.
594 Lombard 2003, p. 104-107.

7

CONCLUSIONS

What is 'zār jewellery'? That is the question I started out with. After perusing hundreds of jewellery items in the sample collection and many more pages of literature, this exploration into jewellery of the zār has shown that it may be many things.

Jewellery and ritual

Starting with *zār* itself, jewellery can fulfil a number of roles within the ritual. The jewellery with spirit images functioned as power object, embodying the bond between possessed and spirit. These were worn by the possessed, as well as by the ritual specialist, and were created specifically for *zār*. The colourful beaded jewellery items were created for *zār* as well, and enabled a spirit to manifest itself during the trance state of the possessed. Apart from these two categories of purpose-made jewellery, regular jewellery may play a part in *zār* too. Coin jewellery may be employed as material contract of the agreement with a spirit, spirits may request any and all jewellery as a gift to be presented to them, and amulets help keep the wearer safe from the ill intentions of uninvited spirits. But *zār* jewellery can be many other things, when we venture outside its immediate ritual context.

Jewellery as historic source about people

Zār jewellery can be a historic source about people. Catching a glimpse of their world is possible through analysing their visualisation of themselves in those pieces with spirit images on the one hand, and by studying the material changes in this and other jewellery used in *zār* on the other. 'Reading' the images first and foremost requires us to be aware of the nature of the mnemonic capacities of *zār*. *Zār* does not operate as a form of chronological record-keeping, but it alludes to those aspects of the world of its wearers that mattered to them, and so does its imagery. This study into jewellery produces the vantage point of an underrepresented group: the illiterate lower classes. Their view on their world is most visible in the one direct reference they provide: the banishment of Khedive Abbas Hilmi II in 1914 reflects their discontent. While most historic accounts of the Egyptian struggle for independence do take the role of women into account, notably in the subsequent 1919 revolution and its aftermath, these accounts are based in sources about and by middle- and upper-class women. The *zār* jewellery items with spirit images add a hitherto unheard voice to the research into the role of women in Egypt's recent history. Besides this direct reference, the spirit images reflect a world with a permanent military presence that affected everyday life, a world in which its wearers relied heavily on their chances to marry and have children to secure their social position, a world in which religious festivities were celebrated and a world in which the river Nile was both beneficial and dangerous. The body of amulets present in the sample collection emphasises the deeply felt fear of remaining childless or losing children as a result of spirit interference, and shows how *zār* assimilated other elements of interactions with spirits in Egypt.

But the view on that world stagnates as time progresses: the spirit images cease to display variety, dwindle in numbers and become fixed in appearance, as if they are frozen in time. Eventually, jewellery with spirit images disappears altogether. Analysis of this trend shows how this diminishing is slow and constant, and started well before the political, economic and religious changes of the 1950s that are often highlighted as explanation for the perceived loss of popularity of *zār* itself. I argue the steady decline in the jewellery of the *zār* suggests that rather, these changes form the circumstances that fundamentally affected two other, interrelated processes that evolved over the course of generations: the syncretisation of an African cult with Islam, and the changing cultural background of the ritual specialist. Both of these are closely interwoven with *zār*'s origins as an African possession cult, and for this I turn to another role *zār* jewellery can have.

Jewellery as historic source about ritual

Zār jewellery can be a historic source about ritual. As such, it informs us about the ritual it formed part of. Exploring the history of *zār* and its roots in Ethiopia results in a different agency for the pieces with spirit images. Instead of 'amulets', designed to protect from a spirit, they form the <u>personal</u> tangible connection between human and spirit on the one hand, and as we have seen, a historic source for the <u>community</u> that individual belonged in on the other. Here again, it is observing developments in jewellery with spirit images over time which shares more about *zār* itself.

On the personal level, the jewellery with spirit images is a power object, as is widely used in African possession cults: an object that embodies the possessing spirit. Its imagery in the Egyptian *zār* power objects provides an additional outlook on that relation between possessed and spirit. While there is a clear power dynamic in the ritual itself, in which the spirit forces the human to provide it with what it wants, the jewellery with spirit images as well as their beaded counterparts visualise a form of reciprocity in this relationship that is not immediately evident from the ritual otherwise.

On the community level, the disappearance of specifically <u>this</u> type of jewellery is in my view indicative of the assimilation of an African possession cult in an Islamic context, an assimilation driven by both internal and external factors. The external factor are religious changes, notably from the 1970s onwards. During the 1970s, the networks of women that *zār* communities had previously provided, were partly replaced by networks of women studying religion together in mosques. Although *zār* itself did not grow any less popular, being seen by one's peers while buying recognizable *zār* jewellery was increasingly frowned upon. I believe the most ostentatious pieces of *zār* jewellery disappeared as a result of this religious peer pressure: those with spirit images. Other jewellery items could still be purchased, as they were not as clearly linked to *zār* as the pieces with spirit images. But the disappearance of these latter is not simply a result of religious peer pressure <u>only</u>: the imagery on these pieces had already been growing increasingly limited for decades. I would like to recall how the power object not only cemented the personal bond between possessed and spirit, but reflected the cultural memory of the community as a whole. I think its decline in imagery illustrates how this aspect slowly seems to have been disappearing from *zār* as a result of an internal factor: the role of the ritual specialist. I believe this to be much more important than previously assumed.

Much is dependent on her training and abilities: diagnosing the patient, mediating between spirit and human, and tailoring the ritual to fit the specific needs of both. Her interpretations are central, and so it is her world view, her framework of understanding, that directly influences *zār*. As *zār* is not canonical, it differs from specialist to specialist, from village to village, from region to region. Apart from these geographical differences, it changes between generations, too: becoming a ritual specialist is taught in personal apprenticeship, not in a universal 'school of *zār*'. And so, as a result of the changing world every new generation of ritual specialists learns to practice *zār* in, *zār* itself changes over time, too, and its material culture follows suit. While the first generation of ritual specialists was born and raised in Ethiopia, in a cultural environment where possession was closely linked to memory and collective identity, the current generation has been born and raised in Egypt itself under very different circumstances. As a result of new generations of ritual specialists, drifting further away from the spiritual reality of their ancestors and training new specialists that were not of similar descent, the adaptive nature of the collective memory started to fade alongside the notion of a power object. And precisely because these aspects had been fading for some time, letting go of the jewellery items with spirit representations altogether was a relatively small step when circumstances so demanded.

It is also the ritual specialist who will advise her client as to the jewellery needed. This goes beyond the power objects with spirit images: the spirit may request additional jewellery, such as bracelets or earrings, and additional amulets may be advised to protect the attendees from the unwanted attention of uninvited spirits. This dual approach to spirit engagement in *zār* has become visible in the jewellery pertaining to the *zār* spirit that was invited, and in that aimed at keeping other spirits out. That dual approach is in line with the use of *madīh* songs, the uses of general incense and colours that are known to avert evil on the one hand, and the spirit songs, the use of specific incense and colours following the predilection of the *zār* spirits on the other. The central role of the ritual specialist determines what '*zār* jewellery' is, to a certain extent: the power objects and beaded jewellery fulfil their own particular role, but other than that, any piece of jewellery desired by the possessing spirit and any amulet that will make the wearer feel safe, can be used in *zār*. The ritual specialist in this respect is a valued business partner of silversmiths, and this is where ritual intersects with the world of commodities.

Jewellery as commodity

Zār jewellery can be a commodity. As all jewellery, *zār* jewellery, too, represents financial value for the wearer and a livelihood for its creator. It was a woman's private property and her financial failsafe in case of divorce or when she became a widow. The value of jewellery was in its content of either silver or gold, and would be sold when needed. As a woman's jewellery often was the only form of savings a family had, it would also be used when costly events occurred such as hospitalisation, major repairs or the wedding of sons. In that respect, jewellery might theoretically be a woman's property, but it would be used for family affairs nonetheless. A noteworthy capacity of jewellery in *zār* in that respect is that this, apparently, could <u>not</u> be sold, lest the spirit would get angry and another costly *zār* had to be organised to reconcile the two. Because having a *zār* was indeed expensive, and it was the jewellery that formed one of the main expenses. Apart from its spiritual significance, women leveraged *zār* as strategy in marriage dynamics in two ways: the high costs of a *zār* effectively inhibited any plans of the husband to take a second wife, and the jewellery obtained during a *zār* would add to the savings of the woman. This would be of considerable relevance if she feared divorce was on the horizon when the marriage remained childless: itself a reason to have a *zār* if the cause is suspected to be spirit possession.

The jewellery would be obtained from a silversmith, who himself was not part of the immediate *zār* community, but catered to their needs. Based on the observation of dr. el-Hadidi, cited before, that in the 1960s and 1970s about two third of the wares of silversmiths in Sohag governorate was *zār* jewellery, I conclude that *zār* jewellery must have been visible in everyday life: whenever a woman or her family would go to buy silver, *zār* jewellery would have been there, too. It is through its status as a commodity, created, present and visible, that *zār* jewellery formed part of a larger community than just that of *zār* itself. From the moment of its purchase, *zār* jewellery with spirit images became a singularity, something that cannot be sold or parted with. Discarding of this jewellery will have taken place around 40 to 50 years later, upon the death of the owner or when the economic need arose to sell jewellery: most *zār* ceremonies seem to have been held in the early years of marriage, so when the wearer would have been in her late teens or early twenties. This estimated period of use corresponds with the appearance and disappearance of *zār* jewellery items on the market for cultural outsiders. From the late 1950s onwards, jewellery with spirit representations became not only visible but available to cultural outsiders. In the 1980s, an abundance of *zār* jewellery was readily available, coming from *zār* devotees who had acquired these in the 1930s and 1940s, but perhaps also from unsold jewellers' stock. The last few items in the sample collection to be hallmarked stem from 1978, and have been making their appearance in the last decade.

To explain this, I argue that here, economic factors add to the religious changes and the slow disappearance of the collective mnemonic capacity of *zār* that led to its eventual disappearance altogether: when purchasing and owning jewellery with spirit images becomes increasingly expensive and is frowned upon by the direct social network, they disappear from shop windows and wearers start trading them in for money. And that is how they transition into yet another role: that of collectors' items.

Jewellery as collectors' item

Zār jewellery can be a collectors' item. Whether by museums or private collectors, *zār* jewellery is avidly collected. In these collections, they acquire new meanings, that become visible in the way they are handled. Where the original wearers would wear the pendants with spirit images with the text side outward (mirrored in the beaded pendants worn by the spirits during a possession episode), the new wearers do the opposite. Jewellery items worn with the spirit side outward, and that is also how they are displayed in museums. Apart from being a commodity again, offered for sale in stores and online, they take on a meaning they did not have that emphatically before: that of actual jewellery in its connotation of decorative adornment. Jewellery items with spirit images are reworked in Egypt itself into earrings and necklaces for the tourist trade, or used as elements in new designs by jewellery designers all over the world. And while they are loved and cared for, their existence as collectors' items makes them vulnerable to losing part of their particular history, because they are slowly moving into the field of jewellery and adornment. Which brings me to my final observation on the merits of the study of collected jewellery.

Studying collected jewellery

This has been a study into a body of collected jewellery that has been become detached from its cultural context. Moreover, this is collected material culture of which a significant part resides with private collectors all over the world. Just like the pieces themselves are scattered over the globe, my exploration into the available knowledge about these items has shown that this is growing increasingly scattered, too. It is, in my view, possible to reconnect collected jewellery to its cultural context in order to understand it better, as I hope this thesis has shown. But the real challenge will be how to ascertain that this reconnection is sustainable on the long term, particularly given the fact that jewellery owned by private collectors often ends up for sale again. My findings are that the current private custodians of *zār* jewellery do not have access to academic sources, and do not actively seek those out either. They depend on information that is offered to them, and while that may not be academically validated, it may very well hold value. Especially older collectors who searched for *zār* jewellery during the 1970s and 1980s, may possess a wealth of 'grey information' that never finds its way into the academic discourse. And while this thesis zooms in on *zār* jewellery, there is an abundance of old jewellery from North Africa and Southwest Asia in general currently spending its life in shoeboxes and showcases, separated from its cultural context. It is here I see a beautiful opportunity for public outreach and engagement by museums that curate collections of what is often called 'ethnic jewellery'. When studied closely as material culture of a given society, jewellery can be an additional historic source. Reversely, understanding that society in question may add to our understanding of the many roles jewellery can have. *Zār* jewellery for example has the potential to remedy the underrepresentation of people under colonial rule in museums and collections in the Western world. Embarking on this type of research, engaging with both collectors and the communities of origin the jewellery comes from and sharing the results in both academic and popular media (including social media, where many collectors convene) may bring these different worlds together, secure the potential of jewellery as a historic source and as such ensure the silver of the possessed continues to speak for a long time to come.

BIBLIOGRAPHY

'Abd er-Rasoul, K. 1955. Zar in Egypt, in: Wiener Völkerkundliche Mitteilungen, vol. 3 no. 1, pp 80-89.

Adly, S. el 1984. The 'Zar', in: *Folklore in Africa Today*, (1982-1984), pp. 655-686.

Alpers, E.A. 1984. Ordinary Household Chores : Ritual and Power in a 19th-century Swahili Women's Spirit Possession Cult, in: *The International Journal of African Historical Studies*, vol. 17, no. 4, pp. 677-702.

Alsop, J.W. 1982. *The rare art traditions: the history of art collection and its linked phenomena wherever these have appeared.* Harper & Row, New York.

Appadurai, A. 1988. Commodities and the politics of value, in: Appadurai, A. (ed) 1988, *The Social Life of Things. Commodities in cultural perspective.* Cambridge University Press, Cambridge, pp. 3-63.

Appadurai, A. 2006. The Thing Itself, in: *Public Culture* vol. 18, no. 1, pp. 15-21.

Aswad, S. el 2002. *Religion and Folk Cosmology: scenarios of the visible and invisible in rural Egypt,* Praeger, Westport.

Bachinger, R. & P.W. Schienerl 1984. *Silberschmuck aus Agypten.* Galerie Exler & Co., Frankfurt.

Bakker, M.C. & K. McKeown, 2021. From Cradle To Grave: A Life Story in Jewelry, in: *All Things Arabia,* Brill, Leiden.

Baron, B. 1989. Unveiling in Early Twentieth Century Egypt: Practical and Symbolic Considerations, in: *Middle Eastern Studies*, vol. 25, no. 3, pp. 370-386.

Battain, T. 1993. La divination dans le ritual du zar égyptien, in: *Egypte/Monde arabe*, 30 juin 1993, pp. 103-112.

Beck, S. 2018. *Excorcism, illness and demons in an ancient Near Eastern context. The Egyptian magical Papyrus Leiden I 343 + 345.* PALMA 18, Sidestone Press, Leiden.

Beeman, W.O. 2015. The Zar in the Persian Gulf: Performative Dimensions, in: *Anthropology of the Contemporary Middle East and Central Eurasia* 3 (1), pp. 1-12.

Behrend, H. & U. Luig (eds), 1999. *Spirit possession, modernity & power in Africa,* James Currey, Oxford.

Biasio, E. 1998. *Beduinen im Negev. Vom Zelt ins Haus.* Verlag Neue Zürcher Zeitung, Zürich.

Blackman, W.S. 1924. Some beliefs among the Egyptian Peasants with Regard to 'Afarit, in: *Folklore*, vol. 35 no. 2, pp. 176-184.

Blackman, W.S. 1926. The Karin and Karineh, in: *The Journal of the Royal Anthropological Institute of Great Britain and Ireland*, vol. 56, pp. 163-169.

Blackman, W.S. 1927. *The Fellahin of Upper Egypt*, The American University in Cairo Press (2000), Cairo.

Blackman, W.S. 1931. Magic and Medicine among the Egyptian Fellahin, in: *The Journal of the Royal Anthropological Institute of Great Britain and Ireland*, vol. 31, p. 279.

Bliss, F. 1998. *Artisanat et artisanat d'art dans les oasis du desert occidental egyptien*, Rüdiger Köppe Verlag, Köln.

Boddy, J. 1988. Spirits and Selves in Northern Sudan: The Cultural Therapeutics of Possession and Trance, in: *American Ethnologist*, vol. 15, no. 1 Medical Anthropology, pp. 4-27.

Boddy, J. 1989. *Wombs and Alien Spirits. Women, Men and the Zar Cult in Northern Sudan*. The University of Wisconsin Press, Madison/London.

Boddy, J. 1994. Spirit Possession Revisited: Beyond Instrumentality, in: *Annual Review of Anthropology*, vol. 23, pp. 407-434.

Boddy, J. 2007. *Civilizing Women. British Crusades in Colonial Sudan*. Princeton University Press, New Jersey.

Bogner, G. & L. Klein-Wisenberg (eds) 1979. *Volksglaube im Islam. Schmuck und Amulettwesen im heutigen Ägypten*. Arbeitskreis Islam, Universität Wien, Wien.

Bohak, G. 2011. The magical rotuli from the Cairo Genizah, in: Shaked, S., Y. Harari and G. Bohak 2011, *Continuity and Innovation in the Magical Tradition*, Brill, Leiden.

Bonotto, G.C. 2010. *Magic in Egypt. Jewellery and amulets of the desert and oases*. Celid, Turin.

Booth, M. 2001. Woman in Islam: Men and the 'women's press' in turn-of-the-20th-century-Egypt, in: *International Journal of Middle Eastern Studies* 33, pp. 171-201.

Borghouts, J.F. 1978. *Ancient Egyptian Magical Texts*. Brill, Leiden.

Bos, J. 2016. *Egypt's Wearable Heritage*. BLKVLD Publishers, Zandvoort.

Brun, E. le. 1902. *Harems et Musulmanes*. F. Juven, Paris.

Buskens, L. 2016. Scènes de la vie privée et publique des bijoux marocains, in: G. Barthèlemy, D. Casajus, S. Larzul & M. Volait (eds) 2016, *L'orientalisme après la Querelle. Dans les pas de François Pouillon*. Editions Karthala, Parris.

Carman, B. & J. McPherson (eds) 1983. *Bimbashi McPherson. A Life in Egypt*. British Broadcasting Corporation, London.

Chalcraft, J.T. 2005. *The Striking Cabbies of Cairo and other stories. Crafts and guilds in Egypt, 1863-1914*. State University of New York Press, Albany.

Chiffoleau, S. & A. Madoeuf 2005. *Les Pelerinages au Maghreb et au Moyen-Orient: Espaces publics, espaces du public*. Institut Francais du Proche Orient, Beirut.

Chidester, D. 2018. *Religion: material dynamics*. University of California Press, Oakland.

Coker, E.M. 2009. Claiming the Public Soul: Representations of Qur'anic Healing and Psychiatry in the Egyptian Print Media, in: *Transcultural Psychiatry*, vol 46 no 4, pp 672-694.

Colleyn, J-P. 1999. Horse, hunter & messenger: the possessed men of the Nya cult in Mali, in: Behrend, H. & U. Luig (eds), 1999. *Spirit possession, modernity & power in Africa*, James Currey, Oxford.

Colyer Ross, H. 1981. *The Art of Bedouin Jewellery. A Saudi Arabian Profile*. Arabesque, Fribourg.

Constantinides, P. 1991. The history of zar in the Sudan: theories of origin, recorded observation and oral tradition, in: Lewis, I.M., A. al-Safi and S. Hurreiz 1991, *Women's Medicine. The Zar-Bori cult in Africa and beyond*. International African Seminars New Series, no. 5. Edinburgh University Press, pp. 84-99.

Cooper, A. 1995. *Cairo in the War 1939-1945*. Penguin Books, London.

Crecelius, D. and Daly, M.W. 1998. Egypt in the eighteenth century, in: *The Cambridge History of Egypt*, Vol. 2, pp. 59-86.

Cuno, K.M. 2010. Egypt to c. 1919, in: Cook, M. & C.F. Robinson 2010. *The new Cambridge History of Islam*, Cambridge University Press, Cambridge, pp 79-106.

Cury, A. 1942. *Cairo: how to see it*. World Wide Publications, Cairo.

Darmody, L. 2001. *The Egyptian Zar-Ceremony: Silver Amulets from a Private Collection. A Catalogue and Interpretation*. Unpublished M.A. thesis, Macquarie University, Sydney.

Danielson, V. 1998. *The Voice of Egypt. Umm Kulthum, Arabic Song and Egyptian Society in the Twentieth Century*. Chicago Studies in Ethnomusicology, Chicago.

Derchain, Philippe 2008. Possession, transe et exorcisme: les oubliés de l'égyptologie. *Göttinger Miszellen* 219, 9-18.

Del Vesco, P. 2015. Jewels from the Nile. The Ethnographical Collection of Winifred Blackman, in: *RAWI Egypt's Heritage Review*, Issue 7, retrieved online at https://rawi-magazine.com/articles/winifred_blackman/.

Dobrowolska, A. and J. Dobrowolski, 2006. *Heliopolis. Rebirth of the City of the Sun*. American University in Cairo Press, Cairo.

Drieskens, B. 2006. L'art de le dire. Une réflexion méthodologique sur les histoires de djinns et autres sujets, in: *Égypte/Monde Arabe* 3, pp. 61-78.

Drieskens, B. 2006 (b). A Cairene way of reconciling, in: *Islamic Law and Society* 13,1, pp. 99-122.

Drieskens, B. 2008. *Living with Djinns. Understanding and dealing with the Invisible in Cairo*. Saqi Press, London/San Fransisco/Beirut.

Drieskens, B. & R. Lucarelli 2002. Untying the magic of the Pharaoh, in: *Egyptological Essays on State and Society, Serie Egittologica 2*, Università degli Studi di Napoli "L'Orientale", Napels.

Duff-Gordon, L. 1902. *Letters from Egypt*. McClure, Phillips & Co, New York.

Dunn, J.P. 2011. Clothes to Kill For: Uniforms and Politics in Ottoman Armies, in: *The Journal of the Middle East and Africa* 2:1, pp. 85-107.

Early, E. 1993. *Baladi women of Cairo: playing with an egg and a stone*. American University in Cairo Press, Cairo.

Edelstein, M.D. 2002. Lost Tribes and Coffee Ceremonies: Zar Spirit Possession and the Ethno-Religious Identity of Ethiopian Jews in Israel, in: *Journal of Refugee Studies* vol. 15, no. 2, pp. 153-170.

Edwards, J (ed), 2007. *Historians in Cairo. Essays in honor of George Scanlon*. American University in Cairo Press, Cairo.

Ejibadze, N. 2011. The Zar-ceremony in Egypt, in: *Bulletin of the Georgian National Academy of Sciences* Vol. 5 no. 2, pp. 137-143.

Ejibadze, N. 2014. One Fragment of the Ethnographic Picture of Egypt (Zār Ceremony), in: *Linguistics and Literature Studies* 2 (4), pp. 115-119.

Ellis, M.H. 2018. *Desert Borderland. The making of modern Egypt and Libya.* Stanford University Press, Stanford.

Elkins, J. 1999. *The Domain of Images*, Cornell University Press, Ithaca/London.

Endrawes, G., L. O'Brien & L. Wilkes 2007. Mental illness and Egyptian families, in: International Journal of Mental Health Nursing 16, pp. 178-187.

Eng, J. 2003. Sample Size Estimation: How Many Individuals Should Be Studied?, in: *Radiology* 2003, 227:309-313.

Erman, A. 1883. Die Bentreschstele, in: *Zeitschrift* für Ägyptische *Sprache und Altertumskunde* Vol. XXI, pp. 54-60.

Fahmy, A. 2007. Enchanted Jewelry of Egypt. The traditional art and craft. American University in Cairo Press, Cairo.

Fahmy, K. 2003. *All the Pasha's Men. Mehmed Ali, his army and the making of modern Egypt.* American University in Cairo Press, Cairo.

Fakhouri, H. 1968. The Zar Cult in an Egyptian Village, in: *Anthropological Quarterly*, vol. 41, no. 2, pp. 49-56.

Fakhouri, H, 1972. *Kafr el-Elow. An Egyptian Village in Transition.* Holt, Rinehart and Winston, New York.

Fisher, A. 1996. *Africa Adorned.* The Harvill Press, London

Flaherty, C. 2012. *E-Notes WW1 Turkish Headgear,* www.ottoman-uniforms.com, accessed November 4, 2020.

Frankfort, H. 1948. *Ancient Egyptian Religion*, Columbia University Press, New York.

Frankfurter, D. 2010. Where Spirits dwell: Possession, Christianization, and Saints' Shrines in Late Antiquity, in: *Harvard Theological Review* vol 103 no 1, pp. 27-46.

Garcia Probert, M.A. & P.M. Sijpesteijn (eds) 2022. *Amulets and Talismans of the Middle East and North Africa in Context. Transmission, Efficacy and Collections.* Brill, Leiden.

Garzouzi, E. 1936. The Zaar of Egypt, in: *Man* Vol. 36, pp. 188-190.

Gell, A. 1998. *Art and Agency. An Anthropological Theory.* Clarendon Press, Oxford.

Gerber, S. 2008. *Die Sammlungen Peter W. und Jutta Schienerl.* University of Vienna, thesis.

Gerber, S. 2012. Die Sammlungen Peter W. und Jutta Schienerl. Rezente orientalische Kultur und Kunst in Wien und Dresden, in: *EOTHEN. Münchner Beiträge zur Geschichte der Islamischen Kunst und Kultur* 5 (2012).

Goeje, de, M.J 1890. Zar, in: *Zeitschrift der Deutschen Morgenländischen Gesellschaft*, Vol. 44(3), p. 480.

Goffman, E. 1959. *The Presentation of Self in Everyday Life.* Doubleday & Company, Garden City N.Y.

Gordon, D.H. 1929. The Zar and the Bhut: A Comparison, in: *Man*, vol 29, pp. 153-155.

Gordon, J. 2010. Egypt from 1919, in: Cook, M. & C.F. Robinson 2010. *The new Cambridge History of Islam*, Cambridge University Press, Cambridge, pp. 372-401.

Gouy, A. (ed) 2023. *Textiles in Motion. Dress for dance in the ancient world.* Oxbow Books, Oxford.

Granzow, T. 2008. *Zār-Rituale in Cairo. Zwischen Tradition und Medialisierungen.* Eberhard Karls Universität Tübingen, Fakultät für Kulturwissenschaften, Institut für Ethnologie (thesis).

Grotberg, E.H. 1990. Mental Health Aspects of Zar for Women in Sudan, in: *Women & Therapy*, 10:3 pp. 15-24.

El-Guindi, F. 1978. The Angels in the Nile: A Theme in Nubian Ritual, in: Kennedy, J.G. (ed) 2005. *Nubian Ceremonial Life. Studies in Islamic Syncretism and Cultural Change*, American University in Cairo Press, Cairo, pp. 104-113.

El-Hadidi, H. 2006. *Survivals and Surviving: Belonging to Zar in Cairo.* PhD Dissertation, University of North Carolina.

El-Hadidi, H. 2016. *Zar. Spirit possession, Music and Healing Rituals in Egypt.* American University in Cairo Press, Cairo.

Halloy, A. 2013. Objects, Bodies and Gods. A Cognitive Ethnography of an Ontological Dynamic in the Xangô Cult (Recife, Brazil), in: Esipirito Santo, D. and N. Tassi 2013. *Making Spirits: Materiality and Transcendence in Contemporary Religions*, Library of Modern religion 20, I.B. Tauris, London/New York p. 133 – 158.

Hansen, N.B. 2006. *Motherhood in the Mother of the World. Continuity and change of reproductive concepts and practices in Egypt from ancient to modern times.* PhD-thesis, University of Chicago.

Harding, A. 2016. Biographies of Things, in: *Distant Worlds Journal* (1), pp. 5-10.

Haverhals-Werkman, J.M. 1991. *Egyptische zilveren sieraden, hun vorm, functie en betekenis.* Unpublished paper, Leiden University.

Haverhals-Werkman, J.M. 1996. *In blijde verwachting? Volksgebruiken rond voortplanting, zwangerschap en geboorte in Egypte.* Unpublished MA-thesis, Leiden University.

Henkesh, Y. 2016. *Trance dancing with the Jinn. The Ancient Art of Contacting Spirits Through Ecstatic Dance.* Llewellyn Publications, Woodbury.

Hermann, A. 1969. *Die Welt der Fellachen.* Hamburgisches Museum für Völkerkunde und Vorgeschichte, Hamburg.

Herschlag, Z.Y. 1964. *Introduction to the Modern Economic History of the Middle East.* Brill, Leiden

Hoodfar, H. 1999. *Between Marriage and the Market: intimate politics and survival in Cairo.* American University in Cairo Press, Cairo.

Houlbrook, C. and N. Armitage (eds) 2015. *The Materiality of Magic. An artefactual investigation into ritual practices and popular beliefs.* Oxbow Books, Oxford/Philadelphia.

İhsanoğlu, E. 2012. *The Turks in Egypt and their Cultural Legacy.* American University in Cairo Press, Cairo.

Inhorn, M.C. 1994. Kabsa (a.k.a. mushahara) and threatened fertility in Egypt, in: *Social Science & Medicine* Vol. 39 (4), pp. 487 – 505.

Innes, M. 1986. *In Egyptian Service: the Role of British Officials in Egypt, 1911-1936.* PhD thesis, Oxford University.

Insoll, T. 2009. Materiality, belief, ritual – archaeology and material religion: an introduction, in: *Material Religion* vol 5, no 3, pp 260 – 265.

Ishaq, S. 2016. *The whisperings of the devil; Muslim individuals' experiences of waswaas.* Unpublished doctoral thesis, University of London.

Jomier, J. 1953. Le Maḥmal et la caravane Egyptienne des Pélérins de la Mecque (XIII-XXe siècles). Impremerie de l'Institut Français d'Archéologie Orientale, Cairo.

Jong, F. de 1976. Cairene Ziyâra-days. A Contribution to the Study of Saint Veneration in Islam, in: *Die Welt des Islams*, XVII, 1-4, pp 26-43.

Kahle, P. 1912. Zâr-Beschwörungen in Agypten, in: *Der Islam* Vol. 3 (1), pp. 1-41.

Kalter, J. 1992. *The Arts and Crafts of Syria*. Thames & Hudson, London.

Kapteijns, L. and J. Spaulding 1994. Women of the Zār and middle-class sensibilities in Colonial Aden, in: *Sudanic Africa*, vol. 5, pp. 7-38.

Keane, W. 2008. The evidence of the senses and the materiality of religion, in: Journal of the Royal Anthropological Institute, pp. 110-127.

Kennedy, J.G. 1967. Nubian Zar Ceremonies as Psychotherapy, in: *Human Organization* vol. 26, no. 4, pp. 185-194.

Kennedy, J.G. (ed) 2005. *Nubian Ceremonial Life. Studies in Islamic Syncretism and Cultural Change*, American University in Cairo Press, Cairo.

Kenyon, S.M. 1995. Zar as Modernization in Contemporary Sudan, in: *Anthropological Quarterly*, vol. 68, no. 2 Possession and Social Change in Eastern Africa, pp. 107-120.

Kenyon, S.M. 2004. *Five women of Sennar. Culture and change in central Sudan*. Waveland Press, Illinois.

Kenyon, S.M. 2007. 'moveable feast of signs': gender in zar in central sudan, in: *Material Religion* vol 3 issue 1, pp. 62-75.

Kenyon, S.M. 2012. *Spirits and Slaves in Central Sudan. The Red Wind of Sennar*. Palgrave Macmillan, New York.

Kholoussy, H. 2005. *For Better, For Worse. The Marriage Crisis that made Modern Egypt*. American University in Cairo Press, Cairo.

Khouri, N. 2005. L'aliénation mentale et la maladie mentale: les fondements d'une circulation des savoirs en Egypte au XIXe siècle, in: *Outre-Mers*, tome 92, no. 346-347, La santé et ses pratiques en Afrique, pp. 103-122.

Khoury, R. 1980. Contribution à une bibliographie du zār [avec 2 planches], in: *Annales Islamologiques* 16, pp 359-374.

Khoury, R. 1981, Représentation de la Huppe (Upupa Epops) sur une amulette du Zar [avec 1 planche], in: *Annales Islamologiques* 17, pp 395-400.

Khoury, R. 1988. Notes sur l'origine du zār et ses rapports avec le vaudou haïtien, in: *Annales Islamologiques* 24, pp 295-301.

Klunzinger, C.B. 1878. *Bilder aus Oberägypten, der Wüste und dem Rothen Meere*. Levy & Müller, Stuttgart.

Koenig, Y. 1979. Un Revenant Inconvenant? (Papyrus Deir el-Medineh 37), in: *Bulletin de l'Institut Francais d'Archéologie Orientale* 79, pp. 103-119.

Kopytoff, I. 1986. The cultural biography of things; commoditization as process, in: Appadurai, A. (ed) 1986, *The Social Life of Things. Commodities in cultural perspective*. Cambridge University Press, Cambridge, pp. 64-91.

Koutrafouri, V.G. & J. Sanders (eds) 2013. *Ritual Failure. Archaeological Perspectives*. Sidestone Press, Leiden.

Kramer, F. 1987 (1993). *The Red Fez*, Verso, London.

Kriss, R. & H. Kriss-Heinrich, 1962. Volksglaube im Bereich des Islam. Band II. Amulette, Zauberformeln und Beschwörungen. Otto Harrassowitz, Wiesbaden.

Kruk. R, 1996. Zār amuletten, in; P. Faber, C. Huygens, F. Ros en M. Rullman (eds) *Dromen van het Paradijs. Islamitische kunst van het Museum voor Volkenkunde Rotterdam*, Snoeck-Ducaju & Zoon, pp 147-150.

Kruk, R. 2005. Harry Potter in the Gulf: Contemporary Islam and the Occult, in: *British Journal of Middle Eastern Studies* Vol. 32 No. 1.

Kruk, R. 2005. *The cutting sword. Challenging the evil sorcerers. Translated from the Arabic by Remke Kruk* (downloaded from www.remkekruk.nl).

Kruk, R. 2011. Een schaal in de maneschijn, in: *Phoenix* 57, 1-2, pp. 53-67.

Lababidi, L. 2008. *Cairo's Street Stories. Exploring the City's Statues, Squares, Bridges, Gardens, and Sidewalk Cafés*. American University in Cairo Press, Cairo.

Lane, E.W. 1842. *An Account of the Manners and Customs of the Modern Egyptians. The Definitive 1860 Edition*. The American University in Cairo Press, Cairo (2003).

Lane, E.W. 1860. *An Account of the Manners and Customs of the Modern Egyptians. The Third Edition*. Charles Knight & Co., London.

Lang, S. 2002. Sulha Peacemaking and the Politics of Persuasion, in: *Journal of Palestine Studies*, 31:3, pp. 52-66.

Lévi Strauss, C. 1962. *The Savage Mind*. University of Chicago Press.

Lewis, I.M., A. al-Safi and S. Hurreiz 1991, *Women's Medicine. The Zar-Bori cult in Africa and beyond*. International African Seminars New Series, no. 5. Edinburgh University Press.

Littman, E. 1950. *Arabische Geisterbeschwörungen aus Ägypten*. Otto Harrassowitz, Leipzig.

Lockwood, A. 2003. Duff-Gordon, Lucie, in: Speake, J. 2003. *Literature of Travel and Exploration. An Encyclopaedia. Volume I*. Routledge, London, pp. 350-352.

Loewenthal, K.M. 2012. Spirit possession: Jews don't do that, do they? Paper given at Royal College of Psychiatrists. [https://www.rcpsych.ac.uk/docs/default-source/members/sigs/spirituality-spsig/jews-don%27t-do-that-do-they-kate-loewenthal.pdf]

Lombard, L. G. 2003. *Ethiopian Prayer Scrolls: an Iconographic and Archetypal Study*. PhD-thesis, Union Institute and University, Cincinnati, Ohio.

MacDonald, D.B., Massé, H., Boratav, P.N., Nizami, K.A., and Voorhoeve, P. 'Ḏjinn'. In *Encyclopaedia of Islam, Second Edition*, edited by P. Bearman, Th. Bianquis, C.E. Bosworth, E. van Donzel, W.P. Heinrichs, P.J. Bearman (Volumes X, XI, XII), Th. Bianquis (Volumes X, XI, XII), et al. Accessed February 23, 2023. DOI: 10.1163/1573-3912_islam_COM_0191

Madoeuf, A. 2006. Mulids of Cairo: Sufi Guilds, Popular Celebrations, and the 'Roller-Coaster Landscape' of the Resignified City, in: Singerman, D. & P. Amar 2006. *Cairo Cosmopolitan. Politics, Culture and Urban Space in the New Globalized Middle East*. The American University in Cairo Press, Cairo, pp. 465, 488.

Mahmood, S. 2006. Feminist Theory, Agency and the Liberatory Subject: Some Reflections on the Islamic Revival in Cairo, in: *Temenos* vol. 41 no. 1, pp. 31-71.

Marçais, G., '"Amūd", in: *Encyclopaedia of Islam, Second Edition*, Edited by: P. Bearman, Th. Bianquis, C.E. Bosworth, E. van Donzel, W.P. Heinrichs. Consulted online on 15 January 2023. DOI:10.1163/1573-3912_islam_SIM_0644

Masquelier, A. 2008. When Spirits Start Veiling: The Case of the Veiled She-Devil in a Muslim Town of Niger, in: Africa Today, Vol. 54 no. 3, pp. 39-64.

Al-Masih, B. 2008. *Al-Zar* in Upper Egypt: a Missiological Perspective, in: Journal of Adventist Mission Studies Vol. 4, No. 2, Art. 7, pp. 73-88.

Mayer, W. 2021. *Silberschmuck aus Nubien. Ein fast verlorenes Kulturgut*. Edition esefeld & traub, Stuttgart.

Mayeur-Jaouen, C. 1998. Saints coptes et saints musulmans de l'Egypte du XXe siècle, in: *Revue de l'histoire des religions* tome 215 no 1, pp. 139-186.

McKale, D. 1997. Influence without Power: The Last Khedive of Egypt and the Great Powers 1914-1918, in : *Middle Eastern Studies* Vol. 33 no. 1, pp. 20-39.

Megerssa, G. and A. Kassam 2019. *Sacred Knowledge Traditions of the Oromo of the Horn of Africa*, Fifth World Publications, Durham/Finfinnee

Mehrez, S. 2023. *Costumes of Egypt. The Lost Legacies. Vol. 1. Dresses of the Nile Valley and its Oases*. IFAO, Cairo.

Mellor, N. 2015. *The Egyptian Dream. Egyptian National Identity and Uprisings*. Edinburg University Press, Edinburgh.

Mercier, J. 1996. Les Métaphores nuptial et royale dus zar: Contributions à l'étude critique de la relation entre le dieu et son adepte dans les cultes de possession, in: Northeast African Studies, New Series, vol. 3, no. 2, pp. 127-148.

Mershen, B. 1987. *Amulette als Komponenten des Volksschmucks im Jordanland*, in: Volger, G. (red) 1987. Pracht und Geheimnis. Kleidung und Schmuck aus Palastina und Jordanien, Rautenstrauch-Joest-Museum, Koln.

Meyer, B. et al 2011. Introduction: key words in material religion, in: *Material Religion* vol 7 no 1, pp 4-9.

Meyer, B. 2011. Medium, in: Material Religion vol. 7, issue 1 pp. 58-65.

Meyer, M.W. & R. Smith (eds) 1999. *Ancient Christian Magic. Coptic Texts of Ritual Power*. Princeton Paperbacks, Princeton, New Jersey.

Meyerhof, M. 1916. Beiträge zum Volksheilglauben der heutigen Ägypter, in: *Der Islam* vol 7 no 4 pp 307-344.

Mianji. F. & Semnani, Y. 2015. Zar Spirit Possession in Iran and African Countries: Group Distress, Culture-Bound Syndrome or Cultural Concept of Distress? in: *Iranian Journal of Psychiatry* 10:4, pp. 225-232.

Mitchell, T. 1991. *Colonising Egypt*. University of California Press, Berkely/Los Angeles.

Mols. L. 2013. *Verlangen naar Mekka. De hadj in 100 voorwerpen*. Rijksmuseum Volkenkunde, Leiden.

Mörike, T. 2021. Magische Materielle Kultur aus Agypten. Die Amulett-Sammlung from Peter W. Schienerl im Museum für Völkerkunde Dresden, in: *Abhandlungen und Berichte der Staatlichen Ethnographischen Sammlungen Sachsen*, Band 55, pp. 27-50.

Moffitt, L.B. 2003. *Anna Young Thompson: American Missionary, Cultural Ambassador and Reluctant Feminist in Egypt, 1872-1932*. PhD-thesis, Georgia State University.

Morsy, S.A. 1978. Sex Differences and Folk Illness, in: Beck, L. & N. Keddie (eds) 1978. *Women in the Muslim World*, Harvard University Press, Cambridge/London, pp. 599-616.

Most van Spijk, M. van der 1982. *Who cares for her health? An anthropological study of women's health care in a village in Upper Egypt*. Women and Development Series Egypt, Cairo/Leiden.

Most van Spijk, M. van der, H.Y. Fahmy & S. Zimmerman 1982. *Remember to be firm. Life histories of three Egyptian women*. Women and Development Series Egypt, Cairo/Leiden.

Mostyn, T. 2006. *Egypt's Belle Epoque. Cairo and the age of the hedonists*. Tauris Parke Paperbacks, London.

Motta, R. 1998. Le sacrifice, la table et la fête. Les aspects «néo-antiques» de la liturgie du candomblé brésilien, in: RELIGIOLOGIQUES, 17 (printemps 1998) NOURRITURE ET SACRÉ pp.75-84.

Motta, R. 2019. Candomblé, in: Callan, H. (ed) 2019. *The International Encyclopedia of Anthropology*. John Wiley & Sons Ltd.

Motta, R. 2005. Body Trance and Word Trance in Brazilian Religion, in: *Current Sociology*, vol. 52 no. 2, pp. 293-308.

Nabhan, M. 1994. *Der zār-Kult in Āgypten. Rituelle Begegnung von Geist und Mensch – Ein Beispiel komplementärer Gläubigkeit*. Peter Lang, Frankfurt am Main.

Naguib, S.-A. 1993. *Miroirs du Passé*. Cahiers de la Société d'Égyptologie, vol. 2.

Nalder, L.F. 1926. The influence of animism in Islam (review), in: *Sudan Notes and Records*, vol. 9., no. 1, pp. 75-87.

Natvig, R. 1987. Oromos, Slaves and the Zar Spirits: A Contribution to the History of the Zar Cult, in: *The International Journal of African Historical Studies*, Vol. 20, no.4. pp. 669-689.

Natvig, R. 1988. Liminal rites and female symbolism in the Egyptian zar possession cult, in: Numen, vol. XXXV, pp.57-68.

Natvig, R. 1991. Some notes on the history of the *zar* cult in Egypt, in: Lewis, I.M., A. al-Safi and S. Hurreiz 1991, *Women's Medicine. The Zar-Bori cult in Africa and beyond*. International African Seminars New Series, no. 5. Edinburgh University Press, pp. 178-188.

Natvig, R.J. 1998. Arabic Writings on Zār, in: *Sudanic Africa* 9, pp. 163-178.

Natvig, R.J. 2010. Zar in Upper Egypt: Hans Alexander Winkler's Field Notes from 1932, in: *Islamic Africa* vol. 1, no. 1, pp. 11-30.

Natvig, R.J. 2014. 'I saw the Prophet in my Dream': Prophet Songs from a *zār* ceremony in Lower Egypt, in: British Journal of Middle Eastern Studies, 41:3, pp 306-321.

Natvig, R.J. 2018. Umm Gumyāna and the *Zār*, in: P. Steiner, A. Tsakos and Eivind Heldaas Seeland 2018, From the Fjords to the Nile. Eassays in Honour of Richard Holton Pierce on his 80th birthday, Archaeopress Publishing LTD, Oxford, pp. 88-97.

Nelson, C. 1971. Self, spirit possession and world view: an illustration from Egypt, in: *The International Journal of Social Psychiatry*, vol 17 no 3, pp. 194-209.

Niclewicz, D. 2016. *World Hallmarks. Volume II. Asia, Middle East, Africa*. Hallmark Research Institute, San Francisco.

Nöldeke, Th. 1890. Zâr, in: *Zeitschrift der Deutschen Morgenländischen Gesellschaft* vol. 44, no. 4, p. 701.

Nünlist, T. 2011. Von Berittenen und Gerittenen: Aspekte des Dämonenglaubens im Bereich des Islams, in: *Asiatische Studien / Etudes Asiatiques* 65 (1), pp 145-172.

Öhrig,B, S. Nützsche. & I. Godenschweg 2005. Vorläufiger Bericht über eine umfangreiche Schenkung an das Museum für Völkerkunde Dresden: Der Nachlass des

Orientforschers Peter W. Schienerl. In: *Abhandlungen und Berichte der Staatlichen Ethnographischen Sammlungen Sachsen*, Band 52.

Okasha, A. 1966. A Cultural Psychiatric Study of El-Zar Cult in U.A.R., in: *British Journal of Psychiatry* 112, pp. 1217-1221.

Paine, S. 2004. Amulets. A World of Secret Powers, Charms and Magic. Thames & Hudson, London.

Pely, D. 2010. Honor: The Sulha's main dispute resolution tool, in: *Conflict Resolution Quarterly*, vol. 28, issue 1, pp. 67-81..

Pely, D. 2011. Women in Sulha – excluded yet influential: Examining women's formal and informal role in traditional dispute resolution, within the patriarchal culture of Northern Israel's Arab community, in: *Conflict Resolution Quarterly*, vol. 22, issue 1, pp. 89-104

Pielow, D. 1997. Dämonenabwehr am Beispiel des „Zars" und den islamischen Amulettwesens, in: *Zeitschrift der Deutschen Morgenländischen Gesellschaft* vol. 147, no. 2, pp. 354-370.

Porter, V. 2010. The use of the Arabic script in magic, in: M.C.A. Macdonald (ed) 2010. *The development of Arabic as a written language* (Supplement to the Proceedings of the Seminar for Arabian Studies 40). Archaeopress, Oxford.

Prandi, R. 2000. African Gods in Contemporary Brazil. A sociological introduction to Candomblé today, in: *International Sociology* Vol. 15:4, pp. 641-663.

Raafat, S.W. 2003. *Cairo, the Glory Years. Who built what, when, why and for whom.* Harpocrates Publishers, Alexandria.

Raby, J. (ed) 1997. *The Nasser D. Khalili Collection of Islamic Art. Vol. XII*. The Nour Foundation, New York.

Rashed, M.A. 2015. From Powerlessness to Control: Psychosis, spirit possession & recovery in the Western desert of Egypt, in: *Health, Culture and Society* Vol. 8 no. 2, pp. 10-26.

Rasmussen, R. H. 2021. *Resilient Immanence in Candomblé. Afro-Brazilian strategies of Ritual Safeguarding*. Talk presented on Sept. 2, 2021 at EASR 2021 'Resilient Religion'.

Raven, M. 2012. *Egyptian Magic. The Quest for Thoth's Book of Secrets*. American University in Cairo Press, Cairo.

Raymond, A. 2001. *Cairo, City of History*. American University in Cairo Press, Cairo.

Redman, J, 2020. Written in silver: protective medallions from inner Oman, in: Baird, I. & Yagcioglu, H. (eds) *All Things Arabia*, Brill, Leiden.

Reeve, J. 2010. Material religion, education, and museums: introduction, in: Material Religion vol 6 no 2, pp. 142-155.

Reid, D.M. 2002. *Whose Pharaohs? Archaeology, Museums, and Egyptian national identity from Napoleon to world War I*. American University in Cairo Press, Cairo.

Reynolds-Ball, E.A. 1907. *Cairo of to-day: a practical guide to Cairo and the Nile*. Adam and Charles Black, London.

Rock-Singer, A. 2019. *Practicing Islam in Egypt. Print Media and Islamic Revival*. Cambridge University Press, Cambridge.

Rodenbeck, M. 1999. *Cairo, The City Victorious*. American University in Cairo Press, Cairo.

Roode, S.M. van 2017. *Desert Silver. Understanding traditional jewellery from the Middle East and North Africa*. Blikveld Uitgevers Publishers, Zandvoort.

Ruete, E. 1886. *Memoirs of an Arabian Princess from Zanzibar.* Translated by Lionel Strachey 1907, Dover edition 2009.

Rugh, A.B. 1986. *Reveal and Conceal. Dress in Contemporary Egypt.* American University in Cairo Press, Cairo.

Russell, M. 2001. Creating al-Sayyida al-Istihklakiyya: Advertising in Turn-of-the-Century Egypt, in: *The Arab Studies Journal*, Vol. 8/9, no. 1-2, pp. 61-96.

Ryzova, L. 2015. Boys, Girls and Kodaks. Peer albums and middle-class personhood in Mid-Twentieth-Century Egypt, in: *Middle East Journal of Culture and Communication 8*, pp. 215-255.

Ryzova, L. 2021. Hemlines and Aspirations. Western influences on Egyptian dress, in: *RAWI Egypt's Heritage Review* Issue 11, pp. 88-95.

Sadiq, H. 2014. *Arab Costumes & Jewelry. A Legacy Without Borders.* National Press, Amman.

Sanua, V.D. 1965. Healing Practices and Prevention of Illness among Egyptian Fellahin, in: Transcultural Psychiatric Research, pp. 120-124.

Sauneron, S. 1960. Les Possédés, in: *Bulletin de l'Institut Francais d'Archéologie Orientale* 60, pp. 11-115.

Savage-Smith, E. 1997. Amulets and related talismanic objects, in: Raby, J. (ed) 1997. The Nasser D. Khalili Collection of Islamic Art. Vol. XII. The Nour Foundation, New York.

As-Shahi, A. 1984. Spirit Possession and Healing: the ZAR among the Shaygiyya of the Northern Sudan, in: *Bulletin (British Society for Middle Eastern Studies)* vol. 11, no 1, pp. 28-44.

Schielke, S. 2007. Hegemonic encounters: criticism of saints-day festivals and the formation of modern Islam in late 19th and early 20th century Egypt, in: *Die Welt des Islams* 47, 3-4, pp. 319-355.

Schienerl, P.W. 1976. Materialen zur Schmuckforschung in Ägypten II. *Archiv für Völkerkunde 30*, Museum für Völkerkunde, Vienna.

Schienerl, P.W. 1976b. Die gebräuchlichsten Schmuckformen in der Oase Fayoum (Ägypten), in: *Acta Ethnographica Academiae Scientiarum Hungaricae*, Tomus 25 (3-4), pp. 297-320.

Schienerl, P.W. 1980a. Eisen als Kampfmittel gegen Dämonen. Manifestationen des Glaubens an seine magische Kraft im islamischen Amulett-wesen, in: *Anthropos* Vol 75 no.3-4, pp. 486-522.

Schienerl, P. W. 1980b, Egyptian Zar-Amulets, in: *Ornament* 4 (3).

Schienerl, P.W. 1980c. Female Jewelry from Siwa Oasis (Egypt), in: *Acta Ethnographica Academiae Scientiarum Hungaricae*, Tomus 29 (1-2), pp. 167-180.

Schienerl. P.W. 1982. Spanish/Mexican Dollars in Egypt: Currency-Raw material for Silversmiths – Ornament – Amulet, in: *Ornament* 5 (3).

Schienerl, P. W. 1983. Amulets in modern Egypt, drawn from the collection of the Ethnographic Museum in Cairo, in: *Ornament* 6 (4).

Schienerl, P.W. 1984. *Tierdarstellungen im Islam*. edition herodot, Göttingen.

Sengers, S. 2003. *Women and Demons. Cult Healing in Islamic Egypt*. Brill, Leiden/Boston.

Shoshan, B. 1993. *Popular culture in medieval Cairo*, Cambridge University Press, Cambridge.

Sirico, J. 2013. The "Social Lives" of Tuareg Bracelets and Tent Posts in the Collection of the Spencer Museum of Art. M.A.-thesis, University of Kansas.

N.N., approx 1940's. *Services Guide to Cairo*. The Co-ordinating council for Welfare Work in Egypt.

Slyomovics, S. 1990. Ritual Grievance: the language of woman?, in: *Women & Performance: a journal of feminist theory* Vol. 5 no. 1, pp. 53-60.

Speake, J. 2003. *Literature of Travel and Exploration. An Encyclopaedia. Volume I*. Routledge, London.

Sonbol, A. 2006 (ed). *The last Khedive of Egypt. Memoirs of Abbas Hilmi II*. American University in Cairo Press, Cairo.

Stanley, N. 1998. *Being Ourselves for You: the global display of cultures*. Middlesex University Press, London.

Stevenson, A.E. 2013. 'Labelling and cataloguing at every available moment': W.S. Blackman's ethnographic collection of Egyptian amulets, in: *Journal of Museum Ethnography* 26, pp. 138-149.

Ter Keurs P.J. 2014. Entanglement: Reflections on people and objects. In: Bampilis T., Ter Keurs P.J. (Eds.) *Social Matters(s): Anthropological Approaches to Materiality*. Wien, Zürich: Lit Verlag, pp. 45-60.

Ter Keurs, P. 2021. Collecting: A multi-layered phenomenon, in: O'Farrel, H. & P. Ter Keurs, 2021. *Museums, Collections and Society. Yearbook 2020*. Universiteit Leiden, Leiden.

Thompson, A.Y. & E. Franke 1913. The Zar in Egypt, in: The Moslem World, vol. IV, no. 3, pp. 275-289.

Thornhill, M.T. 2004. Abbas Hilmi II. *Oxford Dictionary of National Biography*, accessed January 28, 2023.

Toledano, E.R. 2007. *As if Silent and Absent. Bonds of Enslavement in the Islamic Middle East*. Yale University Press, New Haven.

Tubiana, J. 1991. Zar and Buda in Northern Ethiopia, in: Lewis, I.M., A. al-Safi and S. Hurreiz 1991, *Women's Medicine. The Zar-Bori cult in Africa and beyond*. International African Seminars New Series, no. 5. Edinburgh University Press, pp. 19-33.

Tucker, J.E. 1985. *Women in nineteenth-century Egypt*. Cambridge University Press, Cambridge.

Trachtenberg, J. 1939. Jewish Magic and Superstition. A study in Folk Religion. Berhmans' Jewish Book House, New York.

Unger, M. 2019. *Jewellery in context. A multidisciplinary framework for the study of jewellery*. Arnoldsche Art Publishers, Stuttgart.

Vale, M.M. 2011. Sand and Silver. Jewellery, Costume and Life in Siwa Oasis. York Publishing Services, York.

Vogelsang-Eastwood, G.M. 1996. *For Modesty's Sake?* Barjesteh, Meeuwes & Co/Syntax Publishing, Rotterdam.

Volger, G. (red) 1987. *Pracht und Geheimnis. Kleidung und Schmuck aus Palastina und Jordanien*, Rautenstrauch-Joest-Museum, Köln.

Wallis Budge E.A. 2001. *Amulets and Magic*. Routledge, London/New York.

Waterfield, G. 1937. *Lucie Duff Gordon in England, South Africa and Egypt.* E.P. Dutton & Co.

Weeks, S. 1983 (a). Silver Ornaments & Anklets, in: *Cairo Today*, September 1983.

Weeks, S. 1983 (b). Fish of Silver, Fish of Gold, in: *Cairo Today*, October 1983.

Weeks, S. 1984. Silver Zar Amulets, in: *Cairo Today*, February 1984.

Weeks, S. 1984 (b). The Kholkhal, in: *Cairo Today*, May 1984.

Weeks, S. 1986. Not Baubles, Not Bangles, But Beads!, in: *Cairo Today*, November 1986.

Weissenberger, M., 1998. Les bijoux des oasis égyptiennes, in: Bliss, F. 1998. *Artisanat et artisanat d'art dans les oasis du desert occidental egyptien*, Rüdiger Köppe Verlag, Köln.

Wickett, E. 2010. *For the living and the dead. The Funerary Laments of Upper Egypt, Ancient and Modern.* American University in Cairo Press, Cairo.

Wilkinson, J. G. 1867, *A Handbook for Travellers in Egypt.* John Murray, London.

Winkler, H.A. 1936. *Ägyptische Volkskunde*, W. Kohlhammer, Stuttgart.

Winter, M. 1992. Popular Religion, in: *Egyptian society under Ottoman Rule, 1517-1798.* Routledge, London, pp. 98-107.

Witztum, E. et al 1996. The 'Zar' possession syndrome among Ethiopian immigrants to Israel: Cultural and clinical aspects, in: *British Journal of Medical Psychology* 69, 207-225.

Worrell, W.H. 1915. Studien zum abessynischen Zauberwesen, in: *Zeitschrift fur Assyriology und vorderasiatische Archaeologie*, Vol. 29 (1-2), pp. 85-141.

Young, A. 1975. Why Amhara get "kureynya": Sickness and Possession in an Ethiopian "zar" Cult, in: *American Ethnologist*, vol. 2, no. 3, pp. 567-584.

Young, A. 2017. *Transforming Sudan. Decolonization, Economic Development and State Formation.* Cambridge University Press, Cambridge.

Yousef, H.A, 2018. Pleading for a place in modern Egypt: negotiating poverty and patriarchy, 1908-1913, in: *British Journal of Middle Eastern Studies* Vol. 47, issue 2 (published online July 09, 2018).

Yousef, T.M. 2002. Egypt's Growth Performance Under Economic Liberalism: A Reassessment With New GDP Estimates, 1886-1945, in: *Review of Income and Wealth*, Series 48, No. 4.

El-Zein, A. 2009. *Islam, Arabs and the Intelligent World of the Jinn.* Syracuse University Press, Syracuse/New York.

Zeitlian, S. 2006. *Armenians in Egypt. Contribution of Armenians to Medieval and Modern Egypt.* Hraztan Sarkis Zeitlian, Los Angeles.

Zuhur, S. 1992. *Revealing Reveiling. Islamist Gender Ideology in Contemporary Egypt.* State University of New York Press, Albany.

Zvenkovsky, S. 1950. Zar and Tambura as practised by the women of Omdurman, in: *Sudan Notes and Records*, vol. 31, no. 1, pp. 65-81.

Zwemer, S.M. 1920. *The Influence of Animism on Islam. An account of popular superstitions.* The MacMillan Company, New York.

CAPTIONS TO THE PHOTOGRAPHS AT THE BEGINNING OF EACH CHAPTER

Chapter 1. Introduction
Old silver jewellery for sale in Cairo's Khan el Khalili. The triangular amulet box in the centre and the bracelets with dangles to the left are often associated with *zār*. Photo S. van Roode.

Chapter 2. Spirits and women in Egypt
A woman in Sohag, Egypt, 1900-1901. She wears a necklace of beads and a silver pendant. Similar disc-shaped pendants from this timeframe carry the text of the Throne Verse, images of mermaids or geometric patterns, and were believed to help protect the wearer from interference from the spirit world. Photo: Hallwylska Museet/SMH (PDM).

Chapter 3. Collected Objects
A collection of *zār* pendants. Photo S. van Roode.

Chapter 4. Living Objects
Drumming in a candomblé ritual, Brazil. Photo C. Silva, licensed via Canva.

Chapter 5. Historic Objects
Zār spirit images reflect historic realities. A 1944 military parade in Downtown, Cairo. Original photograph in the collection of S. van Roode.

Chapter 6. The world of *zār* jewellery
The Egyptian Nile Valley landscape, enclosed by mountain ranges on either side, is also reflected in the spirit images. Water spirits form a significant category, and many of the pendants with human shapes show the mountainous landscape on either side. Photo Getty Images, licensed via Canva.

Chapter 7. Conclusions
An old pigeon tower in Egypt. These structures could be of considerable height and dotted the rural landscape of the Nile Valley and the oases. Photo Getty Images, licensed via Canva.

APPENDIX 1

THE COSTS OF A *ZĀR*: A CASE STUDY FROM 1913

Not only does *zār* show similarities to a wedding, it is often claimed that having a personal *zār* can also be as expensive as a wedding.[595] Of all types of dealing with spirit possession, *zār* is the only one Blackman explicitly speaks out against because of the costs.[596] Clothes, jewellery, food, incense and payment of the *zār* staff amount to a considerable sum.[597] Already in the earliest report from 1877, *zār* is described as expensive: instead of the elaborate jewellery sets of later date, only a thick silver ring is mentioned with 'occasionally anklets and bracelets', yet according to the author 'many would give their last penny to afford this jewellery'.[598] In fact, the costs could rise so high that in 1903 Muhammad Hilmi Zayn ed-Din included a poignant motto in his pamphlet 'The Harmfulness of the *Zār*',[599] which in the translation of Zwemer reads as:

> Three things good luck from the threshold bar
> A wedding, a funeral and the *zār*.[600]

The motto itself however does not speak of merely 'barring good luck', but rather of 'ruining', referring to the cost of all three ceremonies.[601] In order to gain more insight into the relative cost of *zār*, I have attempted a comparison between the necessary items for one *zār* as listed in a report from 1913[602], the silver prices of the

---

595 See for example Adly 1984 p. 663 or Fakhouri 1968, p. 53. Le Brun differentiates in 1902, p. 263 between *zars* for which one spends as much as for a wedding, and cheaper ones that do not cost as much.
596 Blackman 1927, p. 200.
597 In 1929 it was noted that only the rich could afford a *zār* in Muscat, Oman, by Miss Luton of the American Mission. See Gordon 1929, p. 154.
598 Klunzinger 1877, as quoted by Littman 1950, p 41.
599 The publication is titled *Madar al-Zār*. Kahle 1912, p. 3 and Mitchell 1991, p. 100.
600 Zwemers translation in Zwemer 1920 p. 228.
601 As translated by Kahle 1912, p. 3. For the investment in a wedding, see Kholoussy 2010. For the investment in a funeral, see the elaborate description given by Wickett 2010.
602 I chose this report, because it is one of the most detailed listing the various goods needed. Kriss & Kriss-Heinrich also include a list of necessities for their event in 1957, but as their *zār* might to a certain degree be orchestrated, these might not be representative for an average *zār*.

period and the income of an average Egyptian household in the lower classes. The results, presented in the following paragraphs, indicate that having a private *zār* would indeed have been a very costly affair and that 'ruining' is certainly not too strong a word.

Items needed for *zār*

The description from 1913 lists the arrangement for a *zār* involving a Sudanese spirit[603]: different kinds of nuts, parched peas, sesame seed, parsley, coffee in a paper package, two heads of sugar, two bowls of sour milk, two pieces of soap, a plate of oranges, one of feast cakes, another of Turkish delight, candy and sugared nuts, cucumbers and apples, all of which were covered with a piece of red cloth, three small candles and two large ones on the floor. In addition, incense was burnt and two white hens and a cock were used as sacrificial animals. Salt and flour were sprinkled around during the dancing and a bottle of rosewater was present to quench thirst. In terms of staff the ritual specialist was present with a team of women that played two darbuka drums, two smaller drums and a barrel drum, adding up to five musicians. The patient and other women were wearing 'blue and white Sudan charms, silver chains, anklets, bracelets etc'.[604]

Cost of items needed for *zār*

Historic silver prices are available only since 1915[605], but in January of that year the silver price was $12.45 per ounce. With an average weight of 10 grams, one *zār* pendant would have cost around $4,5,[606] the equivalent of which in Egyptian pounds was circa LE 1.[607] In addition to at least one pendant, the patient would need other jewellery: in the case from 1913, necklaces, anklets and bracelets are mentioned with a rather ominous 'etcetera'. Assuming from the description this patient would need one necklace, two anklets, two bracelets, a *zār* pendant and some smaller items like a ring or another charm, the amount of silver jewellery alone would around 530 grams[608], costing a little under LE 50. This alone constituted nearly a year's income, as I will illustrate in the next section.

In addition to the silver, the elements for the *kursī* had to be provided for as well. A new white *gallābīya* would cost around LE 2. In a time when a family would have only one spare set of clothes for celebrations, buying a new *gallābīya* would have been a significant purchase.[609]

---

603 Thompson 1913, p. 278, also cited in Zwemer 1920, p. 230.
604 Zwemer 1920, p. 234 also adds that the patient is dressed in white and ornamented with special charms.
605 To establish silver prices during the period of interest for this study, http://www.macrotrends.net/1470/historical-silver-prices-100-year-chart has been used. Up until 1914, the pound reflected the Gold Standard. Egypt adopted an official hallmarking system only in 1916.
606 An ounce is 28,3 grams.
607 From 1914 until 1962, the Egyptian pound (LE) was pegged to the British pound at a rate of LE 0,975 for 1 pound sterling, as Egypt was all but formally a British protectorate. Kholoussy 2010, p. xi. The exchange rate LE to dollar was around LE 0,25 to $ 1. Young 2017, p. 52, note 17.
608 As weighed from examples from 1913 in my own collection.
609 Chalcraft 2005, p. 129.

Sugar, produced in abundance in Egypt, was cheap[610], coffee was a luxury product.[611] Local *baladī* soap, made of cottonseed oil, was on the cheaper end, imported soap from Nablus would have been costlier. Candles were also made from cottonseed oil. Incense was again an expensive product.[612] Local produce such as parsley, sesame seed, dried nuts and peas, cucumbers, apples, oranges and milk would not have been too expensive. The three sacrificial animals, two white hens and a cock, would have cost more. Add to that the wages of the ritual specialist and her assistants, and I imagine the total cost for this *zār* could be estimated to be in the ranges of LE 60-80.

Average income in 1913

In 1913 local labour was very cheap and wages were low.[613] For a breadwinner in the lower classes, wages of 14 piastres a day would be the minimum required to clothe and feed a family. Female garment makers, working from home, earned around 1-2 piastres a day, male tailors could just about reach the minimum subsistence level of LE2 per month. Shoemakers on the high end reached an income of 15 to 19 piastres per day, weavers were left with around 5 piastres a day, carpenters and masons hauled in 8 to 10 piastres a day. Higher wages were earned by mechanics, electricians, brick workers and other specialist jobs in the construction industry: these would vary between 15 and 40 piastres a day. The remaining population mainly worked in agriculture, a field where inequality was high and about 70% of the peasant population barely got by.[614]

This would leave a family in the lower classes with an average monthly income of LE 1,5 to LE 5, rising to LE 10 in the better rewarded jobs. In 1913, a reader of newspaper al-Ahram sent a letter to the editor, mentioning that young men in Egypt earned only a maximum of LE 5 per month.[615] An average annual household income in 1913 can be estimated to have been around LE 60.[616]

---

610 See Herschlag 1964, p. 127 for the economic developments on the sugar market in Egypt.
611 A cup of coffee in a coffeehouse cost around 0,5 piastre, as inferred from the Baedeker travel guides from 1902 and 1929. This *zar* was held however when Egypt was still part of the Ottoman Empire, recovering from a major crisis in 1907, on the brink of World War I and before the Americas started exporting coffee on the large scale we are accustomed to nowadays. Chalcraft 2005, p. 129 describes how coffee was a luxury product in 1907.
612 Khoury 1980, p. 363 specifies incense from the incense tree, *oudh*, benzoin, myrrh and camphor: all expensive, imported products.
613 The following wages have been gathered from Chalcraft 2005, p. 107 ff.
614 Cuno 2010, p. 98.
615 Kholoussy 2010, p. 25. The letter was sent to express concern about traditional dowry demands, which could not be met by prospective grooms due to their low income.
616 Yousef 2002, table A1, lists the real GDP per capita in 1913 at 9.04 LE.

APPENDIX 2

GLOSSARY OF ARABIC TERMS

'arūsa
Bride. In the context of *zār*: the patient.

baraka
Blessing, good luck.

ḥaḍra
Visiting day for the shrines of saints and other important figures. In the context of *zār*: regular public *zār*, usually held weekly.

fiḍḍa
Silver

ḥijāb
Veil, barrier. In magical context: an amulet.

jalājil
Small globular dangles

kabsa
Infertility caused by the presence of certain polluting materials or people that have been in contact with these during the period that a woman is considered ritually vulnerable on account of blood after the main crisis-events of circumcision, defloration, childbirth or miscarriage. Also known as *mushāhara*.

kursī
Seat, throne. In the context of *zār*: an altar.

maulid
Festival in honour of the birthday of the Prophet or of saints.

mushāhara
Infertility caused by the presence of certain polluting materials or people that have been in contact with these during the period that a woman is considered ritually vulnerable on account of blood after the main crisis-events of circumcision, defloration, childbirth or miscarriage. Also known as *kabsa*.

qarin
Jinn born together with every human, considered a companion that may either protect or harm its human counterpart.

qarina
Female jinn causing miscarriages or stillbirths, known to harm or kill babies and young children, too.

šaika
Shaykha, in the context of *zār*: the ritual specialist.

ṣulḥ
Reconciliation; method of settling disputes.

ukt
Sister. In the context of spirit engagement: female companion spirit. See also *qarin*.

SUMMARY

This thesis examines Egyptian *zār* jewellery. The jewellery associated with the Egyptian *zār* is no longer employed in the ritual itself. Instead, it has been collected by individuals and museums. The main research question is what *zār* jewellery is: both in terms of outward appearance and definition, and in terms of agency and function.

Chapter 1 discusses the theoretical framework and sources I used for this research. The primary foundation of this research is a sample collection of collected jewellery items, housed in both private and museum holdings. In addition, I have also used the limited written evidence of jewellery in the context of *zār*. This chapter scrutinizes the strengths and drawbacks of the available sources, offering a critical evaluation of potential biases and limitations. I also present the main theoretical framework against which I have studied these objects.

In chapter 2, I explore the world of *zār* in Egypt itself. *Zār* is a possession cult, that entered Egypt in the late 19th century through the slave trade, gained immense popularity across all strata of Egyptian society, and integrated with existing practices for dealing with spirit possession. Within the sample collection, numerous pieces of jewellery are indistinguishable from regular amulets designed to ward off interference from spirits. Based on that observation, I broadened the scope to encompass not just spirit possession in the context of *zār*, but also the engagement with the spirit world by women in general. What did they use these amulets against? This excursion showed that women feared spirits most because of their ability to impede pregnancy, cause miscarriages or kill young children. Because of this fear, the goal of informal rituals in general strongly focuses on avoiding and averting the attention of spirits. Yet, *zār* actively invites spirits. I argue that the jewellery of the Egyptian *zār* demonstrates that while *zār* actively invites spirits, women also used regular amulets to seek protection from any other spirit or negative influences that may appear during *zār*. Upon closer inspection, this dual approach towards spirits in *zār* is also evident in songs and incense.

Chapter 3, 'Collected Objects', zooms in on the collection and publication history of *zār* jewellery. As the foundation of this study lies in collected jewellery, understanding how these collections came into being is crucial. The publication history of *zār* jewellery, in turn, influences our understanding of these items, and is closely tied to their collection history. From this analysis it appears that the most recognizable form of *zār* jewellery, items with spirit images, was not published until the mid- 20th century. Examining the hallmarks on the collected items however reveals their existence from the early 20th century onwards. In my view, this is telling about their visibility. The first publications discussing these jewellery objects with spirit images at length date from the 1960s and take the form of jewellery catalogues rather than studies into ritual. In this chapter, I trace the publication history of *zār* jewellery and argue that they have always been presented as collected objects; they have rarely been observed in an actual *zār* ritual. The biases, personal choices, goals and financial means of the collectors have resulted in a set of publications that subsequently formed the basis for other collectors. With the rise of Internet platforms, the little background known about these pieces was further diluted. As a result, *zār* jewellery became a decontextualised group of material culture.

Chapter 4, 'Living Objects', attempts to restore context to *zār* jewellery, considering both its ritual and everyday contexts. For its ritual context, I turn to the African origins of *zār* and investigate the use of objects in African possession cults. Given that *zār* is a cult of African origin, merged with a monotheistic religion, I use candomblé as an experimental case-study to explore how objects and humans interact in such a syncretized framework. Building on this reassessment, I propose that the jewellery items with spirit images are comparable to 'power objects', sealing the bond between a human host and possessing spirit. The beaded jewellery items are akin to 'manifestation objects' that the spirit needs to manifest itself. The sample collection, however, holds more jewellery than just that with spirit images and beaded jewellery. I propose the sample collection as a whole demonstrates the integration of an African possession cult with the Egyptian cultural background of spirit engagement and suggest roles for jewellery as contracts, as gifts requested by the possessing spirit, and as amulets.

Shifting to the everyday context of *zār* jewellery, I examine its economic aspects. I estimate the cost of a *zār* to be in the range of year's wages. Jewellery forms a significant part of those costs. These high costs then can be leveraged in marriage dynamics. I also reconstruct how the '*zār* business' was intertwined with everyday life; jewellery was prominently featured in silver shops and a substantial part of the creating of *zār* costume and dress likely undertaken by seamstresses working from home.

Chapter 5, 'Historic Objects', investigates the community aspect of *zār* jewellery. Where I have examined the roles and meaning jewellery on a personal level in the previous chapters, here I observe jewellery as a historic source on a community level. Like many African possession cults, *zār* itself works as a form of collective memory, passing on this memory through oral tradition and performance. The uniqueness of Egyptian *zār* jewellery lies in its materialisation of these performances in their spirit images; while live performances are transient, the spirit images serve as records of the community's conceptualisation of the spirits' appearances. These conceptualisations may potentially reflect historical realities. First, I scrutinize the challenges that previous researchers faced in interpreting images. For this, I combine the literature study of chapters 3 and 4, as well as the theoretical framework of the Oromo worldview as a case-study. Utilizing Goffman's concepts of the 'personal front' and the 'collective representation', I then explore the self-image of the *zār* community. Through analysis of dress details, hairstyles, setting and attributes carried by the spirits, along with a statistical analysis of the sample collection over time, I reconstruct the collective representation of the people who used these items. I present three case studies in this chapter to illustrate how we may understand these images as a historic source. These include a case study with a clear direct reference to the banishment of the Khedive Abbas Hilmi II, a case study of the *maḥmal* festivities as indirect references to historic events that may be placed in a particular timeframe, and finally indirect references to the world of women in general. Combining the approaches to fertility and motherhood as presented in chapter 2 with literature study, I propose that several of the images would have been recognised in a fertility context by the women participating in *zār*.

Chapter 6, 'The world of *zār*', consolidates the elements discussed earlier into a comprehensive portrayal of the *zār* community and an analysis of changes in *zār* over the course of approximately 80 years.

The collective representation of the people emerging from these silver jewellery items is that of a rural, illiterate population under military control. The greatest variety in detail is present at the beginning of the 20th century. However, over time, that collective representation becomes increasingly standardized, and out of sync with contemporary dress and preferences. The pendants themselves undergo a transformation, becoming smaller, lighter, thinner, and eventually disappearing altogether. I attribute those gradual changes to three factors.

Firstly, the political and economic developments of the 20th century impact both the nature of *zār* and its economic aspects. *Zār* deals with 'otherness', and as Egypt transitioned from a nation under foreign rule to an independent republic in the 1950s, a new search for 'own' values as opposed to those of 'others' ensued. Economic reforms caused Egypt's economy to decline, potentially making the silver discs too expensive. Ultimately, the economic aspect of jewellery outweighed its ritual connotation: older, heavier *zār* pendants began to appear on the market at a time where household economies increasingly struggled to make ends meet, prompting individuals to sell their jewellery to cover expenses.

Secondly, religious peer pressure among women is another catalyst for the disappearance of *zār* jewellery. From the 1970s onwards, Islamic revival gained widespread ground among Egyptian women. The growing number of religiously involved women exerted social peer pressure that directly affected the use of jewellery with spirit images: publicly being seen with *zār* jewellery, buying and owning it became increasingly problematic.

A third pivotal factor in the change and disappearance of the jewellery with spirit images is the crucial role of the ritual practitioner herself and the changes in that role over the course of two to three generations. This amalgamation of factors, evident in jewellery, illustrates the gradual absorption of an African cult into a monotheistic framework under the influences of political, economic and religious developments.

All these lines of inquiry meet in the final chapter with conclusions. This study into *zār* jewellery shows how this group of collected and decontextualised material culture may still hold information value. Vital to this information value is their collection history: when, how and where were these objects collected? Observing them in both large numbers and a diachronic setting allows us to understand these objects not just in their ritual, but also in their economic and social contexts. When studied in these contexts, collected *zār* jewellery is an additional historic source about the ritual they served in, but also about their wearers: the women who purchased and wore these objects, and the world they lived in.

ACKNOWLEDGEMENTS

As with all independent research endeavours, it takes a village of guidance and support behind the scenes. I extend my sincere gratitude to my promotor prof. dr. Léon Buskens. His faith in me and his critical, yet always encouraging guidance over the years have made this into a profoundly enjoyable journey. I deeply appreciate the personal involvement of prof. dr. René Cappers, my second promotor, and his generosity in sharing his collection and his time with me.

Undoubtedly the most pleasurable part of researching collections has been engaging with their collectors. Many invited me into their homes and graciously shared their treasures: the hours we spent together talking over a table with silver have been not only instrumental to this research, but also forged friendships. In particular, I would like to honour the memory of Marion Crince Le Roy, who passed away before the completion of this research. These encounters with kindred spirits include the digital world. I am very grateful to all collectors I could not meet in person, who sent me photos of their pieces and engaged in online discussions.

In addition to private collections, museums responded to my requests with great hospitality, assistance and kindness. I would like to thank dr. Sylvia Dolz (Staatliche Kunstsammlung, Dresden), dr. Axel Steinmann (Weltmuseum, Vienna), dr. Ursula Warnke (Landesmuseum, Oldenburg) and Cindy Zalm (Wereldmuseum, The Netherlands) for granting me access to their collections. Dr. Emily Bryant (Indiana Museum of Archaeology and Anthropology) generously shared their collection with me. Special thanks go to Hussein Gouda, Usama Dawood and Alaa Abdou, all from Cairo, for their kind assistance with my questions regarding the silver trade.

Beyond jewellery, I have been welcomed to peruse archives and other collections. Dr. Sabine Happ (Münster University), Stefan Sienell (Austrian Academy of Sciences), Franziska Jenni (Museum der Kulturen, Basel), dr. Sofia Häggman (Medelhavsmuseet, Stockholm), Leonie Neumann (Weltkulturen Museum, Frankfurt am Main) all shared invaluable details from their archives with me. Dr. Hager el Hadidi generously shared her time and knowledge of *zār*, and invited me as speaker on the Resilient Religion conference in 2021. Jolanda Bos (Wearable Heritage, Zandvoort) provided me with the opportunity to inspect her fabulous collection of face veils. Salua Qidan (Tiraz Centre, Amman) has been a great help with my endless questions on *zār* jewellery in the Tiraz Collections. Ingrid Langerak (Utrecht) and Martina Dempf (Berlin) both shared their knowledge on Rashayda traditions with me, and dr Rita Lucarelli (University of

California) and em. prof. dr. Hans Schneider (Leiden University) provided me with their views on possession in ancient and modern Egypt. Thank you all!

I wholeheartedly thank Yasmine el-Dorghamy (Cairo) for translating texts on *zār* pendants. Salma Ahmad Caller (UK) invited me to join the discussion in her Postcard Women's Imaginarium-group. I am very grateful to her for indulging my request to use the artwork 'Red Wind: Fire' on the cover of this book.

As an external candidate with a job, finding an academic community to bounce ideas around, encourage and celebrate together is not straightforward. I found mine in the most unlikely of places: the social media platform Instagram. Valerie, Sophia, Rebecca, Laura, Matilda – thank you for your encouragement, time and friendship.

This research brought me much joy in a period that came with challenges of its own. Early on in this project, I was diagnosed with breast cancer, and a few weeks later the COVID-19 pandemic hit the world. I am tremendously grateful for the friendship and support I have experienced during these strange times. The encouragement of Léon and René, along with the support of my family and friends, made it easy for me to continue once the brain fog had cleared.

The pandemic brought new opportunities too. As online talks became popular, I endeavoured to create a digital course on jewellery, the proceeds of which sustained this self-funded project. Thank you to all who enrolled! I would like to sincerely thank the Juynboll Stichting, who graciously awarded me a grant to enable me to focus on writing the final chapters of this thesis, and Karsten and Corné of Sidestone Press, who, upon hearing of my course project, offered to cover the costs of this publication. This generous gesture allowed me to offer this book as full open access. Provincie Gelderland actively encouraged me to pursue this research: thank you, Liesbet and Edwin, for your support!

Finally, two more people have been instrumental in the completion of this research. Nefertari Tadema shared her knowledge, collection, books and passion for jewellery with me for the better part of two decades. She passed away during the final stages of this research, and it is my great honour to dedicate this book to her in loving memory and gratitude for our friendship. My largest debt of gratitude is to Wim, who travelled this winding road with me, and always kept my spirits up.

CATALOGUE

The catalogue presents examples of jewellery used in the Egyptian *zār*, with an emphasis on *zār* jewellery with spirit images. Additionally, I have included examples of coin jewellery, regular jewellery and amulets often associated with *zār* by collectors, curators and vendors. For a complete overview of the types of jewellery used and the roles this jewellery may have played, please refer to chapter 4 and Figure 4.9.

This catalogue contains only a small selection of the jewellery studied for this volume, but as it presents these chronologically for the first time, this allows us to appreciate the developments in jewellery over time as outlined in chapter 5. The majority of these are pieces in private collections, which have never been published before.

Measurements are given for the body of the jewel, excluding dangles and bail. Dates given are the date of the hallmark; if no hallmark is present, a date-range of a decade is given based on stylistic criteria.

ZĀR JEWELLERY WITH SPIRIT IMAGES 1900-1920

The earliest jewellery with spirit images. Pendants from this timeframe are generally 5-6 cm in diameter, carefully executed with flowing lines and a great level of detail.

Water spirits

Mermaids

001. Amulet with mermaid. Date: 1913-1916. H. 6,5 cm. Collection Qilada Foundation – Eric and Marion Crince Le Roy, inventory number 53a.

002. Amulet with mermaid and fish. Date: early 20th century, hallmarked in 1952-1962 (see chapter 5.3.2 for a discussion). H. 6,5 cm. Collection S. van Roode.

003. Pendant with mermaid. Date: 1913-1916. Diameter: 5,5 cm. Collection S. van Roode.

004. Pendant with mermaid. Date: 1913-1916. Diameter: 5,2 cm. Collection Qilada Foundation – Eric and Marion Crince Le Roy, inventory number 25i.

005. Pendant with mermaid. Date: 1913-1916. Diameter: 5,7 cm. Collection Qilada Foundation – Eric and Marion Crince Le Roy, inventory number 63b.

006. Pendant with mermaid, possibly wearing a necklace. Dangles missing. Date: 1913-1916. Diameter: 5,6 cm. Collection S. van Roode.

007. Pendant with mermaid and fish. Date: 1913-1916. Diameter: 5,4 cm. Collection Qilada Foundation – Eric and Marion Crince Le Roy, inventory number 63f.

008. Pendant with mermaid pair. Date: 1913-1916. Diameter: 5,2 cm. Collection Qilada Foundation – Eric and Marion Crince Le Roy, inventory number 17d.

009. Pendant with mermaid pair and fish. Date: 1913-1916. Diameter: 5,2 cm. Collection Qilada Foundation – Eric and Marion Crince Le Roy, inventory number 63n.

Human-headed fish

010. Pendant with human-headed fish and garbled version of Throne Verse. No dangles. Date: early 20th century. Diameter: 5,4 cm. Collection S. van Roode.

011. Pendant with human-headed fish in frame. Date: early 20th century. Diameter: 5,6 cm. Collection S. van Roode.

012. Pendant with human-headed fish in frame and two additional fish. Date: early 20th century. Diameter: 5,2 cm. Collection S. van Roode.

013. Pendant with human-headed fish flanking a fish. Date: early 20th century. Diameter: 6,0 cm. Collection Qilada Foundation – Eric and Marion Crince Le Roy, inventory number 22a.

Male spirits

014. Pendant with male bust, possibly a military spirit. Date: 1913-1916. Diameter: 5,3 cm. Collection S. van Roode.

015. Pendant with male bust in military uniform. The text reads 'Abbas Hilmi'. Date: 1913-1916. Diameter: 6,2 cm. Collection Qilada Foundation – Eric and Marion Crince Le Roy, inventory number 23.

016. Pendant with male bust in military uniform. The text reads 'Abbas Hilmi'. Date: 1913-1916. Diameter: 5,4 cm. Collection S. van Roode.

017. Pendant with male bust in military uniform. Two fish above his shoulders. Date: 1920-1921. Diameter: 5,4 cm. Collection Nefertari Tadema.

018. Pendant with male bust in military uniform. Two plants above his shoulders. Date: 1920 – 1921. Diameter: 5 cm. Collection Qilada Foundation – Eric and Marion Crince Le Roy, inventory number 63a.

Human spirit pairs

019. Pendant with spirit pair, flanking a pigeon tower. Hills on both sides. Geometric design on the lower part. Next to the male spirit, a text has later been added. Date: 1916-1918. Diameter: 5,7 cm. Collection Nefertari Tadema.

020. Pendant with spirit pair, flanking a fish. Hills on both sides, two stars in the sky. Date: 1918-1919. Diameter: 5,7 cm. Collection Nefertari Tadema.

021. Pendant with spirit pair, flanking a fish. Hills on both sides, two stars in the sky. Date: 1919-1920. Diameter: 5,2 cm. Collection Nefertari Tadema.

ZĀR JEWELLERY WITH SPIRIT IMAGES 1920-1940

The pendants from the 1920s form the majority: from the 1930s onwards, their number steadily declines. As time progresses, the pendants become slightly smaller, around 5 cm in diameter. The carefully executed styles of the earlier periods continue during the early 1920s. From the second half of the 1920s onwards, the images become slightly less detailed. This is notably visible in the eyes and hairstyles of the spirits: instead of individually detailed, wide open eyes, the eyes are rendered through a series of more or less parallel lines, and the wavy hairstyles of the early 1920s become more uniform.

Water spirits

Mermaids

022. Pendant with mermaid. Possibly wearing necklace. Date: 1921 – 1922. Diameter: 4,9 cm. Collection Qilada Foundation – Eric and Marion Crince Le Roy, inventory number 63d.

023. Pendant with mermaid. Date: 1922 – 1923. Diameter: 5,5 cm. Collection Nefertari Tadema.

024. Pendant with mermaid. Hills on one side. Date: 1926 – 1927. Diameter: 5,1 cm. Collection S. van Roode.

025. Pendant with male mermaid, wearing a type of pointed headgear. Date: 1926 – 1927. W. 3,8 cm. H. 2 cm. Collection S. van Roode.

026. Pendant with mermaid. Hills on one side. Date: 1929 – 1930. Diameter: 5,4 cm. Collection Qilada Foundation – Eric and Marion Crince Le Roy, inventory number 63c.

027. Pendant with mermaid. One star in the sky. Date: 1933 – 1934. Diameter: 4,7 cm. Collection S. van Roode.

Human-headed fish

028. Pendant with two human-headed fish, flanking a fish. Date: 1921 – 1922. Diameter: 5,3 cm. Collection S. van Roode.

CATALOGUE | 183

029. Pendant with two human-headed fish, flanking a male spirit. Three stars in the sky. Date: 1926 – 1927. Diameter: 5,4 cm. Collection Qilada Foundation – Eric and Marion Crince Le Roy, inventory number 23.

030. Pendant with two human-headed fish with a moustache. Date: 1928 – 1929. Diameter: 5,3 cm. Collection Qilada Foundation – Eric and Marion Crince Le Roy, inventory number 63a.

Male spirits

031. Pendant with male spirit, holding a sword, between a plant and a fish. Date: 1921 – 1922. Diameter: 5,6 cm. Collection S. van Roode.

032. Pendant with male bust. Two plants above his shoulders. Bail missing. Date: early 20th century. Diameter: 6 cm. Collection Qilada Foundation – Eric and Marion Crince Le Roy, inventory number 25-13.

033. Pendant with male bust in military uniform Two plants above his shoulders. Date: 1922 – 1923. Diameter: 4,9 cm. Collection Qilada Foundation – Eric and Marion Crince Le Roy, inventory number 25-10.

034. Pendant with male spirit, wearing a turban, arms outstretched in a whirling (?) pose. One black glass bead added to the dangles. Date: 1922 – 1923. Diameter: 5 cm. Collection S. van Roode.

035. Pendant with male spirit, holding a plant, between a plant and a fish. Dangles refurbished. Date: 1922 – 1923. Diameter: 5,7 cm. Collection S. van Roode.

036. Pendant with male bust in military uniform. Two flags behind his shoulders. Date: 1923 – 1924. Diameter: 5,3 cm. Collection Nefertari Tadema.

037. Pendant with male bust in military uniform. Two plants above his shoulders. Date: 1924 – 1925. Diameter: 5,1 cm. Collection Nefertari Tadema.

038. Pendant with male spirit, holding a plant. Date: 1925 – 1926. Diameter: 5,2 cm. Collection S. van Roode.

039. Pendant with male bust, holding two swords. Two plants above his shoulders. Date: 1926 – 1927. Diameter: 4,9 cm. Collection S. van Roode.

040. Pendant with male spirit in Arab dress, holding a sword, flanked by two fish. Two stars in the sky. Date: 1926 – 1927. Diameter: 5,7 cm. Collection S. van Roode.

041. Pendant with male spirit, holding a plant, flanked by two plants. Chain added later. Date: 1926 – 1927. Diameter: 5,2 cm. Collection S. van Roode.

042. Pendant with male spirit, holding a plant. Hills on one side, fish on the other. Date: 1926 – 1927. Diameter: 5 cm. Collection Qilada Foundation – Eric and Marion Crince Le Roy, inventory number 63h.

043. Pendant with male spirit, holding a plant. Hills/water on one side, a plant on the other. Date: 1928 – 1929. Diameter: 5,3 cm. Collection S. van Roode.

044. Pendant with male spirit, arms outstretched in a whirling (?) pose, holding two unidentifiable objects. Date: 1930 – 1931. Diameter: 4,5 cm. Collection S. van Roode.

045. Pendant with male spirit, hands folded in lap, wearing a wide garment in a whirling (?) pose. Flanked by two plants. Date: 1930 – 1931. Diameter: 5,4 cm. Collection Qilada Foundation – Eric and Marion Crince Le Roy, inventory number 63g.

046. Pendant with male bust, possibly military. Two plants above his shoulders. Dangles missing. Date: 1930 – 1931. Diameter: 5,4 cm. Collection S. van Roode.

047. Pendant with male spirit in Arab dress, holding a sword, flanked by hills. Date: 1930 – 1931. Diameter: 4,8 cm. Collection Qilada Foundation – Eric and Marion Crince Le Roy, inventory number 63l.

048. Pendant with male bust in military uniform. Two plants behind his shoulders. Date: 1931 – 1932. Diameter: 5,4 cm. Collection Nefertari Tadema.

049. Pendant with male bust in military uniform, wearing headgear with a double plume. Two plants behind his shoulders. Date: 1935 – 1936. Diameter: 5,9 cm. Collection S. van Roode.

050. Pendant with male bust in military uniform, wearing headgear with a plume. One plant behind his shoulder, hill on one side. Date: 1937 – 1938. Diameter: 4,5 cm. Collection Nefertari Tadema.

051. Pendant with male bust in military uniform. Two plants behind his shoulders. Secondary loop through drilled hole. Date: 1937 – 1938. Diameter: 6 cm. Collection S. van Roode.

052. Pendant with male bust in military uniform. Two plants behind his shoulders. Date: 1939 – 1940. Diameter: 4,9 cm. Collection S. van Roode.

Female spirits

053. Pendant with female spirit, wearing a long head veil, holding a plant and carrying a basket on her head. Dangles missing, multiple signs of reuse (two worn through suspension holes, two holes for fastening the pendant on fabric with the image facing inward). Date: early 20th century. Diameter: 5,2 cm. Collection S. van Roode.

054. Pendant with female spirit. Hills on either side. Date: 1927 – 1928. Diameter: 4,9 cm. Collection S. van Roode.

055. Pendant with female spirit, wearing a long head veil, carrying a jug on her head, flanked by two plants. Outer border cut off, traces of zigzag border remain, new dangles. Date: 1928 – 1929. Diameter: 4,8 cm. Collection S. van Roode.

056. Pendant with female spirit, carrying a jug on her head, flanked by two plants. Date: 1928 – 1929. Diameter: 4,3 cm. Collection Qilada Foundation – Eric and Marion Crince Le Roy, inventory number 25-6.

057. Pendant with female spirit. Hills and stars on either side. Date: 1928 – 1929. Diameter: 4,9 cm. Collection Qilada Foundation – Eric and Marion Crince Le Roy, inventory number 53b.

058. Pendant with female spirit, wearing a long head veil, carrying a jug on her head, flanked by two plants. Date: 1929-1930. Diameter: 5,5 cm. Collection S. van Roode.

CATALOGUE

059. Pendant with female spirit, hands folded in lap, wearing a wide garment in a whirling (?) pose. Flanked by two plants. Date: 1930-1931. Diameter: 5 cm. Collection Nefertari Tadema.

Human spirit pairs

060. Pendant with spirit pair. Male spirit leaning on a stick, female spirit holding a distaff (?). Cotton plants on lower end. Date: 1921-1922. Diameter: 6,5 cm. Collection Nefertari Tadema.

061. Pendant with spirit pair. Male spirit leaning on a stick. Date: 1921-1922. Diameter: 5 cm. Collection Nefertari Tadema.

062. Pendant with spirit pair. Male spirit leaning on a stick. Date: 1921-1922. Diameter: 4,9 cm. Collection Qilada Foundation – Eric and Marion Crince Le Roy, inventory number 63c.

063. Pendant with spirit pair. Male spirit leaning on a stick, female spirit holding a distaff (?). Dangles missing. Date: 1921-1922. Diameter: 5,4 cm. Collection S. van Roode.

064. Pendant with spirit pair flanking a pigeon tower. Hills on either side. Date: 1922-1923. Diameter: 5,5 cm. Collection Qilada Foundation – Eric and Marion Crince Le Roy, inventory number 63o.

065. Pendant with spirit pair flanking a pigeon tower. Hills on either side. Date: 1922-1923. Diameter: 4,9 cm. Collection S. van Roode.

066. Pendant with spirit pair flanking a fish. Hills on either side. Date: 1924-1925. Diameter: 5,5 cm. Collection Qilada Foundation – Eric and Marion Crince Le Roy, inventory number 63b.

067. Pendant with spirit pair holding a plant. Hills on either side, one star between the pair. A text has been added later, reading Mashallah. Date: 1925-1926. Diameter: 4,7 cm. Collection S. van Roode.

068. Pendant with spirit pair flanking a fish. Hills on either side, two stars in the sky. Date: 1926-1927. Bar pin added later. Diameter: 5,6 cm. Collection Qilada Foundation – Eric and Marion Crince Le Roy, inventory number 63b.

069. Pendant with spirit pair holding a plant. Hills on either side. Date: 1927-1928. Diameter: 4,9 cm. Collection S. van Roode.

070. Pendant with spirit pair, hands folded in lap, single fish on the left and a plant between them. Date: 1931-1932. Diameter: 5 cm. Collection S. van Roode.

071. Pendant with spirit pair, hands folded in lap, a plant between them and on either side. Date: 1931-1932. Diameter: 4,4 cm. Collection Qilada Foundation – Eric and Marion Crince Le Roy, inventory number 63j.

072. Pendant with spirit pair holding a plant. Date: 1932-1933. Diameter: 5 cm. Collection Qilada Foundation – Eric and Marion Crince Le Roy, inventory number 24e.

073. Pendant with spirit pair flanking a fish. Date: 1934-1935. Diameter: 4,4 cm. Collection S. van Roode.

Camels

074. Pendant with a camel carting a canopy. One star in the sky. Date: 1927-1928. Diameter: 5,4 cm. Collection Qilada Foundation – Eric and Marion Crince Le Roy, inventory number 63i.

075. Pendant with a camel carting a canopy. One star in the sky. Date: 1929-1930. Diameter: 4,9 cm. Collection Nefertari Tadema.

ZĀR JEWELLERY WITH SPIRIT IMAGES 1940-1960

From the 1940s onwards, the spirit images become increasingly stylized. The setting with hills, stars, and plants is no longer present, the images themselves become less detailed and more crudely executed. Their diameter is around 3-4 cm. In the 1950s, the first stamped pieces with spirit images appear. These showcase great detail again.

Water spirits

Mermaids and fish

076. Pendant with small fish and plants. Date: 1943-1944. Diameter: 3,8 cm. Collection Nefertari Tadema

077. Pendant with mermaid, holding a plant. Date: 1945-1946. Diameter: 4,4 cm. Collection S. van Roode.

078. Pendant with mermaid. Date: 1953-1959. Diameter: 5,2 cm. Collection S. van Roode.

Male spirits

079. Pendant with male spirit, holding a sword or stick, with a plant on one side. Date: 1941-1943. Diameter: 3,4 cm. Collection S. van Roode.

080. Pendant with a male bust, possibly military. Date: 1940-1950. Diameter: 3,9 cm. Collection S. van Roode.

081. Pendant with male spirit in Arab dress, holding a sword. Date: 1940-1950. Diameter: 4,8 cm. Collection S. van Roode.

Human spirit pairs

082. Pendant with spirit pair, holding a plant. Date: 1945-1946. Diameter: 4,3 cm. Collection Nefertari Tadema.

083. Pendant with spirit pair, holding a plant. Date: 1946-1947. Diameter: 4,3 cm. Collection S. van Roode.

084. Pendant with spirit pair, stamped. Date: 1953-1959. Diameter: 3,3 cm. Collection Qilada Foundation – Eric and Marion Crince Le Roy, inventory number 23.

Camels

085. Pendant with camel. Date: 1953-1959. Diameter: 3,2 cm. Collection S. van Roode.

ZĀR JEWELLERY WITH SPIRIT IMAGES 1960-1980

The use of small, light pendants continues. Hand engraved pendants are also still made, but in a crude, schematic manner. As pendants with spirit images from this decade are less attractive, they have not been collected as avidly as the pendants of the 1920s (see chapter 5.3.2).

086. Pendant with a male bust, stamped. Date: 1965-1968. Diameter: 3,9 cm. Collection Qilada Foundation – Eric and Marion Crince Le Roy, inventory number 25-12.

087. Pendant with woman sitting in front of a brazier with incense (?), stamped. Date: 1965-1968. Diameter: 3 cm. Collection S. van Roode.

088. Pendant with spirit pair, stamped and goldwashed. Date: 1970s-1980s. Diameter: 3,1 cm. Collection S. van Roode.

089. Pendant with spirit pair. Date: 1978-1979. Diameter: 3,9 cm. Collection S. van Roode.

JEWELLERY WITH SPIRIT IMAGES, DIFFERENT ICONOGRAPHY

As mentioned in chapter 5.3.6, the sample collection also holds several pieces with spirit images in a very different iconography. Whether these belong to *zār* is unclear, and most of them cannot be dated due to a lack of hallmarks and comparable imagery. Several of these are shown here: please refer to chapter 5.3.6. for a discussion.

090. Pendant with two figures and what looks like a plant between them. The image resembles that of a spirit pair, holding a plant. Diameter: 5,8 cm. Collection Nefertari Tadema.

091. Pendant with a male bust, with two plants above his shoulders. The image resembles a military bust. Diameter: 6,5 cm. Collection Nefertari Tadema.

092. Pendant with a male bust. Diameter 5,4 cm. Collection Qilada Foundation – Eric and Marion Crince Le Roy, inventory number 27d.

093. Pendant with a bull. Diameter 6 cm. No parallels; possibly another type of amulet? Date: early 20th century. Collection S. van Roode.

094. Pendant with images on both sides: a person standing in a boat with a sail, and a sailing boat without people. No parallels. Collection Nefertari Tadema.

JEWELLERY OFTEN ASSOCIATED WITH *ZĀR*, BUT NOT EXCLUSIVE TO *ZĀR*

In recent years, many pieces of jewellery have been described as '*zār*-jewellery' that certainly may have been used in *zār*, but that have not been produced exclusively for this purpose. They are regular jewellery pieces, often of an amuletic nature, that would have been worn in everyday life and whose use is well attested outside the ritual.

Coin jewellery

Coin jewellery serves many purposes. It communicates the affluence of the wearer, and may also function as an amulet. Coins are often worn as jewellery, or attached to face veils or dresses. Coin jewellery like this may have been used in *zār*, but is by no means exclusive to it. In *zār*, notably the pillar dollar is important, as noted in chapter 2, but this coin is equally important outside a ritual context. It is a general amulet, popular in Egypt.

095. Pillar dollar, fashioned into a pendant. Date: 1817. Diameter: 3,7 cm. Collection S. van Roode. See chapter 2 for the function of this coin as an amulet.

096. Maria Theresia Thaler (1780 restrike), fashioned into a pendant with dangles. Pendants like these were worn in Egypt, but also in Sudan, Ethiopia and Yemen. Noteworthy is that the dangles are positioned in such a way that the pendant would be worn with the head of the empress visible. This is unusual (compare for example to cat. nos. 097 and 110), and may indicate alteration for a foreign buyer. Date: unknown. Diameter: 3,9 cm. Collection Nefertari Tadema.

097. Imitation pillar dollar, fashioned into a pendant with dangles. Date: unknown. Diameter: 3,6 cm. Collection Nefertari Tadema.

098. Twenty piaster coin with King Farouk, fashioned into a pendant with dangles. Noteworthy is that the dangles are positioned in such a way that the pendant would be worn with the head of the king visible. This is unusual (see cat. no. 097), and may indicate alteration for a foreign buyer. Date: mid-20th century. Diameter: 3,1 cm. Collection Nefertari Tadema.

099. Twenty-five piaster coin, fashioned into a pendant with dangles. Date: 1957. Diameter: 3,4 cm. Collection Nefertari Tadema.

Regular jewellery

Regular jewellery is sometimes also associated with *zār* jewellery. This may be because it also exists in a *zār* variety. The most recognisable example of this are the upper arm bracelets presented in chapter 4: as they exist in a *zār* variety, the regular jewellery pieces as they were worn on the Red Sea coast are increasingly ascribed to *zār* as well. Other pieces of jewellery ascribed to *zār* are notably pieces from southern Egypt and northern Sudan. As the emphasis remained on southern Egypt during the early decades of *zār* in Egypt, and the ritual specialist is often mentioned to be a woman of the south in the early accounts, jewellery from this region may have engrained itself in the collective memory as belonging to *zār*. All the types of jewellery shown here are not exclusively made for *zār*, but may very well have been used in the ritual too. An adapted form may have been created for *zār* specifically, but this is difficult to ascertain.

100. Upper arm bracelet as worn on the southern Red Sea coast. These exist in a *zār* variety as well, as shown in Fig. 4.2. Date: 1913-1916. Bracelet diameter: 9,5 cm. Plaquette: 3,5 cm (h) x 8,5 cm (l). Collection Nefertari Tadema.

101. Pair of anklets from southern Egypt. Because of their dangles, these are often associated with *zār*. Date: early 20th century. Anklet diameter: 11 cm. Collection S. van Roode.

102. Pair of anklets from southern Egypt. Because of their dangles and the additional red beads, these are often associated with *zār*. Date: early 20th century. Anklet diameter: 12 cm. Collection Karel Innemée.

103. Bracelet (not silver) from southern Egypt. Egypt. Because of their dangles, these are often associated with *zār*. Date: early 20th century. Bracelet diameter: 6,5 cm. Collection S. van Roode.

104. Ring from southern Egypt, with a solid silver band and geometric designs on the central square. Associated with *zār* but equally used in everyday life. Date: 20th century. Ring diameter: 1,5 cm. Collection S. van Roode.

105. Ring from southern Egypt, featuring geometric designs on the band and a worn red glass stone. Associated with *zār* but equally used in everyday life. Date: 20th century. Ring diameter: 1,7 cm. Collection S. van Roode.

106. Ring from southern Egypt, featuring a small brass dome. Associated with *zār*, but equally used in everyday life. Date: 20th century. Ring diameter: 1,6 cm. Collection S. van Roode.

107. Ring from southern Egypt, with solar motifs on the polyhedral central element. Associated with *zār*, but equally used in everyday life. Date: 20th century. Ring diameter: 1,9 cm. Collection S. van Roode.

108. Ring from southern Egypt, with three-piece band and geometric designs on the central cube. Associated with *zār*, but equally used in everyday life. Date: 20th century. Ring diameter: 1,7 cm. Collection S. van Roode.

109. Ring from southern Egypt with three granules. Associated with *zār*, but equally used in everyday life. Date: 20th century. Ring diameter: 1,6 cm. Collection S. van Roode.

110. Necklace from southern Egypt, featuring a crescent embellished with geometric design and red and green glass, and a pendant fashioned from a Maria Theresia Thaler (1780 restrike). Associated with *zār*, but equally used in everyday life. Date: undated, but with recurring signature of the silversmith, probably early 20th century. Length of necklace 84 cm. Collection Nefertari Tadema.

111. Necklace from southern Egypt, featuring a crescent embellished with geometric design, and a pendant fashioned from an Egyptian imitation of a pillar dollar. Associated with *zār*, but equally used in everyday life. Date: mid-20th century. Length of necklace 88 cm. Collection Nefertari Tadema.

112. Necklace with three amulet boxes. The text on the triangular boxes reads 'Allah', and the text on the middle box reads 'Mashallah'. These box pendants in repoussé display influence from the Ottoman period; they are also worn in Palestine and Syria. Associated with *zār*, but equally used in everyday life. Date: 1924-1925. Length of necklace 49 cm. Collection Nefertari Tadema.

113. Headdress pendant in filigree with gold-coloured appliques and turquoise. These headdress pendants display influence from the Ottoman period; they are also worn in Palestine and Syria. Associated with *zār*, but equally used in everyday life. Date: early 20th century. 2,3 cm (h) x 4,9 cm (l). Collection Nefertari Tadema.

CATALOGUE | 205

114. Pair of headdress pendant/earrings in filigree with turquoise. These pendants display influence from the Ottoman period; they are also worn in Palestine and Syria. Associated with *zār*, but equally used in everyday life. Date: early 20th century. 1,9 cm (h) x 2,4 cm (l). Collection Nefertari Tadema.

Regular amulets

Finally, many amulets that were worn in everyday life were also used in *zār*. The reasons for this are discussed in chapters 2 and 4. The sample collection holds many of those: in this section, I present a selection of these amulets. None of these are produced exclusively for *zār*, but all of them may have been used in the ritual.

115. Pear-shaped amulet in repoussé, featuring floral motifs and the word 'Allah'. These pendants display influence from the Ottoman period; they are also worn in Palestine and Syria. Associated with *zār*, but equally used in everyday life. Date: early 20th century. 7 cm (h) x 3 cm (l). Collection Nefertari Tadema.

116. Pendant with red glass and an image of the pyramids with a palm tree. The red glass has been reused: it has been placed upside down in the pendant. Pendants with red glass may feature in *zār*, but are equally often worn as regular amulet. Date: early 20th century. 6 cm (h) x 1,5 cm (w). Collection Nefertari Tadema.

117. Pendant called *zur'a*. These are used by pregnant women, as well as small children. They feature in *zār*, but are equally often worn as regular amulet to protect pregnant women and young children. Date: early 20th century. Diameter: 3,5 cm Collection Nefertari Tadema.

118. Pendant called *zur'a*. These are used by pregnant women, as well as small children. They feature in *zār*, but are equally often worn as regular amulet to protect pregnant women and young children. Date: early 20th century. 4,7 cm (h) x 2,3 cm (w). Collection Nefertari Tadema.

119. Pendant in the shape of a Christian cross. They feature in *zār* as jewellery for Christian spirits, but are equally often worn as regular amulet by Christians. Date: early 20th century. 3,2 cm (h) x 2,1 cm (w). Collection S. van Roode.

120. Headdress pendant in the shape of a fish. These are regular amulets to protect against water spirits, and may also feature in *zār*. Date: early-mid 20th century. L. 4,1 cm. Collection Nefertari Tadema.

121. Pendant in the shape of a fish. These are regular amulets to protect against water spirits, and may also feature in *zār*. Date: early-mid 20th century. L. 6 cm. Collection Qilada Foundation – Eric and Marion Crince Le Roy, inventory number 66f.

122. Tubular amulet container. These are regular containers and can be opened to hold specialized content. Their style points to Ottoman influence. These are increasingly associated with *zār*, but were equally often used in everyday life. Date: 1930-1931. L. 8 cm. Collection Nefertari Tadema.

123. Headdress pendant in sheet silver, with the word 'Mashallah' cut out. These are increasingly associated with *zār*, but were equally often used in everyday life. Date: 1929-1930. 4 cm (w) x 2 cm (h). Collection Nefertari Tadema.

124. Headdress pendant in stamped sheet silver, with the text 'In the name of God, the Merciful, The Compassionate. There is no God but God.' These are increasingly associated with *zār*, but were equally often used in everyday life. Date: after 1950s. 3 cm (w) x 1,5 cm (h). Collection S. van Roode.

125. Amulet pendant in the shape of a writing board, with the text 'In the name of God, the Merciful, The Compassionate', followed by the beginning of the Throne Verse, which continues on its other side. The three faceted carnelian beads have been added later, given that they all have different caps. These are regular amulets, whose shape has extended into *zār*. Amulets like these may have been used in *zār* but were not exclusively made for it. Date: 1929-1930. L. 6 cm. Collection Qilada Foundation – Eric and Marion Crince Le Roy, inventory number 22d.